THE
ICARUS
SYNDROME

RAND Studies Published with Transaction

The Gradual Revolution:
China's Economic Reform Movement
Hui Wang

The Icarus Syndrome:
The Role of Air Power Theory in the Evolution
and Fate of the U.S. Air Force
Carl H. Builder

In Pursuit of Prestige:
Strategy and Competition in U.S. Higher Education
Dominic J. Brewer, Susan M. Gates, and Charles A. Goldman

Linking Economic Policy and Foreign Policy
Charles Wolf, Jr.

Snow Job?
The War Against International Cocaine Trafficking
Kevin Jack Riley

Troubled Partnership:
A History of U.S.-Japan Collaboration on the FS-X Fighter
Mark Lorell

CARL H. BUILDER

THE
ICARUS
SYNDROME

THE ROLE OF AIR POWER THEORY IN THE EVOLUTION AND FATE OF THE U.S. AIR FORCE

TRANSACTION PUBLISHERS
NEW BRUNSWICK (U.S.A.) AND LONDON (U.K.)

Library of Congress Catalog Number: 93-31554
ISBN: 978-0-7658-0993-3
Printed in the United States of America

                    Library of Congress Cataloging-in-Publication Data
Builder, Carl H.
    The Icarus syndrome: the role of air power theory in the evolution and fate
of the U.S. Air Force / Carl H. Builder, p.   cm.
    Includes bibliographical references and index.
    ISBN 0-7658-0993-1 (alk. paper)
        1. United States Air Force—Unit cohesion. 2. Air power—United States.
    I. Title.

UG633.B79   1993
358.4'03—dc20   93-31554

This is a RAND study.

RAND books are available on a wide variety of topics. To obtain information on
other publications, write or call Distribution Services, RAND, 1700 Main Street,
P. O. Box 2138, Santa Monica, CA 90407-2138, (310) 393-0411, ext. 6686.

Dedication

To Gabriele,
who shared in all the risks,
knowing this Dædalian adventure
could so easily come to an Icarian fate.

Contents

*It is the customary fate of new truths
to begin as heresies and
to end as superstitions.*

—Thomas Henry Huxley

Foreword

The legend of Icarus aside, our experience with manned flight is brief. As this is written, some still living were present at the Earth's surface when the Wright Brothers first managed to lift free from it. An independent U.S. Air Force has existed for only half this brief period. Nevertheless, the impact of airpower has been so emphatic that today few military professionals would like to contemplate active operations undertaken without its benefits. Thus, no recent trend has had more important military consequences than the increasing importance of air and space power.

The rise of air and space power has taken place against the background of international violence that has characterized the 20th century. As we approach the end of this century, we see, in retrospect, regional conflicts too numerous to list and three great world wars. We do not yet fully understand the implications of Western victory in the last of these great wars, which we call the Cold War. As a consequence, we have no clear view of what the nation will ask its armed forces to do in the years ahead. One thing does seem clear: the Air Force must prepare to meet whatever security challenges arise while at the same time undergoing a rapid drawdown in every dimension of resource availability. This is the central problem facing the contemporary Air Force.

Many serving airmen are convinced that we can best prepare for an uncertain future by attending to institutional fundamentals—to our sense of identity and purpose. These can provide a steady frame of reference as we work our way through an otherwise bewildering set of changes. Enter Carl Builder.

Mr. Builder has been thinking about institutional fundamentals for some years. In this latest effort, he traces the ideas and fortunes of airpower's most influential advocates—Billy Mitchell, Hap Arnold, and others who shaped the growth and employment of our Air Force. He also looks to the future, to the shifting nature of warfare and to the impact today's trends may have on our organization.

I do not agree with all that Mr. Builder has to say in these pages. But I do believe that he has raised the right questions. Has the Air Force abandoned air power theory over the years? Have the fundamentals of air and space power changed in a world of new technologies and new challenges? Does the Air Force, as an institution, grasp these fundamentals? So I commend *The Icarus Syndrome* to you. These issues are important.

—Merrill A. McPeak
24 August 1993

Preface

All that is written here has relatively short roots in time; but like a vine, it has traveled a long distance from where it started. It started out as an essay to remind midcareer Air Force officer-students of the fundamentals of their profession. It ended up, instead, as a call for their institution to return to *its* basics—to its historic devotion to air power theory.

My original plan for an essay turned into an analysis of the institution that had requested it. The analysis centered on the role air power theory had played in the early development of the Air Force and the role it might still play in a host of problems that have come to plague that institution. Was air power theory more important to the Air Force than even the Air Force realized? The theory, of course, explained what air power could do and how it must be wielded to be effective; but was it also the glue that bound the Air Force together and inspired its direction? Those are the questions pursued here. The thesis that has emerged is that

- air power theory was a crucial element in the evolution and success of the Air Force as an independent military institution; but

- the subsequent abandonment of air power theory in the face of competitive means (missiles and space) and ends (deterrence theory) cast the Air Force adrift from precisely those commitments that had propelled it to its institutional apogee in the 1950s.

Supporting that thesis is the burden of the analysis presented in the following two dozen chapters. But a brief explanation of how the original enterprise was transformed from a simple essay to an analysis of an institution is appropriate here, if only to reveal what motivated those who instigated and executed the analysis.

Genesis

At the end of 1990, my colleague Ted Warner approached me about my interest in fulfilling a request he had from the Air University located at Maxwell Air Force Base in Alabama. The Air Command and Staff College (ACSC) wanted an essay that would remind incoming students of the obligations of the profession of arms, their heritage in history, and where those obligations might carry them with the future of the Air Force. Ted knew my interests in military history, values, and speculation about the future; he didn't have to bait the hook.

In the early months of 1991, through a series of phone conversations with Major John Loucks and Colonel Rod Payne of ACSC, I assembled a terms of reference and an outline for the essay, which they could take to their commandant, then Brigadier General Phillip Ford, for approval. When we seemed to have a meeting of minds, I made plans to visit the Air University (AU) and try out some of my ideas in the form of a briefing, before putting them to paper.

My briefing, in March 1991, was deliberately designed to provoke. I wanted to put ideas in front of the ACSC faculty, much as a fisherman might cast flies on the water for trout. I didn't think all of the ideas would "fly," but I wanted to find out how the faculty saw things and where they were coming from in approaching the subjects I had agreed to write about. Thus, I loaded my briefing with one-liners about the history and future of the Air Force and about the significance of its heritage.

To my surprise and disappointment, the faculty was polite and very quiet. I couldn't seem to cast anything on the water before them that would provoke much argument or disagreement. I couldn't get a bite, even though I knew they couldn't agree with everything I was saying. I was almost glad when the allotted time for the briefing and discussion came to an end.

The faculty had arranged for me to meet with a group of students—one representative student from each of the class (seminar) rooms—so that I might learn some of the student views about the subjects to be covered in the essay. It quickly became apparent to me that the students, typically majors, didn't think they needed to be told what the Air Force was about after having served in it for a dozen or more years. As one of them put it, "If we don't understand the profession of arms and the Air Force by this time, we never will."

I had some doubts about that statement, but adopted a less direct approach. I began asking them what they thought was the most important Air Force problem they would address if they were magically made chief of staff tomorrow. Suddenly, the group became very animated, and they started to talk as if I wasn't there. They agreed—without exception as I remember—that they would set out to fix the promotion system. I asked what was wrong with it. The answers were quick and ratified with much nodding of heads:

- The promotion system doesn't work as advertised.

- The difference between how it is supposed to work and actually works is so large as to invite contempt.

- Having a flag officer as a mentor is an invisible but widely acknowledged prerequisite to the good jobs and, hence, to promotion.

- Just when junior officers have figured out how they need to get their tickets punched (i.e., the successful career paths), someone changes the rules and promising careers are sidetracked.

- Some careers are dead ends from the beginning because they don't involve wearing a flight suit or wings.

None of these complaints were new to me; however, their force and approbation were quite unexpected. This was, in contrast with my previous briefing for the faculty, a very animated and interesting discussion; but the students' passion for the topic disturbed more than enlightened me about what I needed to write in my essay.

At lunch with a few of the faculty, I related my experience with the students that morning (the faculty had considerately, deliberately chosen to remove themselves from my session with the students, lest they inhibit the student views that might be helpful to me). Instantly, the lunchtime conversation changed; the faculty members became animated and they were unified in their assessment:

- I had just seen a good example of what is wrong with midcareer officers in the Air Force.

- The students are focused on their career tracks and promotions rather than their education or institution.

- The students are constantly on the phone to personnel managers trying to learn or negotiate their next career assignments.

Again, these complaints from the faculty were not so surprising, but their strength and the unanimity of views took me aback.

By the time I went to see the commandant that afternoon, I was disoriented about my mission. Three or four intense hours had revealed very little about what I needed to do when I sat down to write an essay. General Ford put me at ease and I laid out my confusion from the morning's events. He said that I was being exposed to the very problem he wanted me to address; I was seeing, firsthand, the careerism, the "stovepiping,"[1] the loss of professionalism at arms that needed to be changed. He then proceeded to tell me several vivid stories from his own experiences that illustrated the problems the Air Force was having with the values, motivations, and commitments of its officers. These stories, more than anything else, rooted the problems in my mind. One of them will suffice as a concrete example of his concern:

> Taking over as a new wing commander, General Ford was alert to any opportunity to demonstrate to the wing personnel and their families his interest in them and concern for their well-being. While making his first tour of the base with some of his staff, he noticed a set of bleak looking living quarters in naked brick. He asked his facilities manager if those buildings could be painted to improve their looks. The answer was yes. Did the wing have the paint to do the job? Yes. Did the manager think it was practical to paint these brick buildings? Again, the answer was affirmative. How long would it take? Perhaps a week or ten days. As wing commander, Ford said, "Then let's do it."

> Several weeks later, General Ford noticed that the buildings were still unpainted. He called his facilities manager to say, "I thought we had agreed to paint those buildings. What happened?"

> The facilities manager concurred with the wing commander's recollection, but then went on to explain: When the facilities manager had called the facilities staff at the higher command headquarters, they didn't like the idea of painting the naked brick buildings and advised against it. The wing's facility manager took the higher command's staff advice as overriding since he had to deal with them as fellow professionals on facilities issues.

This was an example, in General Ford's view, of how the Air Force had become "stovepiped." Specialists tended to look up the pipe of their own profession rather than the chain of operational command. As specialists, they would be evaluated by fellow specialists; and their loyalties followed their profession rather than the operational mission.

General Ford's vivid examples didn't solve my orientation problem for the requested essay; but they gave me firm footholds on the kinds of problems he wanted addressed in the essay he had requested. And he provided me—although I didn't see it at the time—with two important keys when he used his whiteboard to suggest the two parts of the problem he saw, "air power" and "profession of arms," were somehow related.

I flew home and spent the weekend mulling over what I had heard, but the pieces didn't come together. The problem I was being asked to address was somehow different and larger than the one I had contemplated in my terms of reference and outline for an essay. General Ford called me early the following week, upbeat about our discussion and encouraging me to press on, stressing how important the problem was and how much might be riding on our effort to address it. When I got off the phone and took my noontime walk, the pieces began to "click" into place, one after another. Within an hour, a hypothesis had begun to take form. Within a few days, I wrote a letter to General Ford outlining my new perception of the problem:

> As you indicated, air power is one piece, the profession of arms is the other. One is the heart of the Air Force, the other is its soul. The senior leadership of the Air Force is the trustee of the heart; but everyone in the Air Force is a trustee of its soul. The heart is about organizational purpose or mission—air power—and the soul is about the profession of arms—the absolute and total commitment to mission (what sets the profession of arms apart from other professions is the commitment to mission, even unto death).
>
> The problem, as I see it, is that the two—heart and soul—have failed each other: The senior leadership has failed to keep the heart—the mission of air power—alive and vibrant by keeping it at the forefront of all its actions. And without that mission, the members of the Air Force have had nothing to commit themselves to except their own careers or specialities.
>
> The leadership can't dedicate the organization to its mission just by lip service; its decisions (including promotions and rewards) must reflect that dedication, or its followers soon detect the duplicity. Given that dedication of the organization to its mission, everyone joining the organization can appreciate and elect (or not) to commit to the mission.... To be sure, not everyone who joins an organization will commit to its mission; but those persons are not professionals at arms and they are not the people that the organization should normally seek and reward. If the organization sends out mixed signals about its mission or its dedication to its mission, it can hardly complain if professionalism and commitment to the mission falter among its people.
>
> Thus, I think that both the heart and soul have failed each other in the Air Force. It is kind of like the mutual failure of loyalty, up and down, at CBS, as described

by Peggy Noonan in *What I Saw at the Revolution* (pp. 37, 38). Obviously, I think that dedication has to start at the top and flow downward until people gain confidence and faith that the organization is worthy of commitment.[2]

General Ford's reaction was immediate and positive; he thought these ideas were worth pursuing with a wider audience at the Air University. At the end of May, General Ford sponsored my briefing (which I titled, "In Search of the Air Force Soul, Take II") to the senior leadership of the Air University, including its commander, Lieutenant General Charles Boyd. In that briefing, I advanced the thesis of this analysis: Many of the Air Force's current institutional problems could be laid at the doorstep of its neglect of air power theory as the basis for its mission or purpose.

General Boyd thought that the thesis was worthy of further investigation to see if it could be supported by evidence. He asked me what I would propose to do next in the absence of instructions from him. I asked for time to think about his question and get back to him, which he granted. It became clear that there was more than one essay here; and I started listing them by topic and argument. When the list quickly exceeded five, I knew that there was a book-length analysis lurking in the thesis. And that is what I proposed to General Ford a week later. By early June, I had my marching orders from General Boyd; and this analysis is a direct consequence.

A first draft was available by the first of the following year (January 1992) and distributed to a few in RAND and the Air Force for their comments and suggestions. Even at that early stage, the analysis probably had some influence on the ongoing debates in the Air Force leadership about the future of air power. In a sense, this analysis became a part of the intellectual developments it sought to explain or urge; the analysis and the object of analysis had begun to merge. At that point, an analysis ceases, not because it is completed, but because the analyst has become transformed into a participant.

Hence, this story ends with the recognition, in the final chapter, that the analysis presented here was beginning to influence Air Force policy-making by the spring of 1992. The evolution of air power theory and the fate of the U.S. Air Force are far from resolved, even for the decade just ahead, but this analysis has been carried to a point where it must be exploited to shape those events, not extended simply to chronicle them.

Notes

1. Richard Szafranski, in "Desert Storm Lessons from the Rear," *Parameters*, (Winter 1991–92): 39–49, defines *stovepiping* as "the condition that exists when staff or support personnel forget that they are subordinate to a line commander." With an edge to his humor, Szafranski goes on to observe that *"There's a lot in the stovepipes, but most of it is smoke."* (p. 45, emphasis in the original).

2. Taken from my letter to Brig Gen Phillip J. Ford, USAF, Commandant, Air Command and Staff College, on 12 April 1991. The full citation for Peggy Noonan's book is, *What I Saw at the Revolution: A Political Life in the Reagan Era*, (New York: Ivy Books, 1991), 37, 38. On those pages, Peggy talks about what happened when new management at CBS News shifted the basis for its actions from journalistic professionalism to financial profitability.

Acknowledgments

It was General Phillip J. Ford, then commandant of the Air Command and Staff College at the Air University, who instigated this enterprise. He saw the need, helped me wrestle the problem to the ground, and then enlisted his colleagues and his boss in its support. He was the right person, at the right place, and at the right time, to make it happen.

General Charles "Chuck" Boyd, commander of the Air University, assumed the role of project shepherd. He cleared my way both at RAND and at the Air University, ensuring that the enterprise was supported. He defined the terms of reference or specifications for the work, then counseled and encouraged me along the way. I thought of him as the "gentle intellect" that had been behind the scenes, pursuing something even bigger, even before I took up one of his several challenges.

At RAND, both James Thomson, president, and George Donohue, vice president for Project Air Force, gave immediate and enthusiastic support for the project. George said, "This is something we can and should do, even without Air Force sponsorship." I am indebted to Ted Warner, the project leader, for his early detection of the match between the challenge and my interests, and to David Ochmanek, the program director, for his strong endorsement when the nature of the project shifted and expanded to its final form.

In carrying out the research and writing, I am deeply indebted to four colleagues who did most of the literature searching and combing for pertinent quotes. They are Jerry Stiles, Duane Deal, Lucille Horgan, and Mike Anderson. Duane and Mike are serving Air Force officers, then assigned to RAND as research associates; Jerry is a fellow at the RAND Graduate School, and Lucille is a historian. They used the thesis of this analysis as a comb on the literature, looking for information that might illuminate, support, or refute the concept. Along the way, they contributed their own perceptions and analyses to what is found here.

Joan Schlimgen supported the research from the RAND library, undertaking a long and frustrating search for a particular aircraft accident report that tantalized my memory. My good friend in Britain, David A. Russell, provided valuable help on the legal aspects of aircraft accidents and on European perspectives of the World War II bombing campaigns. Jim Quinlivan freely lent me his considerable knowledge and personal library on Air Force history. I am indebted to David Ochmanek for his considerate and constructive comments and suggestions on the very first, very rough draft of this analysis. Subsequent drafts have benefited from review comments offered by Col. John E. Frisby, Lieut. Gen. Bradley Hosmer, Felix Kozaczka, Robert J. Lempert, and retired Maj. Gen. Perry McCoy Smith.

Cindy Kumagawa, manager of the RAND book program, shepherded the manuscript through the many rituals and agonies of the publication process with confidence and aplomb, despite my chafing and occasional displays of impatience; she knew what she was doing, even when I didn't.

In Praise of Theory

The Air Force is the house that aviators built
On a proud theory of air power, even though, for most,
The affection was really, if truth be known, for the airplane.

They wielded the theory as a sword to gain their independence
And to claim primacy in military power,
Demonstrating it with a stunning monument to Armageddon.

But there were other dreamers abroad who looked to the stars
And made robots that might take them there,
Only to find their tickets had been taken by other robots.

The aviators accepted the robots, as servants, into their house,
Not because they liked them or even understood them,
But because neighbors had eagerly bid for their ownership.

The robots, however, kept challenging the boundaries of the theory
With which the aviators had won their freedom,
Built their house, and enshrined their monument to Armageddon.

The aviators, alas, instead of expanding their theory to the stars
And extending the house to include its new domains,
Revealed by every decision their true affection, the airplane.

Throughout years of plenty, it became accepted throughout the house,
That there was more than enough for all,
Whatever their particular affection for vehicle or trade or domain.

And in those separate devotions, the unity of the house slowly fractured;
To be sure, the aviators continued to own the house,
But no longer the loyalty of its occupants.

For in the absence of the aviator's dedication to the theory,
There was no household commitment to mission
And, ultimately, inevitably, no profession of arms.

Thus, the house is now besieged, from without and within;
The world, once owned, has become hostile;
And both occupants and neighbors are pulling their shades.

—Carl Builder

xxii

PART I

TAKING BEARINGS

1

A View of the Air Force Today

> *The United States has not won a war since the Air Force was established as a separate service in 1947. We ought to do away with the Air Force and give the aircraft back to the Army and Navy.[1]*
>
> *There is a way to get rid of billions of ugly fat in the defense budget without losing an ounce of combat power: Abolish the Air Force.... The US Air Force was created to honor a false premise that should have been discredited long ago; that premise is the efficacy of airpower as an independent war-winning doctrine.[2]*
>
> *Notwithstanding an Air Force general's recent and laughable characterization of it as "our most cherished mission," [close air support] has never enjoyed high priority within the Air Force.... The only times the Air Force has "gotten religion" have been when it feared that the mission would be taken from it and transferred to the army.[3]*

These statements, all made before Operations Desert Shield and Desert Storm, are three of five quotations comprising the frontispiece of a remarkable paper, titled *A View of the Air Force Today*, written by serving Air Force officers in the fall of 1989. The paper (really a draft) was never formally published; but it was circulated first at high levels and then selectively within the Air Force, as an expression of growing concern and frustration by many who serve that institution. The paper is remarkable for its direct criticism of the Air Force and its leadership, for its earnest efforts to be constructive in its criticism, and for its acceptance

3

by many as a view worthy of consideration by Air Force leadership, if only as indications of some institutional problems that needed attention.

That paper is important to this analysis because it was a prior and independently instigated alarm of some unique institutional problems within the Air Force. *A View of the Air Force Today* is a collection of symptoms, partial diagnoses, and tentative prescriptions; and along with other frequently heard complaints, it represents *prima facie* evidence of a problem, like the complaints and speculations of a patient in pain, real or imagined, worthy of being heard and considered. One need not accept the arguments of the paper as *correct* to accept them as *indicators* of some kind of problem worth investigating. They represent an impassioned view of the Air Force as an institution which, even if held by only one in ten, has enough plausibility and conviction to merit treatment as an indictment to be answered.

For those reasons, *A View of the Air Force Today* deserves careful examination. What are the specific charges in the indictment? Do the diagnoses reflect the symptoms? Will the prescriptions match the diagnoses? To answer those kinds of questions, I prefer to resort to analysis rather than summary judgments of the paper. Hence, I have undertaken a content analysis of the paper identical to those I have also made for two other landmark policy papers, *The Maritime Strategy*[4] and *Global Reach —Global Power*.[5]

Those analyses begin with methodical abstracting of the document. The abstract is designed to capture the ideas and arguments with minimum words, shorn of supporting evidence or examples except where those are, themselves, the ideas and arguments. The abstract typically substitutes one sentence (or a few) for each paragraph. All paragraphs are accounted for by at least one sentence. More than one sentence is used only where the paragraph contains more than one idea. Thus, the abstract can be read as a paragraph-by-paragraph topical summary of the original. The headings are as found in the original. The compression achieved in this process is about four-to-one with respect to the original.

With much of the obligatory rhetoric and supporting evidence stripped away, the essential ideas and arguments are laid bare for scrutiny. It is a harsh process, one to which few authors would like to see their writing subjected. Politeness and political sensitivities may be lost in the process.

But significant ideas are not lost, they are revealed; so are the absence of ideas and gaps in logic. But most important, the nature of, and motivation for the document are often revealed.

Here, then, is an abstract of the ideas found in *A View of the Air Force Today*:[6]

An Abstract of the View

The senses of the five quotations in the frontispiece may be stated fairly, if more briefly, as follows:

1. Do away with the Air Force.

2. Air power is not independently decisive.

3. Abolish the Air Force as an institution built on a false premise.

4. Air Force influence in battle is minor.

5. Air Force interest in close air support is phony.

State of Siege

The dominant image for many in the Air Force is of an institution under siege and in disarray. This image would surprise many others because the positive aspects and developments within the institution are so numerous. But, despite the positives, the Air Force seems to have lost its sense of identity and unique contribution. Although the current external environment is a part of the problem, the institution's difficulties are mostly internal. The Air Force may have crippled itself for the decade ahead. Even if disaster is not imminent, the trends are adverse and need to be checked if the Air Force is to fulfill its national security role.

Cultural Clues

There are obvious cultural differences between the services. They can be overdrawn, but these differences can now be felt and deserve our attention. The touchstones for the Army are the art of war and the profession of arms. The Army's separate branches are unified in their concepts and doctrine.

The Navy is oriented with its institution and its traditions which have served it well during challenges to its relevancy. This Navy culture has helped them to formulate the Maritime Strategy to provide integration, coherence, and direction within the Navy.

The Air Force, by contrast, has identified itself with the air weapon, and rooted itself in a commitment to technological superiority. The dark side of this commitment is that it becomes transformed into an end in itself when aircraft or systems, rather than missions, become the primary focus. Identity in the Air Force has become associated with a specific airplane rather than the institution or military art, with a resulting weaker sense of community than the other services.

The Air Force has no integrating vision like the Maritime Strategy or AirLand Battle. The earlier air power theories have been relegated to mythology.[7] While flawed and limited in the light of today's experience, those theories were, nevertheless, powerful integrating blueprints in their time.

The absence of an integrating vision unleashes bad tendencies: weak ties to the institution, loyalties given to airframes or commands, and a focus on systems before missions. The Air Force is fragmented in both how it plans and how it appears to outsiders. Without a unifying theme, there is no basis for tough decisions, so they are pushed off onto others who do the programming and budgeting with their own visions. This lack of a comprehensive strategic vision is the proximate or contributing cause in a variety of current Air Force difficulties.

Roles, Missions and Attitudes

From an Air Force general: The Air Force appears willing to compromise on principles in order to gain its objectives with respect to systems or procedures. This is in sharp contrast to the Navy, which seems never to compromise because of its certainty of the correctness of Navy interests.

From an Army colonel on the joint staff: The other services are more predictable because they act in accordance with well-articulated concepts, while the Air Force usually acts to protect some current interest. The Navy expects to win, while the Air Force is satisfied with being clever. Those two anecdotes are only pertinent as an introduction to discussing why the Air Force is increasingly on the defensive with respect to roles and missions.

Army systems are certainly encroaching on the traditional missions of the air weapon; but more troublesome is the Air Force conceding initiative and control over attack missions to an Army commander, sometimes even to a junior officer on the ground. A substantial part of the Air Force vision is being tied to what a surface commander thinks air power can and should do.

This is the climate that stimulates those outside the Air Force to call for transferring the close air support mission to the Army. This is also a climate that permits even Air Force officers to be confused about the nature of air power and to accept the strategic claims of the other services. All this is exemplified by the initiatives in Europe to use air power to support the close-in battle simply because the Army has devoted too much of its resources to the deep battle. The Air Force has conceded the intellectual high ground to the Army with its AirLand Battle concept. While air power must support the ground commander, it is limited to no more than that if the Air Force has no integrating concept of its own.

Even though the Air Force is the lead military agency for space, space systems will be competing for aircraft roles and missions, posing difficult tradeoffs in budgets and force structure. In the absence of a larger, integrating vision, space becomes a competing faction, devoted to space power, and without much loyalty to the Air Force as an institution.

Even the strategic offensive mission, the well-spring of Air Force institutional independence, appears to be shifting to the Navy and its submarine-launched ballistic missiles. Many people can play in the deterrence game; however the Air Force needs to get its intellectual act together if it expects to play.

An Unusual Conservatism

Because of its focus on systems and commands rather than missions and strategies, the Air Force views innovation more as a threat than as an opportunity. Even new technology tends to be applied only to old ways of doing business.

An example is the ground-launched cruise missile, which was never accepted into the Air Force mainstream. The use of remotely piloted vehicles is not imaginatively considered because it threatens manned penetrating aircraft. The Air Force response to the new initiatives of competitive strategies was to list its top 20 systems in its Program Objectives Memo (POM). In the absence of a broad framework, the Air Force has no compass to guide its position on long-range conventional cruise missiles. The Navy had no trouble finding its position because of the Maritime Strategy.

The Air Force is more likely to be reacting rather than taking the initiative in roles and missions debates. The air power school of thought has not kept pace with events. For an institution on the leading edge of technology, the reactionary posture of the Air Force seems surprising. But what should be more surprising is the vacuum of thought about the promising roles and future of air power. Consensus within the Air Force may not come easily. Some in the Air Force don't even believe that air power should any longer claim to be independently decisive.

Fiscal Storm Clouds

If funding is a measure of institutional success, the Air Force is already in trouble. Air Force spending, as a percentage of the DoD total, has dropped to about two thirds of its 1958 high. During the last half of the 1980s, the Air Force funding cuts were larger than those for the other services. These cuts may not seem large, but they are cumulative and get magnified in their effects.

For example, the National Foreign Intelligence Program accounts are concentrated in the Air Force and are growing, accounting for more than ten percent of Air Force spending. At the same time, Air Force strategic forces spending was down, while Navy strategic forces spending was up. Air Force spending on general purpose forces and on research, development, test, and engineering (RDT&E) has not tracked favorably against the DoD changes in these program areas.

All these trends combine to paint a dismal fiscal picture for the Air Force, as compared with the other services during this time of growing fiscal constraints. During the last half of the 1980s, cuts in the Air Force budget exceeded the combined cuts in the Army and Navy. Worse, because of mandated and protected programs, what was hurt most was the Air Force investments in the future. The Air Force lost $46 billion, while the other two services each lost less than $22 billion.

Some question this gloomy outlook as too narrow a view. But there is a broad consensus that the Air Force is losing with Congress, and this has caused some to blame Air Force marketing efforts. Better marketing may be indicated, but it is clear that Air Force views are not being accepted by Congress and are consequently being overridden. At some point the Air Force must stop blaming others and accept that it has failed to develop and communicate a coherent strategic vision. In the current institutional environment within the Air Force, it may not be easy or even possible to do so.

Its Not Just a Job...Or Is It?

Institutional identity could be a factor in Air Force retention problems. There is a difference between occupational and institutional value systems; and the Air Force is leading the other services in its tendency toward occupationalism.

Surveys support the conclusion that the Air Force is tending toward occupationalism. Unfortunately, those tendencies are stronger with pilots and with time in service. The strong impetus toward occupationalism in the Air Force should not be surprising because of the institution's dependency on technology and on specialists. It will be difficult to slow the tendencies toward occupationalism if the institution has no core identity.

Operational Art

Various causes for the identity problem have been offered: too few operators, too few rated officers, too few heroes, too few war fighters, too many support officers. The prestige of flying has declined in favor of management. Egalitarianism has gutted the elites. But shifting the demographics of the Air Force won't ensure a vision. The complexity of Air Force systems and operations demands specialists and specialized training. What is needed is thinking beyond those demands.

Even if there were more operators, they wouldn't necessarily be thinking about broader strategic issues because current senior Air Force operators see themselves mainly as the suppliers of sorties—unlike their Army and Navy counterparts. This doesn't deny that operators could or should be the source of the needed vision, only that having more operators will automatically provide it. The vision must come from a larger process within the institution and from those who hold power in it.

The following guidelines for a vision are suggested:

1. The needed vision must find the unifying thread in all Air Force tasks. Perhaps it will be found in the third dimension which air power brings to surface warfare. Perhaps that would free the Air Force from measuring its capabilities in terms of the surface battle and to accept all forms or types of Air Force capabilities, whether manned or not, combat as well as support, and regardless of trajectory or penetration.

2. The focus should be on air power as a tool at the operational or theater level of war. Just as the Maritime Strategy focuses on controlling access and the continental strategy focuses on controlling location, perhaps air power can do both.

3. The Air Force heritage should be mined, particularly the work of Kenney in the Southwest Pacific, where air power was used as an integrated whole. All elements—strategic, tactical and transport—were used against the enemy.

4. Jointness, properly interpreted, should be exploited. Kenney, working jointly, brought air power from almost nothing to the dominant instrument in the theater campaign.

The siege mentality within the Air Force can be broken if the disarray is countered with an effective vision. The Air Force has the means within its traditions and culture to address this challenge. The authors are optimistic, but have a sense of urgency.

The Legacy of Desert Storm

Has the "view" changed since the stunning success of air power in the prosecution of the Gulf War? Without a doubt, it has. None of the five quotations used in the frontispiece would be credible "hooks" to gain a reader's attention today. Air power and the Air Force in particular have proven claims that have been challenged since their beginnings. The investments in technology, despite all the hand wringing over complexity and gold plating, did pay off. Air power in all its forms—strategic, tactical, lift, space, aerial refueling, warning, surveillance, interdiction, logistics, close air support, stealth, defense suppression, precision guided weaponry, and air superiority—dominated the conflict. The Air Force stood proud; air power had come of age.

In the final analysis, in its swiftness, decisiveness, and scope, the coalition's victory came from the wise and appropriate application of air power....

Air power found, fixed, fought, and finished the Iraqi military.... This was recognized by Secretary of Defense Dick Cheney who remarked, after the war, that "The air campaign was decisive...."[8]

But were the concerns expressed in the *View* completely invalidated by the triumph of the Gulf War? Did the institutional problems of the Air Force evaporate in the glow of air power's vindication? Few would make the leap. The outside critics of the Air Force fell silent. So did the critics of complex and costly, high-technology weaponry. The "defense reformers" turned their attacks away from what the American military was doing wrong and focused, instead, on how fast the "threat" was evaporating and how fast defense expenditures should be reduced to keep pace.[9]

Moreover, not all the lessons of Operations Desert Shield and Desert Storm are so heartening. We are increasingly reminded that:

- Our military virtuosity, including overwhelming air power, did not resolve the enduring regional problem posed by Iraq and its leadership (one of the principal motivations for prosecuting the conflict beyond the defense of Saudi Arabia);

- Not all future wars are likely to be so permissive as to give us six months for building up and training our forces in the theater;[10]

- Not all conflict venues will have the superb base structure of Saudi Arabia for the projection of air power (much of it built beforehand by the Army Corps of Engineers);[11]

- Our air strategy and plans were not immediate or axiomatic consequences of Air Force doctrine, but had to be improvised and "pushed" by the few who had thought beforehand about theater air campaigns.[12]

- Our air power was so overwhelming that the highly praised "strategic" strikes against command and control targets may not have made that much difference on the outcome (even if Iraq had retained its command and control, to have acted upon it, to have moved in response, would have invited even more effective air attacks);

- What our allies appear to have envied in our forces was not our superb airplanes and precision guided munitions so much as our intelligence, surveillance, communications, and navigation capabilities (not our "shooters," but our AWACS, JSTARS, and extensive space assets);

- We are unlikely ever again to find better circumstances to demonstrate the prowess of air power; and

- History may reveal that Operation Desert Storm was the final expression of an ending military era rather than the prototype for the next one.

Such "revisionist" observations "go with the territory" of the victor when, in war or in philosophy, the outcome is so splendidly one sided. And one of the liabilities given to the victor is the almost irresistible proclivity to prepare to fight that splendid war again.[13]

The Emerging Vision

But the stunning demonstration of air power in Operation Desert Storm was not the only source of change within the Air Force since the *View* was written in 1989:

- New leadership in the Air Force, both in the secretariat and in the chief of staff, was determined to make institutional changes that would better adapt the Air Force to rapidly and drastically changing political, fiscal, threat, and technical environments.

- Even before Desert Storm, the secretariat had published a white paper, *Global Reach—Global Power,* outlining what were perceived to be the unique attributes of air power in the changing world environment.

- Following Operation Desert Storm, the Air Force leadership undertook a radical restructuring of Air Force organization to reduce its headquarters staffs, streamline its chains of command, and vest authority at lower levels.

- And all during this time, the fiscal and personnel projections for the American military were darkening, confronting many people with the prospects of involuntary separations from their service.

These changes, which came at a time of great turbulence and uncertainty about the world's political structure and the nation's economy, were not universally welcomed within the Air Force. They strained existing concerns about career prospects, the fairness of the promotion system, and elitism or favoritism among the traditional Air Force commands. Changes that might have been accepted as appropriate or positive in a more favorable institutional climate were now more likely to be seen as reinforcing or amplifying preexisting complaints and concerns.

Evidence that the Air Force's institutional problems were still festering came in August 1991 with the underground publication of an Air Force "brown paper" satirizing the changes being wrought by the Air Force Chief, General Merrill McPeak. The paper's title, *TAC-umsizing the Air Force: The Emerging Vision of the Future*, was a take-off on an earlier epithet applied when SAC rather than TAC officers dominated the Air Force leadership. As satirical humor, the paper defies fair abstraction, but its thrust has been captured by fascinated observers:

In a biting satire that swipes at Air Force Chief of Staff Gen. Merrill McPeak's sweeping reorganization of air combat units and Washington headquarters, a document circulating inside the service claims the management hierarchy is flavored too heavily with fighter pilot machismo.

Spoofing a purported infusion of Tactical Air Command personnel, the document...tells of the emergence inside the Air Force of the "Manly Man...."

Depending on one's point of view, the well-circulated paper represents "an insurrection" against McPeak's initiatives or poking fun at the boss jibes common to all jobs....[14]

General McPeak's response was in keeping with the comparative openness of the Air Force among the American military services to institutional introspection at all levels:[15]

Far from dismissing the "Brown Paper" as simple high-jinks, McPeak acknowledged during an interview session with reports that *it reflected some discontent with the reorganization....*

"I've been waiting for the Brown Paper to appear. I'm delighted to see that it's there because I was wondering if there was anybody out there listening. They are and they still have their sense of humor," he said.[16]

Several other satirical "guerrilla" papers have been circulating within the Pentagon's air staff: One describes the genesis of the current Air Force reorganization, in biblical style, as a bad idea that became camouflaged by successive levels of bureaucratic polishing as it progressed up the chain of command. Another lampoons officer retention policies in terms of league football teams retaining quarterbacks at the expense of their line and defensive players.

None of these barbs, gripes, and complaints—by themselves—will withstand hostile scrutiny, able defense, or ample counterarguments. As one Air Force general explained, young people in the service are always complaining—he had, too, when he was a young pilot. Like engine knock in a high performance engine, what makes all this noise worthy of attention is not any single "ping," but the damage that may be occurring to pistons, rods, and shafts when engine knock goes unattended too long.

Notes

1. Lt. Col. Stephen Fought (USAF, Ret), faculty, Naval War College, *U.S. Naval Institute Proceedings*, February 1989.

2. Gary Anderson, USMC Battalion Commander, *Washington Times*. (As cited in the original.)

3. Jeffrey Record, *Baltimore Sun*, 8 March 1989.

4. Carl H. Builder, *The Masks of War: American Military Styles in Strategy and Analysis* (Baltimore: Johns Hopkins University Press, 1989), 82.

5. See Chapter 23 of this analysis.

6. One of the authors of the original has reviewed the abstract to ensure its fairness as to content and tone.

7. The reference to mythology is poignant, given the title of this analysis.

8. Richard Hallion, *Reaching Globally, Reaching Powerfully: The United States Air Force in the Gulf War, A Report* (Washington D.C.: Department of the Air Force, September 1991), 52, with the quotation referenced to "Meet the Press," CBS News, 14 April 1991.

9. See, for example, David H. Hackworth, "Amputation, Not Pedicure," *Newsweek*, 9 December 1991, 35.

10. General Merrill McPeak, Air Force chief of staff, put it this way: "Let's face it. We never came under significant attack. We really don't know whether the command structure was really tough enough, durable enough, to really survive really difficult combat conditions...." Those observations are quoted by Tony Capaccio in "USAF Chief Pans War's Command Chain," *Defense Week*, vol. 12, no. 49, 2 December 1991, 1.

11. Some of the facilities were brand new. There were instances where the arriving American personnel found themselves unwrapping new equipment they found in place before they could put the facilities into operation for the first time.

12. One Air Force general told me that the air campaign planning was a distressingly close thing: At the very beginning of Operation Desert Shield, the Tactical Air Command was prepared to wait on the theater ground commander to define his ground plan so they could, in turn, develop their corresponding plans for his air support. At the same time, the Strategic Air Command was prepared to carpet (and obliterate) any designated area of Iraq (or Kuwait) with bombs. That was pretty much the extent of the tactical and strategic thinking in the principal combat commands of the Air Force. Fortunately, we had the time so that such reflexive reactions could give way to a more thoughtful process of air campaign planning.

13. Force levels are already being defended in terms of the ability to undertake another contingency like Operation Desert Storm. That is more than a conveniently familiar reference point, considering one never heard a defense of military force levels in terms of their being able to undertake another contingency like Vietnam.

14. Tony Capaccio, "'Brown Paper' Satire Pans McPeak Initiatives," *Defense Week*, 30 September 1991, 3.

15. Builder, *The Masks of War*, 104, 105.

16. Tony Capaccio, "McPeak Welcomes 'Brown Paper' Barbs," *Defense Week*, 5 October 1991, 5 (emphasis added).

2

Is There a Problem?

Metaphor [is seen by most scientists] as a pejorative term, something inexact and therefore unscientific. In truth, real science is riddled with metaphor. Science grows from imaginary models in the mind and is sharpened by measurements that check the fit of the models with reality.[1]

Despite the 300-year effort...to confine them to the English classroom, metaphors are suddenly inescapable in technical prose.... Metaphors survived...if for no other reason than scientists, like the rest of the world, think in them.[2]

Clearing Off the Coffee Tables

We all know that our perceptions of problems are drawn from much more than objective facts or analysis. Facts are always subject to interpretation or a larger context. Analyses can be selective in their purposes and in their use of evidence. I had this brought home to me most dramatically in an experience, which I remember as "clearing off the coffee tables."

A colleague and I spent 1981 working with the government agency responsible for controlling air pollution in the Los Angeles basin, trying to help them formulate a new strategy after they had exhausted the one that had launched their agency 30 years earlier.[3] The first step in thinking about a new strategy was to have a broad understanding of the air pollution problem—not just in scientific or statistical terms, but how the problem was *perceived* by those who were concerned with its consequences and control. That meant talking to a lot of people—about a hundred interviews, as I recall—who had informed, but diverse viewpoints and interests in air pollution control. After the first dozen or so interviews, it was apparent that the views were polarized:

- Some believed that the air pollution problem in the Los Angeles basin was highly exaggerated. To be sure, smog was a public nuisance, like a smelly meat packing plant. It might make the eyes water; but people who complained of health problems were probably overly sensitive or in a minority that would complain no matter where they were. The problem should be treated as a public nuisance and abated through reasonable regulations.

- Others believed that air pollution in the Los Angeles basin was an immediate danger to life and health. In their view, people were dying every day in Los Angeles due to its polluted air; but the doctors writing the death certificates didn't have the courage to write in the cause of death as smog. The problem should be treated as a threat to public safety, worthy of control by all the emergency powers of government.

While there were still others with views in between these extremes, the distance between these two was so great as to beg some understanding of their coexistence by people who had access to the same information. After the first few interviews revealed these extremes, we began collecting the evidence offered in support of these views. Surely, if a person of one extreme view was confronted with all the evidence and arguments collected from those at the other extreme, we should be able to see some movement or adjustment; perhaps, (a naive thought) we could even draw these disparate views closer together.

After collecting evidence and arguments from both extreme views, we were ready to test our theory. When we found, during the course of an interview, a person holding views close to one of the extremes, we would explain that our interviews had, of course, exposed us to people who held quite different views of the problem. Would they be willing to comment on some of the evidence and arguments offered by those who differed? Without exception, they were most willing, even eager to take on the opposition.

Since many of these interviews were conducted in homes or in gracious office settings, I have the visual recollection of the evidence or arguments being laid out on or over coffee tables. We would lay out on the table from our collection what we thought was the best case for the opposing view in the form of a dozen pieces of evidence or argumentation. These pieces might include clinical evidence, research experiments, tests, comparative data, analyses, and closely reasoned theories. Then, the person being interviewed would rise to the challenge and paw through to the collection on the table. Piece by piece, each item would be picked up, examined, and demolished or dismissed. Not one piece would be left.

When the table had been figuratively cleared, we would ask the person being interviewed to fill the coffee table with their evidence and arguments. Again, they would do so with alacrity. Not only did it give them an opportunity to make their case, but it also gave us the pieces of evidence and argumentation that we needed to fill the coffee table for someone of the opposing view. What we took from one coffee table, we put in our figurative wheelbarrow, to be trundled to the next coffee table, where it was dumped out, only to be dismissed and demolished with ease. This clearing of the coffee table was repeated so many times, by so many reasonable and well-informed people, that it had to be taken into account in the design of strategies for air pollution control.

The lesson I learned from these interviews was not that people could be polarized in their views; I knew that going in. What I learned is that people of differing views could look at precisely the same evidence, including considerable amounts of scientific evidence, and come reasonably to completely different conclusions. Clearly, more scientific evidence was not going to change these views; the views could be sustained by the ways in which the ample evidence could be interpreted—accepted or dismissed.

> We have found…different views of the problem held and articulated by very well informed, intelligent, and responsible people…. When we see how they interpret and reconcile the commonly available data and arguments with their individual convictions and values, we see little prospect that those views will change simply because of additional data or arguments of like kind. Their views seem to be driven as much by privately held values as by the ambiguous evidence.[4]

However both sides in this controversy were calling for more scientific tests and analyses. What they were able to do with the existing evidence strongly suggested that they could assimilate any new data and still retain their views. More scientific evidence might have swayed some of those whose views were not so highly polarized, but I am not even certain of that modest benefit.

Alternative Views

Applying that lesson to the issues raised in *A View of the Air Force Today*, I am sure there is some polarization of views within the Air Force about the nature and severity of the institution's problems:

- Some believe that the Air Force is not facing any extraordinary institutional problems beyond those faced by the other services at this time. These are tough budgetary times for the entire American military. The American culture has changed; and the attitudes and values of those in the Air Force will naturally reflect those changes. Young people have always expressed concern (griped or groused) about their institution and its leadership. The problem, if there is one, is not significant or unique within the Air Force.

- Some believe that the Air Force, as an institution, is in trouble and needs to find and take corrective actions to ensure its future viability. The Air Force is losing its competitiveness, its principles, and its sense of direction. Many of the nation's leaders may no longer understand or appreciate the relationships between air power and U.S. national security.[5] Air Force people are increasingly favoring their own careers and interests over that of the Air Force mission or institution. These problems are more severe in the Air Force than in the other services; and in these tough times, the Air Force could be severely hurt.

Although I have not conducted anything near 100 interviews with Air Force officers on this subject, I have encountered extreme views and the same clearing of the coffee tables. From my prior experience with views about air pollution, I am convinced that the presentation of additional evidence or argumentation will not change those views. Those views come from deeply held perspectives of the world, how the world works, and values much more than they do from objective evidence. Although that admission may sound unscientific, such contradictions are the norm when science and policy meet.

Therefore, the hypothesis developed in this analysis proceeds not from generally accepted facts but rather from the following three premises of faith:

1. That the Air Force may, indeed, be facing some serious institutional problems;

2. That some of these problems appear to be unique to the Air Force among the American military services; and

3. That these unique problems deserve a better understanding so that we have a basis for debating or undertaking proposed actions.

I do not think these three premises can be proven to the satisfaction of those who are skeptical of them. *The Icarus Syndrome* is simply not their coffee table.

Nevertheless, I have learned that opposing views must be recognized and respected. If those who do not accept the premises of *The Icarus Syndrome* are even to entertain—let alone consider—the ideas and arguments of this analysis, they must first be recognized and their views given some standing. Here are some alternative interpretations of the evidence that they might have laid out on their coffee tables:

- If there was a problem of confidence, it was dissolved by the experience of Operation Desert Storm. Whatever the questions about the decisiveness of air power before, whatever the doubts of the military reformers about performance of the American military, they were completely dispelled by the story of Operation Desert Storm. There has been a complete turnaround in the confidence of the Air Force, the American military, and the American public's attitude about the military.

- If the Air Force has an institutional problem, it won't be made better by wallowing in it. The more the Air Force questions its purpose or its effectiveness, the more it will sap its own confidence and make its concerns into a self-fulfilling prophesy. What is needed is not more questioning or analysis, but pride in, and dedication to, the institution.

- The entire nation is caught up in a self-induced crisis of purpose and vision. The "vision thing" has become an national pastime. This is a fad, like the "yuppies," that will pass when economic times change again. If everything started going well for the nation and its institutions, including the Air Force, all this noise about vision and purpose would be quickly quieted.

- The Air Force, as the newest of the American military services, is going through its first identity crisis and transformation—something the other services have gone through several times, given their four-times longer histories. The Navy has gone through periods where its bureaus were corrupt and it would have been hard pressed to put a seaworthy ship into battle. The Army has also gone through tough times, the last being in the wake of the Vietnam War. The Air Force will survive this and come out the better for it.

- The Air Force, as with all of the American military institutions, is a reflection of the American society and its values. Those are changing, not always and everywhere for the best, and some of the problems of the American society are manifested in the Air Force today in such complaints as careerism, selfishness, impatience, self-gratification over altruism, etc. They will get better or change, if and when the American society gets better or changes.

I find elements of truth in these and other arguments or viewpoints. They have plausibility and they point in the direction of the obvious; they are not counterintuitive. The same can be said for the polarized arguments about air pollution in the Los Angeles air basin: For some, air pollution is a nuisance; for others it is a hazard. The pertinent question is not which argument is right—several may have truth—but what are the implications if they were right? Most of the alternative hypotheses listed above imply leaving the institution alone because there is nothing wrong with it, it can only be made worse by meddling, it is already better, it will get better on its own, or it will get better along with the American society or economy. In other words, their implications for intervention are modest, passive, or proscriptive.

The premises of *The Icarus Syndrome*, by contrast, are that the problems of the institution are serious, unique only to the Air Force among the American military institutions, and need to be understood if they are to be wisely corrected. If accepted, they urge informed intervention. Thus, what separates the *Icarus* premises from the alternative views is not the certainty about which premises are right or wrong, but which premises will require affirmative, informed intervention. Intervention is not necessarily to be preferred; but, if required, it needs to be planned and executed competently like surgery. This analysis is offered in that spirit—not so much to prove which diagnosis is right—but to carry the diagnosis that calls for informed intervention through to its logical conclusions of a prescription and prognosis. As with the problem of air pollution in the Los Angeles air basin, the indicated prescription may be one that would not harm the institution regardless of which diagnosis is right—or if all diagnoses have some merit.

Thus, I hope that all who are concerned about the future of the Air Force as an institution will entertain *The Icarus Syndrome* for the time it takes to understand the thesis and its implications, whether or not they have made up their minds about the sources and solutions for their concerns. They can then decide whether the proposed cure for *The Icarus Syndrome* is unsuitable for their concerns or is a healthy regimen for any institution in these difficult times.

Recently, while discussing the troubles of another institution with an organizational psychologist, I tried to put the scope of its problem in some perspective: I offered my estimate that those who were really unhappy with the institution's leadership might be a minority, perhaps only one-third of the staff. The psychologist raised his eyebrows at my denigration of the problem. He said, from his experience, an organization could be in serious trouble even if only a small fraction of the staff was dissatisfied.

A few weeks later, I had the opportunity to relate the conversation to a retired flag officer, expressing my surprise at the psychologist's alarm. The officer confirmed the psychologist's view from his own experiences. When a military unit in his service appeared to have personnel problems, a team of outside experts would come in and canvas everyone in the unit and then provide feedback to the commanding officer. Their rule of thumb was that even ten percent discontents could mean that the commanding officer had a real problem.

If those judgments are correct, then I am certainly willing, from my conversations with Air Force people at all levels, to argue that the Air Force faces a problem which is more than fiscal or common to all the services. It is a problem that could be given many labels—a problem of morale, spirit, vision, heart, soul, direction, purpose, etc. Getting my arms around that problem and putting a label on it is a substantial part of what this analysis is about.

A Basis for Optimism

Over the past several years, in my conversations with both Army and Air Force officers about the prospective development of new visions within their respective institutions, I have offered the following contrasts between the two institutional problems:

- The Army has a vision, but it is more out of step with the changing times. On the other hand, the Army has a longer, sounder heritage available which it can draw on to formulate a new vision.

- The Air Force has lost its sense of vision, but it has a strong affinity toward re-establishing one. More importantly, the Air Force has a better institutional culture for debating these issues at all levels.

Although several institutional observers have described Air Force officers as being less intellectually inclined than those of the other services (some critics have even used the term "anti-intellectual"), I think the term has been misapplied. Air Force officers may not be any more *academically* tolerant or broad as those in other services, but I have found them to be intensely intellectual about their business. I define an intellectual as one who likes to play with ideas, who is comfortable with ideas, even radical ideas. Indeed, I have previously observed that

> the Air Force, consistent with its reverence for technology, has always been the most comfortable of the three services with analysis. The Air Force has relied on analysts from its inception to support operational, developmental, and acquisition decision making at high levels. The airplane, the focal instrument of the theory of air power and independent air forces, was itself conceived and born by means of ...analyses ....
>
> What separates the Air Force from its sister services is how it regards analysis. Air Force officers, as members of an institution whose faith rests on theory and technology, are accustomed to dealing with analysis on every aspect of flight and the application of air power; supporting decisions with analysis is quite natural. Most senior Air Force officers are consumers of, even participants in, the analyses that support internal decision making. Thus, analysis...is often regarded as the most effective medium for debate within the Air Force itself....[6]

I am optimistic because I think this analytical culture—and the intellectual culture it fosters—gives the Air Force a medium to efficiently exchange ideas about the Air Force's institutional problems and their resolution. Whatever the nature and severity of the Air Force's institutional problems may be, it is better equipped with the intellectual tools it needs to expose and resolve them than any of its sister services.

Notes

1. James Lovelock, "Planetary medicine: Stewards or partners on Earth?" *Times Literary Supplement*, 13 September 1991, 7.

2. Anne Eisenberg, "Metaphor in the Language of Science," *Scientific American*, vol. 266, no. 5, May 1992, 144.

3. This research is described by Carl H. Builder and Morlie H. Graubard in *A Conceptual Approach to Strategies for the Control of Air Pollution in the South Coast Air Basin* RAND, R-2917-SCAQMD/RC, (Santa Monica, CA: RAND, September 1982).

4. Ibid. 14.

5. At least to the degree that the Navy has been able to imprint the relationships between naval power and the security of maritime nations upon the American political consciousness. I am indebted to David Ochmanek for this point.

6. Builder, *The Masks of War*, 104, 105.

3

The Icarus Syndrome

Dædalus: a mythical Greek architect and sculptor, who was said to have built, among other things, the labyrinth for King Minos of Crete. Falling out of favour with Minos, he fashioned wings of wax and feathers for himself and for his son Icarus and escaped to Sicily. Icarus, however, flew too near the sun, and his wings melted; he fell into the sea and drowned. The island on which his body was washed ashore was later named Icaria.[1]

Losing the Bubble

Several Air Force personnel who are worried about what is happening to their institution have phrased their concerns to me in the question, "How did we lose the bubble?" Although "the bubble" can be taken as a reference to several different things, all of them imply an indicator of orientation or direction—like the bubble (hemisphere) of visibility from the cockpit, the spirit bubble in a navigational sextant to indicate vertical, or even the bubble in an ordinary carpenter's level. They could have just as well asked, "How did we lose our bearings?"

Metaphors are attractive in circumstances such as these because it is difficult to name precisely what is missing or even to prove that anything is missing. If there is a loss of something, is the loss just in the sense of aim or direction, as provided by a compass? Or, is the disorientation greater and more urgent, such as with the loss of a basic flight control instrument? The risks are quite different. Without a compass, one might lose the way, fail to find the objective, or not reach the destination. Without a basic flight control instrument, such as a turn-and-bank indicator, the pilot risks losing control of the airplane and crashing.

Not everyone, of course, in or out of the Air Force, perceives that the institution is in trouble. For some, the instruments appear to be about normal, the bubble is in sight, and nothing more than a little trimming of the controls is needed. For others, the flight is very bumpy right now, sometimes even disorienting, but it is only because of the weather outside. Nothing is intrinsically wrong with the institution; these are rough times, but they, like the weather, will pass if the Air Force stays steady on its course.

There are too many to ignore, however, who are genuinely concerned about what is happening to the Air Force, as an institution and from within. Their concerns have to do with the vision of the institution, its sense of identity and purpose, its values, and the dedications and loyalties of its personnel. These concerns imply that something intangible has changed within the Air Force, that the change is unfavorable, and that it is affecting the institution's ability to cope effectively with an adverse external environment. That adverse external environment is more than declining resources; it is also declining public appreciation for what the Air Force offers the nation besides pleas for more of its newest "toys." These concerned people seem to be saying, "Yes, these are rough times, but, if we had the bubble in sight, we would know how best to navigate this thing through the storm and into much better air."

Any or all of these views of the Air Force may be correct, from some aspect. Arguing which is more correct may be less useful than thinking about their separate implications.

- If it is just a weather problem, then the focus of the institution should be on the externalities: the changing world which the Air Force must confront in the threats and in the economic, technological, and social enviroments at home and around the world. This demands that the pilot's head be up and looking outside the cockpit to skirt the thunderclouds and reach the clear patches above or below.

- If the bubble has been lost, however, the pilot's eyes belong inside the cockpit, on the instrument panel, until control has been recovered. The focus of the institution should be on the internalities: its goals and priorities, morale and spirit, values and doctrine. With the aircraft under basic control, the weather can be more effectively navigated.

It is obvious that both internal and external factors could pose simultaneous problems for the Air Force at the present time. For a pilot, alone, the question would be, "Which is the more important or urgent in demanding my attention?" However, that question may not be pertinent for cockpits with several crew members or for the Air Force as an institution, where both the externalities and internalities, both the weather and the instrument panel, can be addressed simultaneously. That said, two questions remain:

1. Will both be adequately addressed? Is it easier or more natural to watch the weather rather than the instrument panel?

2. Is institutional introspection more destructive than constructive at this time? Is watching the panel more likely to lead to vertigo than to recovery?

These two questions call for judgments; and it is those judgments that form the premises behind this enterprise:

- The Air Force, as an institution, has developed some internal problems that are adversely affecting its ability to deal effectively with increasingly severe external problems.

- The Air Force's abilities to address its external problems are considerably more developed and routinely applied than those for its internal problems.

- The Air Force will benefit more from addressing its internal problems than it would from ignoring them. Indeed, if the Air Force can "find the bubble" again, it will not only be a much more comfortable airplane to be in, but it will be much easier to navigate through the present rough weather.

Finding the bubble implies something specific that was lost from sight. *I believe the directional bubble was the concept of air power. It wasn't lost, it was abandoned.*

Devotion to Means or Ends?

The theory of air power—the idea of aviators unified in a cause much larger than themselves—was originally conceived around the airplane as a new means to broad and important ends. The theory began with the advent of the airplane as a practical way to provide two important qualities in warfare—speed and vantage point above the ground—and in two traumatic aspects of World War I:

1. the ghastly carnage of stalemated trench warfare on the grounds; and

2. the terrifying bombing of England from the air, first by zeppelins and then by Gotha bombers.

The idea was that air power could be employed, not just as an adjunct to land or sea warfare as conceived by the armies and navies, but as an independent force to bypass bloody, costly and often indecisive engagements by striking directly, quickly, and decisively at the strategic heart of the enemy—the enemy's war-making capabilities. To do that, two additional things loomed as prerequisites:

1. wresting control of the air from the enemy; and

2. wresting control of the airplanes from the land or sea warfare commanders.

Both the control of the air and the use of the air to strike at the heart of the enemy would require fleets of superior airplanes. These prospects presented an opportunity for military aviators, and this idea became their cause.

Whether or not the theory was correct or valid has been in dispute from the very beginning—particularly its claim to decisiveness in war. Even among the military aviators, there were those who doubted that air power could always be used with decisive effect. Even among those who subscribed to the decisiveness of air power, there were some who argued that control of the air could not be achieved quickly by bombers alone but would require a prior battle among opposing fighter or "pursuit" planes. These arguments continue to reverberate today and cannot be disposed of here. One can be skeptical of the validity of the theory or its claims and still marvel at the role it played in history and, more generally, at the power of theories in the evolution of human institutions. Darwin's theory of natural selection and the evolution of species remains disputed; but its significance in the development of the natural sciences and some religions can not be doubted. The validity of air power theory is not the issue examined here; it is how a theory of air power evolved and was used to build and sustain a military institution.

A theory of air power in some form may well have been inevitable, but it could have taken a different form; and for the Germans, with different experiences from World War I, it did. The Germans saw air power as a critical adjunct to land warfare, with local control of the air as a necessary means for conducting land operations. It was the British and Americans who found the concept of victory through independent and strategic employment of air power so compelling. And the development of aircraft in those three countries during the period between the two world wars reflected these differences.

The air power theory was, like most successful ideas, appealing to both its sellers and buyers. Indeed, most means are sold on the basis of their claimed ends, even though the seller's vested interests are often mostly in the means. We even sell ourselves on things, such as a new car, on the basis of ends, such as saving the money "wasted" on repair bills for the old car. If one wants to hear the best arguments couched in terms of ends, go first to those with the greatest vested interest in the means; they are the lightning rods for the articulation of ends served by their means.

For the most part, the sellers of the air power theory were aviators, who were, understandably, always more interested in means (the airplane) than the ends (war). They thought the leverages claimed for air power— speed and vantage point—were uniquely embodied in the airplane; if one accepted the theory and its ends, the airplane was the *only* means for fulfillment of its ends. Therefore, they could afford to sell the theory in the terms of its serious ends rather than its more joyous means.

The buyers were mostly those who had to support politically and financially the buildup and employment of air power. They were not particularly interested in the means, but in the ends—how wars might be won quickly without the hideous bloodshed often seen in land warfare. Air power promised the ends they sought. Could they doubt the theory when the only thing they were uncertain about, the technical means, were so enthusiastically and confidently endorsed by the experts—the aviators?

The contract, steadfastly pursued by air power enthusiasts on both sides (buyers and sellers), became the basis for the buildup and employment of military aviation and, ultimately, a separate institution devoted to air power and run by aviators. But to sell the theory of air power beyond the airplane enthusiasts (who didn't need to be sold) the aviators had several good reasons for sublimating their deeper affections for the means:

- Devotion to the ends was more altruistic or ennobling than the sheer joy of the means;

- The ends of the theory were more appealing than the means to the public which held the purse strings and would have to send its "boys" off to fight in foreign wars; and

- Since the means were unique (the aviators thought) to the ends, acceptance of the ends would (it logically followed) ensure acquisition of the means.

Until the 1950s, the alternatives to the airplane as means to fulfill the ends of air power—such as dirigibles, blimps, and then helicopters—represented only marginal encroachments in terms of their capabilities. The major threats to the theory were challenges to its basic tenets: that air power could be decisive if wielded independently. Just as the advocates of the theory implicitly challenged the utility and necessity of conventional army and naval forces, its skeptics challenged its claim to decisiveness and, hence, its need for independence.

The experience of World War II did not resolve these differences, even though the protagonists and antagonists claimed that it proved the correctness of their original arguments or positions. But the advent of the atomic bomb at the end of World War II made the debate academic; the validity of the theory was accepted as undeniable in the destructiveness of a few airplanes and their bombs: Air power with such enormous destructive capabilities could obviously be wielded decisively. Therefore, it deserved the stature of an independently wielded force. What the aviators had struggled so hard to achieve had been won for them by the nuclear physicists. Indeed, the atomic bomb went so far in its destructive capabilities as to alarm the aviators by undermining their arguments for maintaining large fleets of airplanes.

Competitive Means for Common Ends

The concept of air power gave aviators and those who supported them—technically, logistically, financially and politically—a unifying sense of purpose and a cause far more noble or altruistic than the aviator's abiding love of flight and flying machines. That concept worked to the advantage of all involved so long as the airplane was the only means for fulfilling that concept. But when other means such as unmanned aircraft, guided missiles, and spacecraft became available, it was the aviators who revealed, by deeds more than words, that their real affection was for their airplanes and not the concept of air power.

The first real challenges to the air power theory, *as originally conceived by the aviators, with the airplane as its unique means for fulfillment*, came out of World War II in the form of Hitler's "vengeance" weapons, the V-1 cruise missile and the V-2 ballistic missile. The Navy and Army immediately began to explore the potentials of these weapons from captured samples after the war. Significantly, the Air Force did not; it saw its future in manned jet aircraft carrying the atomic bomb.

Guided missile enthusiasts collected together within each of the three services, just as the aviators had in the Army and Navy almost a half century earlier. And just as the aviators had been treated as rambunctious minorities outside the mainstream of their parent services, the guided missile factions, too, with their often exaggerated claims of the coming revolution, were tolerated more than accepted within their services.

With German rocket scientists as its eager vanguard, the Army pursued the development of ballistic missiles, although the Germans still had one eye on going into space—as they had from their beginnings at Peenemunde. The Navy pursued cruise and ballistic missile applications for submarines and surface ships before discovering a most felicitous marriage of the solid-propellant ballistic missile and the nuclear-powered submarine. The Air Force missile enthusiasts explored a number of applications for cruise and ballistic missiles, but found nothing so revolutionary or effective as to threaten the mainstream of the Air Force in their perception of the primacy of the airplane.

Soviet rocket developments, particularly the orbiting of the first space satellite changed everything. What had been a side show for the three services suddenly became the main arena. The Army, by virtue of the space orientation of its German scientists, had the initial advantage in launching the first American satellite and subsequently provided the cadres who formed the American space program. Under urgent demands to develop medium range ballistic missiles, the Navy found a home for its Polaris program, while the Army and Air Force battled each other for the land-based missile, with their Jupiter and Thor programs. The Air Force Atlas intercontinental ballistic missile program went from the back burner to the front. The next ten years would see the guided missile revolution.

The advents of guided missiles—cruise and ballistic—and space satellites posed significant new capabilities to displace the airplane as the principal means to fulfill many of the ends of air power. Indeed, many of those outside aviation, in politics and the public, who had previously embraced the air power theory for its ends rather than its means, seized upon guided missiles as potentially superior to the airplane for the pursuit of many of the ends they sought.

The concept of air power had, from the beginning, been a means to ends; but it offered different ends for different interests. For its political supporters, it was a means promising to avoid the hideous casualties of stalemated land warfare. For the aviators, those perceived political ends provided the means for securing the fleets of aircraft they wanted so much as ends in themselves. These were symbiotic interests, joined in the means and pursuing high ends that could be comfortably shared in words, even though the aviator's deepest, unexpressed affections were for the means more than the political ends. The symbiosis ended when competitive means for the same high ends appeared; and the aviators were forced to choose between means they had so long cherished and the ends expressed in the concept of air power.

Fateful Choices

The breakdown of the symbiosis was not deliberate or sudden but intuitive and incremental. Although subtle and gentle, the change was detectable, particularly by those who felt injured—the groundlings who were advocating alternatives to the airplane. Like a child who can sense the slightest favoritism of a parent toward a sibling, the groundlings quickly recognized that the aviators who ran the Air Force were really more faithful to airplanes than they were to the concept of air power which could now be served by alternative means. The missile and space advocates, like the aviators before them, had found new means to the old ends of air power, only to find that the institutional leadership was devoted to the old means more than the old ends. The new means would be accepted, but clearly not favored within the institution. The groundlings must have felt much like Andy Rooney did about CBS News when new management revealed greater devotion to the "bottom line" than to the traditions of a news organization: "I think a great many of us are feeling we are loyal to something that no longer exists, and it makes us feel foolish."[2]

Confronted with a significant challenge to the primacy of the airplane within the logic of their own theory of air power, the aviators running the Air Force did two things they did not really want to do:

1. They accepted guided missiles and space satellites as alternative means to some of the broad and important ends of air power; and

2. They revealed—through their decisions more than their words—that their true affection was not for the theory of air power, but for the airplane.

The consequences of those actions upon their institution were profound. In the absence of a unifying cause, the Air Force began to fractionate into factions devoted to missiles, space, and different kinds of airplanes. The aviators, by right of history and seniority, retained control of the institution; but their evident affection for their airplanes created a caste and, hence, competition among the factions. What emerged was an institution devoted to disparate means more than to unifying ends, with destructive effects upon institutional morale, dedication, and values.

The concept of air power, having been well established by its advocates and the Air Force, did not disappear. The aviators still talked about the concept—airplanes were still one means for fulfilling its ends—but not like they had before. Its articulation was softer and more circumspect because the central role of airplanes was no longer axiomatic; it had to be argued and crafted. Instead of arguing for the superiority of the ends of air power, the aviators found themselves arguing over its means: strategic versus tactical aviation, missiles versus aircraft, manned versus unmanned aircraft, sea versus land basing, space versus air vehicles, etc.

The aviator's original sublimation of their affection for the means—in order to advance the ends of air power—ceased. When they found that the means were not (at least to many) unique to the ends, the aviators shifted from selling the ends of air power to selling one of its means. But they had lost the altruistic or ennobling aspects of their cause and, perhaps equally important, they had lost their appeal to that larger audience which had to be convinced to support their preferred means. They had let the neat package unravel.

It became increasingly obvious that the concept of air power was not the *raison d'être* of the Air Force, it was airplanes and flying. Once the concept of air power no longer served as the altar for common worship by aviators and groundlings alike, the unifying sense of mission, purpose, and cause within the institution began to evaporate. People found themselves in an institution because that was the place to do what they wanted to do—to fly airplanes, to work on rockets, to develop missiles, to learn an interesting or promising trade, etc. The institution fractured;

and a hundred mischiefs were turned loose to bedevil the Air Force.

In a sense, the fortunes of the Air Force as an institution rose and fell on its dedication to theory. Air power theory, valid or not, was like the wax that held together the feathers in the wings of Icarus. When the wax melted from the heat of the Sun, the fabric of the wings disintegrated and Icarus fell to his death. When the Air Force leadership abandoned the institution's single unifying theory in favor of the diverse interests of its factions, they allowed the wax to melt. I have called that institutional trajectory *The Icarus Syndrome*. It implies that the Air Force first exploited and later neglected the important ideas that gave the institution cohesive purpose and energy.

What might have been done instead? The aviators might have recognized that technology would eventually provide alternative, competitive means, alongside the airplane, to fulfill the ends of the air power theory. However, they tried to deny that possibility, even as the evidence grew during the 1940s and 1950s. If they had accepted the possibility, before the event, they might have reshaped the institution, the theory, and their affections in several directions. The aviators might have:

- narrowed the ends of the theory and their institution to those which would remain dominated by the airplane as the principal means;

- transferred their affections to the ends of the theory and thereby embraced all new means as they emerged;

- shared the power in the institution with those pursuing other means, thereby keeping the institution's devotion to ends even as they retained their own devotion to narrower means; or

- created some amalgam of the above three in the form of compatible changes in the institution, the theory, and their affections.

Substantiating this thesis of what happened to the Air Force is the principal objective of this analysis. Finding the best way out of the problem, if it has been properly identified, is definitely *not* a burden of the analysis, although I have taken the opportunity to offer the best solution I can find. After developing and documenting the thesis, I have focused on mostly the logic and the parameters—the ingredients and the necessary conditions—for a satisfactory solution, even if those parameters are conflicting or contradictory (as I suspect they may be). The one (if anyone) who solves this problem will undoubtedly have to untie some Gordian knots, pick the winners and losers, and decide who to throw to the wolves. Those choices, of course, are not mine to make.

Notes

1. *The New Encyclopedia Britannica*, Micropedia, vol. 3, 15th ed. (Chicago: Encyclopedia Britannica Co., 1976), 342.

2. As reported by Peggy Noonan in *What I Saw at the Revolution*, 37.

PART II

CREATION

4

The Precursors

From time immemorial man has longed to soar into the sky, but in the distant days...it seemed impossible that this bold dream would ever come true.

And yet, mythology tells us that there was a man who not only believed in human flight but actually achieved it.

His name was Dædalus, and with him flew Icarus, his son.[1]

Air power theory was not the obvious consequence of manned flight or military aviation. It did not spring into the minds of all those who flew. It was not immediately apparent to most military minds that the airplane would revolutionize warfare, any more than it was apparent that the new petrol engines would soon transform war into a clash of machines on land and in the sea and air. Air power theory did not emerge completely and recognizably as such until two decades after the Wright brother's first flight. And during those two decades the roots of air power theory were formed—in the minds of the men who would become its prophets and in the experiences of the publics and politicians who would come to support it.

To understand both the form and significance of air power theory, we need to appreciate the precursors of the theory in people and their experiences. Although air power was a universal theory, it was not universal in its origins; it did not take hold everywhere, even among nations at the leading edge of military aviation. The theory has its deepest roots in Italy, Britain, and America. Only the latter two would transform the theory into practice. And it would take on two distinctive forms in British and American hands because of their different experiences. Yet, by the end of World War II, those two forms would merge into one that would dominate the security structure of the Cold War.

This chapter is the first of a series of ten chapters on the evolution of air power theory and the Air Force. The burden of these historical chapters is to demonstrate the important role of air power theory in the evolution of the U.S. Air Force. That is an argument of my thesis, not a fact; and since history is subject to considerable latitude in its interpretation, I have elected to draw as much as possible on the interpretations of others rather than make my own assertions as to what history reveals.

Several reviewers of this analysis have suggested that I summarize this history more in my own words than by using quotations from others. I have resisted because the interpretations of others collected here are rich in details, perspectives, and contradictions that I wanted to preserve for, and share with, those who might want to analyze the record for themselves. Therefore, I encourage readers to browse through Parts II and III for those historical aspects of interest. Those who are familiar with the development of air power theory and the creation of an independent Air Force may want to proceed directly to Part IV.

In this first chapter, I focus on the experiences and the people from which air power theory sprang. This is not a history of military aviation before Douhet, Mitchell, and Trenchard[2] but of the particular circumstances and events which shaped them and their eventual supporters of air power theory.

Before Theory, Flight

Before there could be a theory of military aviation, there had to be military fliers and aviation. And, in the beginning, the military aviators had other, more immediate concerns besides theory. Michael Sherry describes their precarious situation and pragmatism:

> Among American army and navy fliers...responsible for early developments in military aviation, practical concerns and patterns of improvisation were also dominant. Money was one preoccupation—the army hesitated to fund aviation at all. Staying alive was another—one fourth of the first contingent of flying officers died in training. They crashed too often or left aviation too soon or were too low in rank to worry about doctrine and strategy. Between 1910 and 1912, they were among the world's first aviators to experiment with firing guns and dropping bombs from planes, but they leapt to few conclusions as a result. As for the Signal Corps, interest was limited to the airplane's role in reconnaissance and communications.[3]

Even as the significance of the airplane on warfare began to dawn in some minds before World War I, what should be done or how to do it was not obvious. Americans were certainly as interested as any about aviation and:

> Military aviation was even then a public issue, but political debate did little to clarify conceptions of the airplane's purpose. A struggle over where to place aviation in the military system—one destined to plague military politics for decades—was already beginning. But that struggle did as much to sidetrack thinking about the airplane's purpose as to inform it, partly because it encouraged exaggerated claims from partisans, partly because it focused attention on the organizational forms rather than on the strategic substance of air power.

> True, it was possible to imagine that the airplane would some day be more than "merely an added means of communication, observation and reconnaissance," as the assistant secretary of war characterized it in 1913. By 1916 even the army's general staff, never given to a generous view of the airplane's potential, recommended aviation's eventual separation from the Signal Corps, while Congress was already considering a proposal for a cabinet-level department of aviation. During the war, aviation was finally removed from the Signal Corps' authority and might have become an independent service had the war gone on longer.

> But young airmen like William Mitchell and Henry Harley Arnold, who would later lead the fight for aviation's autonomy, were content before 1917 to remain wards of the Signal Corps, unsure as yet that they had either the doctrine or the political resources to fly on their own....[4]

As a young army first lieutenant, Henry "Hap" Arnold clearly foresaw the possibility of city bombardment from airplanes, but not its significance in terms of air power theory:

> As early as 1913, Arnold began to speculate on the strategic role air power might play in the future. In an article published in the *Infantry Journal* that year, he wrote, "The actual damage that can be done to objects on the ground from an aeroplane is very limited. But if 200 or 300 bombs are dropped in or around a column of troops, there will be some confusion and demoralization even if the damage inflicted is slight." He went on to say, "it is certain, therefore, that some damage can be effected by dropping explosives from aeroplanes." He emphasized that if a powder charge were "dropped into a city it would certainly cause considerable damage." This was the first written analysis, however sketchy, of the role of strategic bombing. [5]

The Legacies of World War I

The experiences of World War I, particularly for the British, gave air power theory both its form and motivation. Air power theory would eventually become one of the war's fractious offsprings, but only a dozen years after the first flight at Kittyhawk, the technology for air power was still too young to make it one of the war's determinants:

> Greater than the impact of air power upon the war was the influence of the war itself on the subsequent development of air power.... During the course of the fighting virtually every theory, attitude, ideal, hope, dream and debate that would mark the course of air warfare a quarter century later had been foreshadowed.[6]

One of the consistent themes to emerge in air power theory was the offensive as opposed to defensive use of aircraft. The importance of the concept of the offensive came early to the Allied airmen, perhaps first to Hugh Trenchard who took over command of the Royal Air Corps in August of 1915.

> Impressed with the military potential of the airplane, Trenchard began formulating the offensive air doctrines that would win him recognition as one of three prophets of air power, with Douhet and Mitchell.[7]

In the fall of 1915, soon after Trenchard took command in France, the Germans effectively challenged the British and French use of the air for reconnaissance over German lines. The German instrument for gaining air superiority was the Fokker M5 *Eindecker,* which incorporated the first successful adaptation of the machine gun synchronized to fire forward through the propeller.[8] After the German Fokkers bested them in the air, Trenchard and the French conferred on how they might react.

> They came at last to the conclusion that the corps aeroplanes could best be protected by what one might call the strategic offensive, that is, by fighting and subduing the enemy airmen far away from the aeroplanes flying in direct cooperation with the army.[9]

The early proponents of air power and, later, air power theory—Hugh Trenchard and Billy Mitchell—were caught up in the idea of the offensive use of air power to break the bloody stalemate of trench warfare. That idea appealed not just to the airmen, but also to statesmen and politicians such as Jan Christiaan Smuts (1870–1950), because it was they who were ultimately accountable to their publics for the costs of the war in treasure and blood. Trenchard was the first of the theorists given the opportunity to convert the idea into practice. The commander of the British forces in France, Douglas Haig (1861–1928) supported Trenchard's ideas for the offensive use of the Royal Air Corps. "One reason why Trenchard enjoyed this support was doubtless his own determination to assist Haig in winning the war by achieving a breakthrough on the western front."[10]

Trenchard's intense belief in the air offensive was his trademark. He insisted that command of the air over the battlefield was possible only through a "relentless and incessant offensive." He thought it best "to exploit the moral effect of the airplane on the enemy, but not to let him exploit it on ourselves.... [T]his can only be done by attacking and continuing to attack." Ground commanders who wanted the RFC merely to hover over their positions, in order to protect them from aerial observation and attack, had taken strong exception to Trenchard's views. General Haig quickly overruled them, and the air offensive became established RFC policy.[11]

The connection between this thinking in Britain and its subsequent appearance in America is not obscure. According to Alfred Hurley, the influence of Trenchard on America's first prophet of air power, Billy Mitchell, began during the war:

The first meeting between Trenchard and Mitchell set the tone for their future relationship. Trenchard, famous for his brusqueness, quickly challenged Mitchell's demands on his time. But Mitchell's reply that Trenchard could well afford to ignore RFC business for a little while because he had organized it so well broke down Trenchard's reserve.... Yet it was Trenchard himself who talked to Mitchell about the role of the air weapon of the present and of the future.[12]

Trenchard must not be included in the "considerable section of British military opinion" whom Mitchell found interested "in a radical air strategy." Only the radicals argued that a strategic bombardment campaign against Germany would end the war more quickly than a continued stress on ground operations. Among these radicals were some of the younger airmen around Trenchard who were trying to interest him in such a viewpoint. At about this time in London, two of the leaders of British aviation, Gen. David Henderson and Sir Sefton Brancker, sought such a policy. The clearest exponent of it, however, was General Jan Christiaan Smuts, the soldier-politician whose report to the British government on strategic bombardment on August 17, 1917, was significant in the formation both of the Royal Air Force and of the nucleus of a strategic bombing effort the following spring.[13]

The fingerprints of Churchill and the Royal Navy are evident in some of the technical and operational groundwork for the offensive use of air power and for Mitchell's subsequent interest, after the war, in demonstrating the use of large bombs against naval targets:

As for Mitchell, his education continued...with a visit to the Royal Naval Air Service Unit at Dunkerque. Its commander was Wing Captain C. L. Lambe....

Lambe and his airmen were primarily engaged in raiding German shipping and attacking the occupied ports on the Belgian Coast. But they also had a more unusual mission—the bombardment of German inland targets. This objective bore the imprint of Winston Churchill's service as First Lord of the Admiralty. In 1915, Churchill had encouraged the naval airmen to attack the sheds housing the airships that were raiding England. A year later, this work temporarily expanded to include strikes on German targets from a base at Luxeuil, in eastern France. The naval airmen were experimenting with bombs and hoped for new aircraft with the range to carry them into Germany. One of their number, Commander Spenser Grey, showed Mitchell their most potent weapon, a 1,650-pound bomb....[14]

Even though the American involvement in World War I was relatively brief, it had a significant and persistent effect upon postwar developments in Army aviation:

World War I established aviation as a combatant arm of the U.S. Army, integrated it with other arms under division, corps, and army commanders, and gave it the mission of supporting ground forces. Aerial operations during the war convinced Army commanders of the value of aviation, and of the need to retain it as an integral part of their forces. This carried over into the postwar organization of the Army Air Service.[15]

The British Experience

If the British were not the only ones to come out of World War I appalled by the bloody carnage of trench warfare, they were the only ones to be traumatized by the effects of air power in the form of strategic bombardment:

Practically every moonless period in 1915 had brought enemy raiders to London and the east coast. Militarily ineffective the zeppelins might be, but their nuisance value could not be ignored. About two hundred people were killed; over one million pounds of damage was caused. It needed only a lengthy bomb-free lull of three months followed by one long night of scattered bombing over the Midlands to alarm the public seriously. This happened...on 31st January, 1916.[16]

If the strategic bombardment had remained limited to the night attacks by zeppelins, its effects might have been soon forgotten, but the Gotha bombers picked up where the zeppelins left off:

The raid [of 13 June 1917] caused minor damage to property, major havoc to morale; nearly 600 people were killed or maimed; none of the fourteen raiders was brought down; and the manifest ineffectiveness of the anti-aircraft defences, to say nothing of the ensuing public outcry, led the Government to react vigorously. Not since early 1916 had this unpleasant aspect of the developing air war been rammed so crudely home.[17]

The psychological shock of this second daylight attack [on 7 July 1917] within a month was prodigious. Alarm and anger re-echoed in the Press, affecting public and politicians alike....[18]

These experiences were to have a profound effect on the way air power would be developed and applied by the British over the next several decades. Because of this "psychological shock" on the British public (and hence the politicians who served it), the perceived effectiveness of aerial bombardment upon cities became exaggerated; and Britain would subsequently emphasize the development of an offensive bomber force rather than a defensive fighter force.

However the diverse experiences of World War I may have inspired the military aviation enthusiasts about their future, two aspects of air power theory had taken firm root in the minds of the British and American leaderships who would build their military aviation establishments after the war:

1. The importance or primacy of the offense in the use of military aviation; and

2. The bombing of cities could have a demoralizing effect upon the populations supporting modern warfare.

Although these two ideas would never become explicit axioms of air power theory, they would lurk behind almost everything the air power prophets and their disciples would do and say for the next four decades.

Notes

1. Menelaos Stephanides, *Dædalus and Icarus*, Stephanides Brothers' Greek Mythology, series B: Gods and Men, no. 11 (Athens: Sigma Publications, 1989), 10.

2. General Giulio Douhet (1869–1930), the Italian prophet of air power; General William ("Billy") Mitchell (1879–1936), the American evangelist for air power; and Air Marshall Hugh Trenchard (1873–1956), air power advocate and institutional father of the Royal Air Force. Clearly, they were members of a common cohort, all born within the span of a decade.

3. Michael S. Sherry, *The Rise of American Airpower: The Creation of Armageddon* (New Haven: Yale University Press, 1987), 10.

4. Ibid., 11.

5. Edgar F. Puryear, Jr., *Stars in Flight: A Study in Air Force Character and Leadership*, (Novato, Calif.: Presidio Press, 1981), 20. The quotes are taken from First Lt. Henry H. Arnold, U.S. Infantry, "Air Corps and War," *Infantry Journal*, vol. 10, (July 1931–June 1941): 229.

6. David MacIsaac, "Voices from the Central Blue: The Air Power Theorists," in *Makers of Modern Strategy*, ed. Peter Paret, (Princeton: Princeton University Press, 1986), 629.

7. Richard P. Hallion, *Rise of the Fighter Aircraft, 1914–1918*, (Annapolis, Md.: The Nautical & Aviation Publishing Company of America, 1984), 15.

8. Ibid., 12.

9. Andrew Boyle, *Trenchard*, (London: Collins, 1962), 154, 155.

10. Alfred F. Hurley, *Billy Mitchell: Crusader for Air Power*, (Bloomington: Indiana University Press, 1975), 26.

11. Ibid., 25, 26.

12. Ibid., 25.

13. Ibid., 26, 27.

14. Ibid., 28.

15. Maurer, *Aviation in the U.S. Army, 1919–1939*, General Histories (Washington D.C.: Office of the Air Force History, 1987), 439.

16. Boyle, *Trenchard*, 160.

17. Ibid., p. 221.

18. Ibid., p. 224.

5

The Prophets

Dædalus stayed and worked in Crete for many years [as the architect for King Minos]. He married Naucrate, a lovely girl from the Cyclades, and she bore him a son, Icarus. But she died when the child was still very young.

From his earliest years Icarus learned to love building, painting and sculpture, and his greatest ambition was to follow in his father's footsteps. When he was coming into manhood he helped in the construction of the labyrinth, the greatest of the works which Dædalus undertook in Crete.

The labyrinth was a building of such complexity, with so many rooms and corridors, that whoever entered it could not find his way out again.

...Dædalus helped Theseus [the great hero of Athens] to overcome the Minotaur imprisoned within the labyrinth, and when the king learned of it his anger was terrible. Overnight, Dædalus found himself a prisoner in the very labyrinth he had created, along with Icarus, his son. Now, the two of them had but one thought in their heads: how to find their way out of the maze and flee from Crete.[1]

The Italian Connection

Before, and immediately after World War I, the Italians played a dominant role in the development of military aviation and in the theory of air power, in part "because their war with the Turks in 1911–12 accelerated their aviation program."[2] More importantly, the Italian

aviation program emphasized offensive force through aerial bombardment. Gianni Caproni is generally

> ...acknowledged as the father of bomber aircraft. His design, manufacture and
> marketing of effective bombardment airplanes over a period of more than a
> quarter of a century earned him great distinction as well as access to high level
> officials in Italy and abroad, including the United States.... He was the first to
> supply planes to the Italian Army in 1911–12. During World War I he built the
> first true bombing airplanes.... From 1916 on, influenced by Douhet and on his
> own, Caproni initiated contact with influential members of the Italian High
> Command, the Bolling Commission and other allied groups to advance the cause
> of strategic bombardment.[3]

Although the prophesy of air power was not singular—there was
remarkable intercourse among the prophets in Italy, Britain, and
America—it was Douhet who first turned the prophesy into explicit
theory and put it into forceful, vivid writing. "Much of what Douhet
propounded was not original with him, but his were perhaps the most
coherent, the most systematic, and the most prophetic airpower writings
of the era."[4] All of the major tenets of air power theory could be found
there:

> At the very least Douhet's arguments in favor of the decisiveness of air attack
> as a means of winning a war, for the establishment of command of the air by air
> attacks against an enemy's airdromes, for "battle cruiser" aircraft that would not
> require fighter escort, and for the development of commercial air transport
> aviation as an adjunct to military aviation proved useful [later] as a corroboration
> of the Air Corps ideas.[5]

This corroboration was not coincidence but rather was evidence that "the
military aviators of the world spoke the same language."[6]

Curiously, the Italian connection and Douhet's role in the development of air power theory were not immediately acknowledged by the
Americans: "In his writings Mitchell never attributed any special
influence on his thought to Douhet, and U.S. Air Corps Officers would
not publicly cite Douhet for several years."[7] Perhaps it was because the
Americans, unlike the traumatized British, faced the problem of selling
air power theory within the context of American altruism and
optimism. Douhet was clearly a scold, and his phrasing might not have
sold air power to an American audience. Douhet was looking ahead
to the needs for aviation in the next war, while the Americans needed
the bloody imagery of the last war to sell aviation for the next war. As
Douhet put it:

In the name of charity, let us forget the last war! Then it was possible to create an air force from the very beginning, by establishing industrial plants and creating the various types of plane. But at that time aviation itself was just being born, and every nation was in the same situation. But in future wars aviation will have grown to adulthood and will know its own value. And that will be a very different matter ....[8]

Indeed, Douhet took a position that was not to appear explicitly in American air power concepts until late in the prosecution of World War II:

It seems paradoxical to some people that the final decision in future wars may be brought about by blows to the morale of the civilian population. But that is what the last war proved, and it will be verified in future wars with even more evidence.[9]

More pertinently, the geographically intimate position of Italy with respect to her adversaries was clearly a part of Douhet's concerns—quite unlike the relative isolation enjoyed by the United States.

The brutal but inescapable conclusion we must draw is this: in face of the technical development of aviation today, in case of war the strongest army we can deploy in the Alps and the strongest navy we can dispose on our seas will prove no effective defense against determined efforts of the enemy to bomb our cities.[10]

Douhet's language was lurid and graphic:

Tragic, too, to think that the decision in this kind of war must depend upon smashing the material and moral resources of a people caught up in a frightful cataclysm which haunts them everywhere without cease until the final collapse of all social organization. Mercifully, the decision will be quick in this kind of war, since the decisive blows will be directed at civilians, that element of the countries at war least able to sustain them. These future wars may yet prove to be more humane than wars in the past in spite of all, because they may in the long run shed less blood. But there is no doubt that nations who find themselves unprepared to sustain them will be lost.[11]

The British Connection

Although Jan Smuts was probably the first visible British leader to recognize the potential of air power, Trenchard can properly be called the father of the RAF—in the same sense that Hap Arnold would later become the father of the U.S. Air Force. Both were institution builders, not just advocates.

Trenchard, an army major general before he was appointed the first Chief of the RAF, was not only convinced that national security required a centralized and independent air arm but he also saw a unique way to prove it to the British public and government—an opening unlike anything available to like minded fliers in the United States. As part of the settlement of World War I, Britain had accepted from the new League of Nations a supervisory "Mandate" for a clutch of new "nations" formed from the territory that had belonged to the Turks. These included Palestine, Transjordan, Mesopotamia, the Lebanon, the Hejaz, and the Yemen, all of which were squabbling with themselves and the outside world as they still do today. In 1920, for example, quelling rebellion in Mesopotamia cost the British 2,000 military casualties and £1,000,000. Trenchard proceeded to demonstrate that the Royal Air Force, even though shrunk from 96 squadrons in France at war's end to only 25-1/2, could handle Britain's problems in the Middle East effectively and at far less cost. He then did the same thing on the troubled Northwest Frontier of India. By 1924, thanks also to a revived role in Home air defense, efforts to disband the RAF had disappeared, and Trenchard was secure in the reputation he carried ever after as its "Founder."[12]

Trenchard believed best way to handle the air arm in World War I was to "...unify all aviation under one commander, to place the minimum number of airplanes necessary for the use of ground troops in action with each army, and to concentrate the bulk of bombardment and pursuit so that he could 'hurl a mass of aviation at any one locality needing attack.' "[13] This concept would re-emerge elsewhere. Although "the two were vastly different in personality and deportment," the influence of Trenchard's thinking was apparent in Mitchell's actions to reserve as much as possible of the air power available to the Americans in a single strike force for the offensive.

Mitchell, U.S. Army Air's top commander in France, managed to achieve aerial unity if not independence when he organized the scattered Air Service units into a single striking force late in 1918. Its cumbersome title, setting an important precedent, was the General Headquarters Air Service Reserve.[14]

But, if Trenchard and Mitchell were concerned about *how* to organize air power most effectively in those early days, Jan Smuts had lept ahead to *what* air power would become."The Smuts Committee in [Britain] found that 'air predominance' would become equally important to sea dominance in the 'defence of the Empire.' "[15] This was much closer to the bottom line of air power theory as it would eventually emerge between the two world wars in both Britain and America.

The Mitchell Legacy

Although clearly influenced by both Douhet and Trenchard, Mitchell appears to have been an advocate and promoter of air power more than theorist or institution builder. "In his early writings...Mitchell had publicized the ideas which would be continued, expanded and refined to become the doctrine of the Air Force."[16]

Mitchell would be remembered most for events—his sinking of the German battleship *Ostfriesland* (1921) as a demonstration of air power for coastal defense and, only four years later, his highly publicized court-martial for insubordination—yet much of his legacy seems to be his zeal for air power and his abiding respect for airmen as the new breed:

> ...Mitchell's fight with the Navy over the battleships was not just a simple fight between the Army, the Navy, and the little Air Force—it was really a battle of ideas, involving air-minded people and non-air-minded people in both services....[17]

To the dismay of many, including both supporters and skeptics of air power, Mitchell went well beyond the theoretical preachings of Douhet. He took his arguments directly to the public by attacking the bureaucracies he perceived as impeding the proper development of air power.

> But he was not vouchsafed a tidy overseas opportunity, as Trenchard had been, to make his case. Instead he plunged into a caustic, continuous attack on both the Army General Staff and the Navy while dramatizing the airplane's potential by his well-publicized feat of sinking captured German battleships. "That man," grumped President Calvin Coolidge, "has talked more in the last three months than I have my whole life." In 1925, after the Navy dirigible *Shenandoah* crashed with the loss of 14 men, Mitchell's tongue carried him too far when he blistered the War and Navy Departments with charges of "incompetency, criminal negligence and almost treasonable administration" of aviation. He was court-martialed for "insubordination and conduct unbecoming of an officer" and resigned on 25 January 1926.[18]

Mitchell's fate may have had a more profound effect than his advocacy on subsequent developments in air power: Two of the American military aviation pioneers who followed Mitchell were clearly chastened by his fate:

> [Ira] Eaker drew important lessons concerning Mitchell and the best way to continue the pursuit of air force independence. About Mitchell, he commented many years later, he:

> invited the court-martial...as one of the methods of bringing before the people at large the neglect of military aviation.... His trial was high-lighted by the suppressions of the General Staff in those days against aviation.... The collapse of his military career was a sacrifice, deliberate, to accomplish his purposes, and he accomplished just exactly the purposes he visualized.... I don't know that it had a favorable effect on public opinion. There wasn't any possibility of anybody doing anything with the General Staff at that time favorable to aviation. They were hostile to it and all its works because it was taking some of their hard-to-get funds for artillery, coast artillery, cavalry, ordnance.... We were looked upon as upstarts, unmilitary, non-military, much too outspoken for our own good and making dramatic claims for aviation and its possibilities—military—that had no basis in fact. The General Staff of that time was absolutely over-age and archaic.... Had it not been for Mitchell and the little group that he inspired and assembled around him, we wouldn't have any aviation of consequence. We'd have had no training or air leaders. We would have had no logical air plans.... Without Mitchell's sacrifice there would have been no military aviation....

But it was many years after the Mitchell trial before the obstreperous "fly-boys," as the General Staff groundlings like to call them, came to accept or reluctantly abide by this *realpolitik*. Arnold was an early casualty. Only a few months after Mitchell's departure Arnold was caught distributing mimeographed material opposing General Staff policies and narrowly avoided a court-martial, being banished instead to an obscure cavalry post in Kansas.[19]

Hap Arnold also "learned his own lesson in military politics in the decade following the Mitchell court martial. He had been exiled to a cavalry post at Fort Riley, Kansas, and served his penance."[20]

Mitchell's New Breed

Mitchell had acted out his image of a new breed of warriors. From the beginning, the military aviators were mavericks:

> In August 1919 the War Department invited from all its general officers comments on the Congressional proposal to create an independent department of Aeronautics. The responses that came in echoed and re-echoed the fundamental propositions set forth by...Pershing...and the other top military brass. There were additional arguments against a separate air service; though rated as secondary points, they loomed large in the minds of the ground generals. Chief among them was the notion of discipline. One respondent wrote:

>> No people in this war needed discipline more than the aviators and none had less. All the attention was given to handling the machines

and but little thought was had of discipline. The result was more or less of a mob with great loss of efficiency, as strict discipline is the foundation stone of military success.[21]

The aviators knew that only those who had the courage to fly could rightfully judge them. In a spirited description of the new class of military aviators, Billy Mitchell tried to establish in the minds of his readers a new community of "air-going people" that only the aviators and younger generation could fully appreciate:

A new set of rules for the conduct of war will have to be devised and a whole new set of ideas of strategy learned by those charged with the conduct of war. No longer is the making of war gauged merely by land and naval forces. Both of these old, well-understood factors in conducting war are affected by air power which operates over both of them. Already we have an entirely new class of people that we may call "the air-going people" as distinguished from the "land-going people" and the "sea-going people." The air-going people have a spirit, language and customs of their own. These are just as different from those on the ground as those of seamen are from those of land men. In fact, they are much more so because our sea-going and land-going communities have been with us from the inception of time and everybody knows something about them, whereas the air-going people form such a new class that only those engaged in the actual development and the younger generation appreciate what it means.[22]

The military aviators could set themselves apart from the "mob" on the ground that had to be prodded into action at the point of a gun.

The air man's psychology of war depends on the action of the individual, he has no man at his elbow to support him; no officers in front to lead him, and no file closers behind him to shoot him if he runs away as in the case in a ground army. The whole system is entirely different from that of troops on the ground where mob psychology has to be used in directing the men in combat.[23]

The intrepid band of military aviators was an exclusive club:

Few people outside of the air fraternity itself know or understand the dangers that these men face; the lives that they lead and how they actually act when in the air.... No one can explain these things except the airmen themselves.[24]

And to make the military aviator's courage explicit for those of faint heart:

In the actual fighting of the aircraft, moral qualities are required that were never before demanded of men. In the first place, they are alone. No man stands at their shoulder to support them. They know that if a flaming bullet comes through their gasoline tank it immediately becomes a burning torch and they are gone. They know that if a wing is torn off there is the same result...that if they fall two hundred or twenty thousand feet, existence is at an end.[25]

But Mitchell pressed the point in an unfortunate expression of elitism and discrimination, which, despite repeated and deliberate claims to the contrary, reverberates with devastating effects even today within the Air Force:

> The work of an air force depends on the men that fly the planes, not primarily on those that remain on the ground.[26]

Notes

1. Stephanides, *Dædalus and Icarus*, 15.

2. Sherry, *The Rise of American Airpower*, 11.

3. Lt. Col. Frank P. Donnini, USAF, "Douhet, Caproni and Early Air Power," *Air Power History*, vol. 37, no. 2, (Summer 1990): 46. The Bolling Commission was created soon after America's entry into World War I for the purpose of establishing objective American goals for military aircraft production.

4. Giulio Douhet, Editor's Introduction, *The Command of the Air*, translated by Dino Ferrari, (Washington D.C.: Office of Air Force History, 1983), vii.

5. Robert Frank Futrell, *Ideas, Concepts, Doctrine: A History of Basic Thinking in the United States Air Force 1907–1964* (Montgomery, AL: Maxwell AFB, Air University, 1974), 35.

6. Hurley, *Billy Mitchell*, 78.

7. Futrell, *Ideas, Concepts, Doctrine*, 21, 22.

8. Douhet, *The Command of the Air*, 131.

9. Ibid., 126.

10. Ibid., 10.

11. Ibid., 61.

12. James Parton, "The Thirty-One Year Gestation of the Independent USAF," in *Aerospace Historian*, (Fall, September 1987), 151, 152. Bruce Hoffman, in *British Air Power in Peripheral Conflict, 1919–1976*, RAND R-3749-AF (Santa Monica, Calif.: RAND, October 1989), 4–35, provides an excellent description of these colonial operations of the RAF.

13. Futrell, *Ideas, Concepts, Doctrine*, p. 11, quoting from Brig. Gen. William Mitchell, *Memoirs of World War I* (New York: Random House, 1960), 103–111.

14. Parton, "The Thirty-One Year Gestation of the Independent USAF," 152.

15. Futrell, *Ideas, Concepts, Doctrine*, 15.

16. *Ibid.*, 30.

17. H. H. Arnold, *Global Mission* (New York: Harper & Brothers, 1949), 100.

18. Parton, "The Thirty-One Year Gestation of the Independent USAF," 152.

19. Ibid., 153.

20. Murray Green, "Hugh J. Knerr: The Pen and the Sword," in *Makers of the United States Air Force*, ed. John L. Frisbee (Washington D.C.: Office of Air Force History, 1987), 101.

21. Thomas H. Greer. *The Development of Air Doctrine in the Army Air Arm 1917–1941* (Montgomery, AL: USAF Historical Division, Maxwell AFB, 1955), 24.

22. William Mitchell, *Winged Defense: The Development and Possibilities of Modern Air Power —Economic and Military* (New York: G. P. Putnam's Sons, The Knickerbocker Press, 1925), 6.

23. Ibid., 160, 161.

24. Ibid., vii.

25. Ibid., 163.

26. Ibid., 31, 32.

6

The Theory

"Slavery is hard to bear," said Dædalus, "but ten times harder for an artist. Yet how can we leave Crete if we can't even find our way out of the labyrinth?"

"Only the birds are free," replied his son. "If we could fly like them, we could escape from here. But, alas, the gods did not give men wings."

"They gave them brains, though, Icarus," replied his father, then suddenly fell silent, wrapped in thought.

"Yes, we have brains," continued Icarus, "but if we had wings, too, how wonderful it would be! We would soar high into the sky, as high as the sun; we would travel like the birds, like the clouds, like the gods themselves."[1]

The Beginnings of Theory

The basic premises of the original air power theory were about the ends of war more than its means. James Fechet, who succeeded Mitchell as assistant chief of the Air Service in 1925, and went on to be chief of the Air Corps (1927–1931), made the distinction between means and ends—and their relative importance—quite clear:

The objective of war is to overcome the enemy's will to resist, and the defeat of his army, his fleet or the occupation of his territory is merely a means to this end and none of them is the true objective….[2]

By separating ends from means and focusing on the ends, air power theory provided the intellectual opportunity to approach the means of warfare from logic rather than tradition. Air power wasn't just a new means for waging war, it could be seen as the most effective means for getting directly to the central objective of war.

Giulio Douhet is generally acknowledged to be the first to advance the air power theory in what he called "command of the air."[3] He posed the first and central premise of the air strategy as an axiom:

> To conquer the command of the air means victory; to be beaten in the air means defeat and acceptance of whatever terms the enemy may be pleased to impose.[4]

To this axiom, he added two corollaries:

1. In order to assure an adequate national defense, it is necessary—and sufficient—to be in a position in case of war to conquer the command of the air.

2. All that a nation does to assure her own defense should have as its aim procuring for herself those means which, in case of war, are most effective for the conquest of the command of the air.[5]

The significance of military aviation in war was not in its enhancement of surface military forces—although it could do that—it was to become the dominant force in war.

> To have command of the air means to be in a position to wield offensive power so great it defies human imagination. It means to be able to cut an enemy's army and navy off from their bases of operation and nullify their chances of winning the war. It means complete protection of one's own country, the efficient operation of one's army and navy, and peace of mind to live and work in safety. In short, it means to be in a position to win. To be defeated in the air, on the other hand, is finally to be defeated and to be at the mercy of the enemy, with no chance at all of defending oneself, compelled to accept whatever terms he sees fit to dictate.[6]

These views would not be foreign to any advocate of air power today.

The primacy of the offense in the air was an integral part of the theory. Douhet said that the nature "of air warfare is offensive...and should be so organized and trained...."[7] The offensive from the air was not to be applied frontally, but selectively, with great care for the ends of war. It is clear that Douhet recognized the logistical nature of modern, mechanized, industrial warfare:

> The maximum returns from aerial offensives must be sought beyond the field of battle. They must be sought in places where effective counteraction is negligible

and where the most vital and vulnerable targets are to be found—targets which are, even though indirectly, much more relevant to the action and outcome on the field of battle. In terms of military results, it is much more important to destroy a railroad station, a bakery, a war plant, or to machine-gun a supply column, moving trains, or any other behind-the-lines objective, than to strafe or bomb a trench. The results are immeasurably greater in breaking morale, in disorganizing badly disciplined organizations, in spreading terror and panic, than in dashing against more solid resistance.[8]

Mitchell joined Douhet by arguing that the defense against aircraft was best waged through offense:

The only defense against aircraft [said Mitchell] is by hitting the enemy first, just as far away from home as possible.[9]

But to bring military aviation to bear effectively in war, aircraft would first have to battle for control of the sky, said the prophets from Italy, Britain, and America:

The purpose of aerial warfare [said Douhet] is the conquest of the command of the air.[10]

[Trenchard's] contention from the beginning had been that air supremacy would sooner or later have to be fought for.... There could be no "standing on the defensive" in the skies. Survival in three-dimensional warfare depended on maintaining the offensive, whatever the odds or the cost.[11]

The principal mission of aviation [said Mitchell] is fighting hostile aviation.... If we give up the air to a foreign power it has been proved during the war that they can cause incalculable damage with their air service alone....[12]

Control of the sky couldn't be accomplished by an "air service" supporting and subordinated to the ground forces. Again, the Italian, British, and American prophets were of one view:

[Douhet said that the] Air Force to do this must be independent....[13]

He [Trenchard] was at one with the joint authors [of the Smuts memorandum which urged a separate Air Force], in accepting without reservation the "almost boundless" potentialities of aircraft as future weapons. Where he disagreed with them was on the expediency of forcing development prematurely, above all through a separate Ministry, at such an hour of acute danger [during World War I].[14]

Therefore [said Mitchell], in order to unite and bring your greatest effect to bear in any one place it is necessary to unite all elements of your aviation at one place where the decision is called for....[15]

And that was exactly what Mitchell had tried to do when he had set up his "General Headquarters Air Service Reserve" force during the war.

Yet the prophets realized that independence did not deny the need for joint operations. Douhet argued:

> To make one [military service] dependent on the other would restrict the freedom of action of the one or the other, and thus diminish their total effectiveness. Similarly, an air force should at all times cooperate with the army and the navy; but it must be independent of them both.[16]

Mitchell used different words, but with the same reasoning:

> [T]he mission of each branch of the national defense must be clearly stated and its powers and limitations thoroughly understood in order to combine its action with the other branches to insure the maximum effect.[17]

The *uniqueness* of air power in striking at the heart of the enemy through the new, third dimension is consistently evident in the theory:

> [F]or now it is possible to go far behind the fortified lines of defense without first breaking through them. It is air power which makes this possible.[18]

> [T]he air has introduced a third dimension into warfare.... Aircraft enables us to jump over the army which shields the enemy government, industry, and people, and so strike direct and immediately at the seat of the opposing will and policy. A nation's nerve system, no longer covered by the flesh of its troops, is now laid bare to attack....[19]

All these arguments were only facets of the air power theory, dressed in the forceful, sometimes lurid rhetoric of the day. What, then, was the essence of the theory in today's language? Air power theory proposed that military aviation had opened up a completely new and dominant dimension of warfare—not just an adjunct to surface warfare—which could produce quick and decisive results in war if exploited through offensive strikes directly at the critical sources of enemy power; but to do those things, military aviation must first be used to control the air and be centrally and independently controlled. That was classical theory—a supposition or conjecture about the relationships between things—in the form, "if this, then that."

The Stirrings of Independence

Even before the arguments for institutional independence would become so evident and divisive, military aviators saw military aviation taking on two important, but different forms or missions.

"Air service" is that part of aviation which works directly with and in conjunction with ground troops, such as observation aviation which regulates artillery fire, conducts Infantry liaison missions, and such other work as is directly connected with ground troops—in other words "service," i.e., "air service."

"Air Force" is that part of aviation capable of independent action without regard to ground operation, such as bombardment, pursuit, and attack. These branches of aviation strike independently at enemy centers such as cities, factories, railroad yards, docks, etc., without regard to location or operation of ground troops. In other words it is a "force" within itself; i.e., "air force."[20]

The theory said that the second part of military aviation was the more significant to the ends of war. More importantly, only that part offered the prospect of independence—in operations and as an institution.

The theory implied an independent air force, but that was easier said than designed or executed. Even Mitchell expressed his qualms:

Air forces are more difficult to organize and put on a sound footing than either an army or navy, because in this newest arm we have no traditions upon which to build except those developed during the war.[21]

The airmen were not alone in their quest for independence. They had developed important allies, probably because their theory of air power spoke to the interests of these allies.

Many, but not all, Army airmen...wanted aviation free from army control, believing that only when divorced from ground forces and given an independent mission would aviation realize its full war making potential. Then, they held, air power would be decisive in warfare. Army commanders clung to their control over aviation, regarding the air arm as just one of several arms comprising a single force to work under a single head toward a single objective. Hence, in the 1920s the War Department vigorously defended the status quo against attacks from airmen *and their allies in Congress and among the general public.*[22]

But the War Department, despite its vigorous defense of the status quo, would end up yielding some crucial ground to the airmen:

Despite the strenuous efforts of aviation enthusiasts to separate aviation from the Army and War Department, the General Staff had retained control over the Air Service during the first half of the 1920s. Having lost part of that power to Assistant Secretary of War for Air Davison in 1926, the General Staff hoped to get it back when he left office. Division chiefs and other General Staff members commonly favored creation of a [centrally controlled] GHQ Air Force. First, however, they wanted to assess the effect it might have. They felt that once established, GHQ Air Force would claim the complete attention of the airmen to the neglect of aviation for direct support of ground forces.[23]

The camel's nose beneath the tent flap was the acceptance by the Army General Staff of the distinction between air service (assigned to ground commanders) and air force (assigned to the command of airmen):

> The composition of [army aviation] changed significantly as emphasis shifted from "air service" (auxiliary to ground forces) to "air force" (a separate element with a separate mission). No one in a position of responsibility in the twenties and thirties—not even Mitchell—challenged the proposition that military aviation consisted of both forms of aviation and...that both were essential. But no consensus existed as to the mission of each, the types of aviation each needed, how total resources should be apportioned between the two, and what form organization should take. In the army reorganization of 1920, the War Department assigned observation, pursuit, and attack [aviation] to ground forces for "air service" in direct support of ground operations. It allocated bombardment aviation to "air force" to work with ground forces or operate as a separate striking force, as directed by the commander in chief in the field. Airmen insisted only observation be designated "air service," and all combat aviation (bombardment, pursuit, and attack) be designated "air force" for independent operations. As a corollary, they would cut back on observation aviation and enlarge the combat air force. By the beginning of World War II, the airmen had gained all these objectives save complete independence.[24]

Once the intellectual separation between air service and air force had been accepted, the rapid evolution of aircraft technologies would favor the air force part of the two because the effectiveness of bombardment aircraft was much more dependent on enhancements in speed, range, and payload than observation aircraft.

> Improvements in aeronautical equipment and techniques during the twenties and thirties made the airplane (particularly the bomber) a powerful weapon, and greatly increased the combat capabilities of the Army's air arm. Army officers in key positions saw these changes taking place. They began to realize air power might be better employed if massed under a single commander rather than dissipated among ground forces. Loath to relinquish control over such a powerful and promising weapon, they created [a centrally controlled] GHQ Air Force as an active component of the Regular Army [on 1 March 1935]. This, as the General Staff hoped, quieted agitation for an independent air force.[25]

The wick on the flame of independence had been turned down for the time being. Any hopes that it might be turned up soon were quickly dashed by President Franklin Roosevelt when he took office:

Denied independence, airmen wanted the power of the Assistant Secretary [of War for Air] strengthened. The General Staff wished to abolish the position that cut into its authority. President Franklin D. Roosevelt resolved the matter when, more as an economy measure than anything else, he left the post vacant after Davison [its first and only incumbent] departed in 1932.[26]

The flame of independence would not burn brightly again in America for another decade, when war would provide the opportunity for its airmen to test their theory of air power.

Dismissing the Defense

If all the prophets of air power theory *emphasized* the offense, Mitchell was the most outspoken in his *dismissal* of the defense available to ground forces.

Any system of defense against aircraft from the ground alone is fallacious and money put into it, if not spent along carefully considered lines, is merely thrown away.[27]

Mitchell's reasoning derived from his consistent theme of airmen as a new class apart from the groundlings who were simply incapable of fathoming the workings or potential of air power.

Ground armies, unfamiliar with the action of air power, are constantly setting up the claim that anti-aircraft artillery is capable of warding off air attack. This is absolutely not in keeping with the facts, and a doctrine of this kind is a dangerous thing to be propagated....[28]

During the past year a great many statements have been made that the anti-aircraft artillery is improving and that the results now would be different from those that occurred during the war. This is most decidedly not the case. The improvements made, which amount to little, are nothing in comparison with the improvements made in airplanes....[29]

A Theory to Build Upon

The early prophets provided a well-formed and articulated theory of air power. It had its roots in Italy, Britain, and America. It was colored by the experiences of World War I—by the carnage of trench warfare and, especially for the British, by the terror bombings from zeppelins and the Gotha bombers. Those experiences provided this theory with motivation (avoidance of bloody stalemates), orientation (the offensive), and focus (the strategic heart of the enemy).

That theory took hold in Britain and America. It didn't need to be sold in Britain because that nation had been doubly hurt—by the loss of a generation of young men in the trenches and by experiencing the terror of aerial bombardment. But it would have to be sold to the American public. Douhet's writings were too tragic and barbaric to do that job, while Mitchell appealed to the dreams and altruism of the American public.

The air power theory of the prophets contained all the seeds for the fruit that was to be harvested over the next several decades: the emphasis on the offensive use of air power, on the battleplane or big bomber, and the drive for institutional independence. Its advocates already exhibited attitudes which would remain its scourge right up to the present: a certitude in the universal decisiveness of air power, a disdain for air defense capabilities,[30] and an elitism among pilots.

From the very beginning, as air power theory first emerged from the minds of its prophets, it seems to have attracted different people for different reasons. It attracted:

- some military professionals who conceived the theory as a more effective way to wage war and to organize its means (Smuts, Douhet, and Trenchard);

- military aviators because it gave a higher purpose to their love of airplanes and flying (Mitchell and his disciples, Spaatz and Eaker);

- many in the public who were dismayed by the bloody stalemate of trench warfare in World War I and who hoped to avoid its repetition; and

- some of those politicians who had to raise the public funds for military forces and who saw in the theory a way to buy defense on the cheap (Roosevelt and Churchill).

These different interests all found a common focus in air power theory—the idea of striking at the heart of the enemy through the third dimension, thereby avoiding the carnage and cost of surface warfare—even though some were attracted by its ends and others mostly by its means. What seems remarkable about this era of air power prophets is not the unanimity of their views in the theory but the *diversity* of interests that found the theory of air power attractive. The prophets had found a theory with broad appeal for British and American audiences who held the purses the airmen needed to tap.

Notes

1. Stephanides, *Dædalus and Icarus*, 15, 16.

2. Futrell, *Ideas, Concepts, Doctrine*, 28, quoting Gen. James Fechet.

3. Douhet, *The Command of the Air*.

4. Ibid., 28.

5. Ibid., 28.

6. Ibid., 23.

7. Ibid., 129.

8. Ibid., 126.

9. Mitchell, *Winged Defense*, 213.

10. Douhet, *The Command of the Air*, 128.

11. Boyle, *Trenchard*, 156.

12. Futrell, *Ideas, Concepts, Doctrine*, 35.

13. Douhet, *The Command of the Air*, 128.

14. Boyle, *Trenchard*, 229.

15. Futrell, *Ideas, Concepts, Doctrine*, 18.

16. Douhet, *The Command of the Air*, 5.

17. Mitchell, *Winged Defense*, 214.

18. Douhet, *The Command of the Air*, 9.

19. Capt. B. H. Liddell Hart, *Paris, or the Future of War* (New York: E. B. Dutton & Co., 1925), 36, 37.

20. Puryear, *Stars in Flight*, 96, referenced to a letter from Maj. Carl Spaatz, A.S., to Gerald Garard, January 29, 1926.

21. William Mitchell. Brigadier General, Air Service, *Our Air Force: The Keystone of National Defense* (New York: E. P. Dutton & Company, 1921), xx.

22. Maurer, *Aviation in the U.S. Army*, 440, (emphasis added).

23. Ibid., 290.

24. Ibid., 441, 442.

25. Ibid., 442.

26. Ibid., 441.

27. Mitchell, *Winged Defense*, 205, 206.

28. Ibid., 206.

29. Ibid., 212, 213.

30. In the beginning of air power theory, during the 1920s and 1930s, the disdain was for *all* forms of air defense capabilities, whether from the ground or in the air—the self-defended bomber was sufficient for the offensive. Today, the disdain for air defenses is more discriminating: Surface-to-air defenses are not as highly regarded as enemy fighter or interceptor aircraft; and bombers may require assistance in suppressing enemy air defenses. Nevertheless, the air offense remains much more highly regarded than air defenses.

7

Prophesy

Dædalus set to work immediately. With great skill and artistry he fitted all together [feathers brought to him by Pasiphae, King Monos' wife], using wax to hold each feather in place. The work was delicate and needed both time and patience, but within a few days the wings had taken shape.

There were four of them, like a bird's wings in every respect, but very much larger, and so beautifully made that even the gods would have envied them.

Using leather straps, Dædalus fastened one pair onto Icarus' arms and shoulders, and then he put on his own.

The time to test the wings had come. Beating his arms up and down, Dædalus rose effortlessly into the air. Icarus did the same, and his wings, too, bore him upwards. All was ready![1]

Selling Air Power

The airmen had a theory, but little more than that. Plausible and attractive as it might be to them, they had no evidence with which to confront their skeptics.

Chief among the many factors preventing airmen from attaining the type of organization they sought was their inability to marshal convincing evidence supporting their views. Neither the World War I experience nor the existing state of technology bore out their assertions concerning air power. So the airmen based their arguments on hopes and wishes, and took their stand on conjecture as to the future capabilities of aeronautical equipment and techniques.[2]

Unfortunately, the audience they had to convince was the Army; and to overcome its skepticism, the airmen would need more than a small measure of public support.

Time and again, the War Department General Staff turned aside the airmen's claims as to the effectiveness of air power by pointing out that "this had not yet been demonstrated." The airmen's efforts to win overwhelming public support proved futile.[3]

The airmen needed resources, but

...working against the airmen was their inability to produce convincing facts to support their views fully.... [W]ith no enemy in sight, and needing proof of efficacy of air power—the nation would not support a powerful United States air force.[4]

In the absence of evidence of the correctness of their theory, the airmen needed some impetus for sponsorship—a desire to believe in the theory despite the absence of evidence—and that would come only when the war clouds gathering over Europe and East Asia could no longer be ignored. Then, many would *want* to believe air power theory, including the most important sponsor of all, the nation's president. General Jimmy Doolittle put it directly: "Basically, the trouble was that we had to talk about air power in terms of promise and prophecy instead of in terms of demonstration and experience."[5]

What the airmen lacked in evidence, they made up for with tantalizing promises of what could be just ahead. Here is how Hap Arnold and Ira Eaker described the future of war in the air from their vantage point in the mid-1930s:

More and more war in the air is becoming a constant threat throughout the world. The Atlantic and Pacific Oceans will shrink in "air-travel size" and present the same flying time and hazard that the Mediterranean Sea and Gulf of Mexico do today. No nation will have but one frontier to guard, for hostile aircraft may approach from any or all directions. Death rays, electric rays for stopping airplane engines, barrages of steel netting, automatically operated anti-air-machine torpedoes, radio-controlled manless fighting planes, gas projectors, all may take their place in the anti-aircraft defenses. The attacking air force may be equipped with planes bearing Diesel engines and thus be unaffected by the electric ray; they may be equipped with radio-controlled bombing planes not influenced by any gas which may be projected into the air; with aerial torpedoes which can be launched from the ground and sent accurately toward their predetermined destinations; or with planes so silent that they cannot be seen or heard on the ground and so will pass overhead at high altitudes and go undetected.[6]

With today's hindsight, some of these visions border on flights of fancy; yet, in them one can see the barest outlines of what we have come to know as air-to-air missiles, surface-to-air missiles, cruise missiles, and stealth aircraft.

Although still limited in scope, the appeal of air power to Americans was in what it promised to *avoid* rather than what it promised to *deliver*:

> Air power derived its appeal by promising to place the glitter of modern technology in service of traditional values, above all the nation's long-standing distrust of standing armies. American security had never been effortless, and especially since the 1890s prominent Americans such as Theodore Roosevelt, moved by visions of empire abroad and unity at home, had forged a stronger army and navy. Mitchell, however, promised something more comforting. Air power, as he usually described it, would provide inexpensive security for a new generation of Americans, leaving them free from militarism and its accompanying evils—taxation, conscription, and tyranny.[7]

The public was clearly drawn into the arguments of the air power advocates and their skeptics. Will Rogers became an early advocate and voice for air power, speaking directly to the public:

> I tell you, any experiment that is being made in the air is not a waste of time or money. Our defense, offense, and all, have got to come from the air.[8]

Or more stridently:

> When we nearly lose the next war, as we probably will, we can lay it onto one thing—the jealousy of the army and navy toward aviation. They have belittled it since it started and will keep on doing it till they have something dropped on them from one, and even then say it wasn't a success.[9]

Rogers was probably making an oblique reference to the Navy's reactions to Billy Mitchell's several demonstrations (1921–1923) of air power against Navy ships, which the Navy had predictably belittled.

The uniqueness of air power—its ability to strike through the third dimension—was a central aspect of its theory and its marketing. Operating through the third dimension was not just novel—a new and strange dimension for military operations—it promised to transform the concept of national frontiers and the security they had heretofore provided.

> In a trice, aircraft have set aside all ideas of frontiers. The whole country now becomes the frontier and, in case of war, one place is just as exposed to attack as another place.[10]

This uniqueness of air power posed special significance for Americans, who, for the first time would be vulnerable even within their vast interior spaces. As Will Rogers put it:

In the next war, you don't want to look out, you want to look UP. When you look up and see a cloud during the next "War to end Wars," don't you be staring to admire its silver lining till you find out how many enemy planes are hiding behind it.[11]

Isolationism, a strong theme in American politics following World War I, would soon become untenable because of air power, Mitchell argued:

The coming of aircraft has greatly modified this isolation [of the United States] on account of the great range and speed which these agents of communications are developing.... The vulnerability of the whole country to aircraft as distinguished from the old conditions that obtained when the frontiers or the coast had to be penetrated before an invasion of the country could be made, has greatly interested the people of the nation.[12]

Mitchell stated the obvious, if not the relevant, when he asserted the vast dominions of the air—a theme that the Navy would echo 60 years later in advancing its "maritime strategy."

[A]s air covers the whole world there is no place that is immune from influence by aircraft.[13]

Moreover, it might not take much of that unique power to paralyze an enemy nation and, therefore, by implication, a nation like the United States. As Mitchell put it:

For attacking cities that are producing great quantities of war munitions that are necessary for the maintenance of an enemy army and country in case of war, the air force offers an entirely new method of subduing them. Heretofore, to reach the heart of a country and gain victory in war, the land armies always had to be defeated in the field and a long process of successive military advances made against it. Broken railroad lines, blown up bridges, and destroyed roads, necessitated months of hardships, the loss of thousands of lives, and untold wealth to accomplish. Now an attack from an air force using explosive bombs and gas may cause the complete evacuation of and cessation of industry in these places. This would deprive armies, air forces and navies even, of their means of maintenance.... So that in the future the mere threat of bombing a town by an air force will cause it to be evacuated, and all work in munitions and supply factories to be stopped.[14]

The "mere threat" might be enough. Thirty years later, the threat would be the centerpiece of the mutation of air power theory as embodied in the theory of nuclear deterrence.

The advocates selling air power argued that the third dimension of air warfare granted to air forces something that ground and naval forces had never known—a domain where supremacy brings omnipresence and omnipotence:

> Armies on the ground or ships on the water have always fought on one surface because they could not get off it. The air force fights in three dimensions.... No missile-throwing weapons or any other devices have yet been created or thought of which can actually stop an air attack, so that the only defense against aircraft are other aircraft which will contest the supremacy of the air by air battles.... Once supremacy of the air has been established, airplanes can fly over a hostile country at will.[15]

And, lest Americans overlook the significance of air power to their pocketbooks:

> The surface ship, as a means of making war, will gradually disappear, to be replaced by submarines that will act as transports for air forces and destroyers of commerce. The advent of air power holds out the probability of decreasing the effort and expense required for naval armaments, not only in the craft themselves, but in the great bases, dry docks, and industrial organization that are necessary to maintain them. Differing from land armies, which are in a stage of arrested development, navies are in a period of decline and change. The air force is the great developing power in the world today.[16]

Not only would air power relegate the surface forces to secondary roles, it would offer great savings to its owner and impose great costs upon its victim.

> The missions of armies and navies are very greatly changed from what they were. No longer will the tedious and expensive processes of wearing down the enemy's land forces by continuous attacks be resorted to. The air forces will strike immediately at the enemy's manufacturing and food centers, railways, bridges, canals and harbors. The saving of lives, man power and expenditures will be tremendous to the winning side. The losing side will have to accept without question the dominating conditions of its adversary, as he will stop entirely the manufacture of aircraft by the vanquished.[17]

The Dirigible Enigma

The reactions of the early prophets to lighter-than-air (LTA) ships are pertinent to the thesis of this analysis because they offer a view of the air power advocates' deeper interests and motivations. If LTA ships could contribute to striking at the heart of the enemy through the third dimension—as they had against Britain during World War I—should they be included in the aspirations of the air power prophets? Or, was the air power theory only a veneer to justify *winged* military airplanes and flying them? As a window on motives, unfortunately, the airmen's attitude toward LTAs is not all that transparent. The theory and its prophets seem to have supported LTAs, but those who would have to pay for them did not.

Significantly, Mitchell seems to have been a proponent of LTA ships after World War I:

> The development of airships has continued; and it will take its place beside the airplane as a coordinate branch of aeronautics. One cannot do its full work in a military way without the other.[18]

Mitchell described the efforts to acquire one of the German zeppelins for the Air Corps after World War I:

> In the meantime, we had tried hard to get one of the largest Zeppelins in Europe. We had sent Colonel Hensley to Germany to obtain one.... The contract had been concluded, the money sent over, and the work started by the Zeppelin people on a ship for this country, when the work was stopped and the whole proposition halted for several years.... We wished to use the great airships for reconnaissance problems, for transporting goods, supplies, and men, for fighting other airships and as an airplane carrier, that is, equip it with airplanes which could fly away from it and return to it, so that it could go any place over the ocean, launch the airplanes, let them do what was desired, and then have them return.[19]

To be sure, those whose careers were already entwined with the LTAs were more certain and positive about their potential, but they were a minority even among airmen and faced too many obstacles to flourish in the contests over scarce resources:

> The balloon and airship men held great hopes for the future of lighter-than-air aviation for both military and civil uses. Dirigibles looked promising for reconnaissance, bombardment, and transportation. But the dirigible's slow speed, poor maneuverability, and high vulnerability to both enemy action and natural elements offset advantages of range and carrying capacity. *The lighter-than-air enthusiasts found little support from other Air Service members, from elsewhere in the Army* (except in the artillery which wanted it's observation balloons), *from members of Congress, or from the general public.* Officers of the heavier-than-air branch occupied key positions in the air arm. And with the money, men, and materiel available for Army aviation severely limited, the tendency was toward building up the heavier-than-air branch. A number of

dirigible disasters, including the Navy's loss of the Shenandoah, Akron, and Macon, retarded and then halted airship programs in both the Army and the Navy. So the Army's lighter-than-air branch declined and virtually disappeared, eclipsed and consumed by heavier-than-air aviation.[20]

Even those Army airmen, like William E. Kepner, who started out in LTA and devoted years to their development, were likely to have much preferred duty in the heavier-than-air craft. When Kepner was first assigned to balloons rather than airplanes for flight training, "He wired an urgent message to the Army's adjutant general pleading that a mistake had been made in his assignment." Despite his subsequent record-setting accomplishments in balloons, Kepner was relieved and delighted when, "At last, he pinned on the coveted airplane pilot wings that had eluded him for some twelve years."[21]

It would probably be fair to say that the majority of the aviators favored winged airplanes over the dirigibles, increasingly as time and events proved the technological limits and relative vulnerabilities of both. Even today, one can find a small group of civil airmen who cling to expansive dreams of LTA ships, but the faction seems to grow smaller with time as the continuing LTA experiments founder, one after the other, on technical and fiscal rocks.[22]

The Battleplane Emerges

The long-range, self-defended, heavy bomber—which was destined to become the centerpiece of so much controversy over the next several decades—had been described early in Douhet's concept of the "battleplane." The battleplane would have all the qualities it needed for command of the air—to carry the attack (the offensive) to the enemy and to defend itself from attack by enemy aircraft (control of the air).

> This type of [battle]plane should have the radius of action, speed, and armor protection as described; but should have armament sufficient both for aerial combat and for offensives against the surface.... If the Air Force were made up entirely of battleplanes, all the planes could take part in the engagement, with full freedom of action. Therefore, from all points of view it is best that the bulk of an Independent Air Force be made up entirely of battleplanes designed for aerial combat and for bombing offensives against the surface.[23]

The early efforts of the Air Corps to acquire battleplanes in the form of long-range bombers met heavy opposition from inside and outside of the

Army. An important impediment was the offensive orientation of bombers at a time when the nation's military was supposed to be devoted to defense: "The Air Corps hoped to use the long-range reconnaissance mission to procure long-range bombers. It wanted them for strategic operations but could not say so when military policy rested on defense."[24]

Coastal defense was the only mission available at the time to the Army Air Corps that might justify long-range bombers. A short-lived agreement between the Army and Navy chiefs (General MacArthur and Admiral Pratt) offered a "plausible justification for long-range bombers to defend against sea attack. One of the significant outcomes of the agreement was War Department approval of projects...that [ultimately] led to the development of the heavy bombers of World War II."[25] The path would be a tortuous one:

> The agreement between the services did not long survive Pratt's retirement on July 1, 1933. His successor as Chief of Naval Operations, Adm. William H. Standley, repudiated it. The Navy developed land-based planes with the aim of assuming the whole coastal defense responsibility. The Army kept on planning and preparing for a role in coastal defense. The Air Corps pursued its quest for long-range bombers.[26]

The battle to acquire the big bombers would soon consume General Frank M. Andrews, Commander of the Army's GHQ Air Force. It was a long quest that would cost him his chance to be chief and that would finally see Hap Arnold win both the bid for the bombers and the role of chief.

Forging Doctrine from Theory

Air power theory was now developed, at least in broad outline. What was needed from the airmen in the mid-1930s was conversion of theory into tactics, doctrine, and concepts for organization and training.[27] While well-grounded in the theory, these airmen were no longer proselytizers so much as patient developers of the ideas needed to exploit the theory. Their end was no longer to gain acceptance of a theory but to provide the means to implement it when war came, as they were quite sure it would, even then. The intellectual challenges had to do with defining the necessary and most effective means—the targets, planes, tactics, doctrine, and organization.

The fixed anvil, provided by the theory, was the primacy of the offense:

> Young Air Corps officers…were being told at the Air Corps Tactical School that "A well organized, well planned and well flown air force attack will constitute an offense that cannot be stopped."[28]

The rapidly moving hammer was the technology for Douhet's battleplane, which now had to be defined. Fighters were seen as adjuncts rather than threats to the big bombers. Haywood Hansell describes how the doctrine for the big bombers evolved at the Air Corps Tactical School at Maxwell Field in Alabama:

> The argument leaned toward the bombers…[and not] the danger to the air offensive posed by enemy fighters. [Nevertheless] the Bombardment Section supported the development of long-range escort fighters, a position vehemently opposed by Chennault as Chief of the Pursuit Section, who favored short-range, high-performance interceptors.

> These questions were debated heatedly in an atmosphere of intellectual ferment that may be hard to imagine today. For the first time an integrated doctrine for the use of air power was emerging, and the technology to support it seemed to be within reach. Strategic concepts and principles of employment were put in writing. Texts were written, revised, and written again…

> The substance of that philosophy as defined at the Tactical School was that "the will and capability of a modern industrialized nation to wage war can be undermined and caused to collapse by destruction of carefully selected targets in the industrial and service systems on which the enemy people, their industries, and the armed forces are dependent; and this method of waging strategic air warfare is, in general, preferable to area attack of cities or industrial areas." Carrying out that strategic doctrine called for a clear definition of national purpose and strategic objectives, collecting strategic intelligence in order to select critical targets, providing air offensive forces that could reach their targets with acceptable losses, improving bombing accuracy, and developing bombs capable of destroying the selected targets…

> It should be remembered that the Air Corps was still part of the Army and that the air power doctrine developed at the Tactical School was not accepted by the War Department. Its General Staff was dominated by ground officers, many of whom believed that the mission of the Air Corps was coastal defense and support of ground force operations. An independent strategic mission for air power was not universally accepted, even after it was tacitly acknowledged through establishment of the General Headquarters Air Force in 1935….[29]

The primacy, even the contribution of the air offensive, did not go unchallenged. Its skeptics in the Army staff kept pointing to the absence of evidence to support the claim.

> Air Force doctrine as enunciated by the Air Corps Tactical School rested on the proposition that

> the principal and all-important mission of airpower…is the attack of those vital objects of a nation's economic structure which will tend to paralyze the nation's ability to wage war and thus contribute directly to the attainment of the ultimate objective of war, namely, the disintegration of the hostile will to resist.

Tactical School taught, and Air Corps officers as a rule believed, aviation could be decisive. The General Staff and officers of other arms could not accept this in the absence of demonstration. As the War Plans Division put it: "So far, well-organized nations have surrendered only when occupied by the enemy's army or when such occupation could no longer be opposed." Aviation could assist but could not itself achieve victory. The Tactical School responded by asserting that the advent of air power gave for the first time in history the ability to bring war immediately to the internal structure of an enemy nation…."[30]

This was unadulterated air power theory from the Tactical School; but the War Plans Division exacted a compromise from the airmen in the form of the following "watered-down" statement for publication:

> The power of air forces has not yet been fully tested. The effect which they are capable of producing and the extent to which they will influence warfare is still undetermined. But it appears certain that skillful use of air forces will greatly affect operations in future wars.[31]

Despite the headwinds provided by the Army General Staff, a sudden wind shift was anticipated by the air power advocates:

> The Japanese were gobbling up East Asia after invading Manchuria in 1931. Hitler came to power two years later, and now he and Mussolini posed a clear danger to the European democracies. Unless they were stopped, another world war was likely. If America became involved, the air advocates, rebelling against the military status quo, did not want another American Expeditionary Force bogged down overseas in the carnage of static trench warfare. They envisioned the long-range strategic bomber as *the* technological breakthrough that could win such a war in less time, with fewer casualties.[32]

The *efficiency* of air power applied to the enemy's critical economic targets appealed to the Americans. The British were still transfixed by the *terror* of air power applied against cities as a deterrent or a breaker of civilian morale. "With Mitchell's voice silenced, the most lurid predictions came from England, where the fear of air war on cities remained greatest."[33] And, the performance of the German aviators in the Spanish Civil War only increased these concerns:

British and American officials thought they were following the Nazis' lead, not pioneering the course toward air war against cities. But it remained the case that, in the 1930s, only England and America seriously developed the concept and instruments of strategic air war....

For reasons of deterrence, the RAF concentrated more on the bomber's role as destroyer of cities than did the Americans, who emphasized precision bombing...

Nonetheless, a fundamental orientation toward strategic bombing arose, however confused its translation into policy. In England, a profound anxiety over exposure to aerial attack fused with an equally powerful sense of England's limited moral and material resources for conventional combat. In the United States, the material resources were ample, but political tolerance for using them was not. In both countries, abhorrence and attraction combined to make air power compelling. What resulted was the apparent paradox, noted by one authority, whereby nations "whose policy was normally defensive tended towards the counter strike deterrent theory, while those with aggressive intentions developed tactical air forces."[34]

Air power in prophesy was about to be converted to air power in being. Over the next few years, the airmen would be directly translating their newly forged doctrine into the development of forces—first a trickle and then a wartime flood—beyond their most ambitious dreams. War would ultimately demonstrate serious flaws in their doctrine, but that wasn't their concern then. What mattered to them as war clouds gathered was the impetus to develop and build an air armada of battleplanes. If that impetus set a course that was slightly off its stated mark, the airmen thought that the error, like wind drift, could and would be corrected with observations over time.

Notes

1. Stephanides, *Dædalus and Icarus*, 18.

2. Maurer, *Aviation in the U.S. Army*, 440.

3. Ibid., 440

4. Ibid., 443.

5. Futrell, *Ideas, Concepts, Doctrine*, 75.

6. H. H. Arnold and Ira C. Eaker, *This Flying Game* (New York: Funk & Wagnalls, 1936), 296, 297.

7. Sherry, *The Rise of American Airpower*, 39.

8. Bryan Sterling, *The Best of Will Rogers* (New York: Crown Publishers, 1979), 117.

9. Ibid., 115.

10. Mitchell, *Winged Defense*, 3, 4.

11. Sterling, *The Best of Will Rogers*, 115.

12. Mitchell, *Winged Defense*, xiii.

13. Ibid., xii.

14. Ibid., 5, 6.

15. Ibid., 8, 9.

16. Ibid., 18, 19.

17. Ibid., xvi.

18. Ibid., 9.

19. Ibid., 38, 39.

20. Maurer, *Aviation in the U.S. Army*, 441, (emphasis in the original).

21. Paul F. Henry, "William E. Kepner: All the Way to Berlin," in *Makers of the United States Air Force*, ed. John L. Frisbee (Washington, D.C.: Office of Air Force History, 1987), 153, 157.

22. Some of the more recent experiments by those who dream of reviving the LTA ships are vividly recounted in Public Broadcasting System program, *The Blimp Is Back*, produced under the *NOVA* television series by WGBH, Boston, first aired on 30 October 1990, transcript available as No. 1714 from Journal Graphics, Denver.

23. Douhet, *The Command of the Air*, 117, 118.

24. Maurer, *Aviation in the U.S. Army*, 289.

25. Ibid.

26. Ibid.

27. The hardware to implement the theory would have to come later. At this stage, the airmen did not have the resources to *acquire* the fleets of battleplanes they would need in war. All that they could do with their meager funds was *develop* prototypes of the planes they wanted; and even the development funding was closely examined and painfully justified.

28. James N. Eastman, Jr., "The Development of Big Bombers," *Aerospace Historian*, vol. 25, no. 4, (Winter, December 1978), 215.

29. Haywood S. Hansell, Jr., "Harold L. George: Apostle of Air Power," in *Makers of the United States Air Force*, ed. John L. Frisbee, (Washington, D.C.: Office of Air Force History, 1987), 78–80.

30. Maurer, *Aviation in the U.S. Army*, 331, 332.

31. Ibid.

32. Green, "Hugh J. Knerr: The Pen and the Sword," 108, 109, (emphasis in the original).

33. Sherry, *The Rise of American Airpower*, 65.

34. Ibid., 72, with the quotation attributed to Robin Higham, *Air Power: A Concise History* (New York: St. Martins Press, 1972), 10.

PART III

EXPLOITATION

8

The Apostles

*Before they set off, Dædalus looked his son in the
eyes and said:*

*"Icarus, my child, the journey we are about to make
is not an easy one. We have a long way to go, but
we shall reach our destination safely if we take
care. We must not fly too low, in case the waves
soak the feathers, but we must not soar too high,
either, for then the sun may melt the wax which
holds our wings together. We must travel slowly
and steadily, like storks, and then we can be sure
of a safe and pleasant flight."*

*"And now the great moment has come—a moment
mankind may never forget. Follow me, and
remember my advice." And with these words he
lifted his great wings and soared into the sky with
Icarus close behind.[1]*

Precision Daylight Bombardment

The era of air power prophets—Trenchard, Douhet, and Mitchell—
and the time of their prophesy was ending. The theory and its conversion
into reality would now pass into the hands of their apostles—Harris in
Britain; Andrews, Eaker, Spaatz, and Arnold in America—as the first
harbingers of another world war appeared in the form of the fascist
adventures in Ethiopia, Manchuria, China, and Spain. The apostles had
been given a well-formed theory of air power and a growing body of
doctrine, but not the physical implements necessary to exercise either.

The skeptics of the theory, both in Britain and America, were now
becoming the minority. What had to be sold was not the theory, but the

physical means to execute air power according to the theory. The physical implements were the design, development, and procurement of the airplanes and trained crews needed to demonstrate the increasingly accepted promises of air power.

In America, Andrews and Arnold used air power theory as their compass to develop the means and form of Army aviation as World War II loomed. They were the institutional logisticians, mostly concerned with acquiring the airplanes and organizing the infrastructures that would allow the theory of air power finally to be expressed. Air power theory had now moved off into the hands of tacticians who had to convert theory to practice if the strategic hopes and dreams of the prophets were to come true. In the hands of these tacticians, a particular concept of strategic bombardment was evolving:

> In their own institutions, most of all at the Air Corps Tactical School in Alabama, Air Corps officers were free to construct their own curriculum and dogma. The leisurely pace of life in the peacetime army gave them plenty of time to do so.
>
> By the 1930s, both the airmen and their institutions were also mature enough to carry on their struggle in more sophisticated ways. A cohort of officers had a decade or two of experience in aviation and had passed beyond the youthful stage of infatuation with the joys of flying. The Air Corps Tactical School had established a body of literature and a tradition of theorizing about aviation. Mitchell's fate had taught airmen that glamorous stunts and daring pronouncements were insufficient to achieve recognition of air power.
>
> The new doctrine of precision bombing was the product of their efforts and the vehicle of their ambitions. Briefly, airmen, especially at the tactical school, argued that strategic air power could contribute to victory or secure it by attacks on the enemy state, especially its economic institutions. These attacks need not be indiscriminate, indeed should be targeted at only a few key components whose destruction would disrupt the functioning of the entire state. The enemy's will or capacity to fight would then collapse.[2]

This American concept of strategic bombardment rested on a logistical concept of war fighting: [At the Tactical School, they] "sought to define what Mitchell and others called the 'vital centers'; that is they planned to discover and then to destroy by determined bombardment those elements in the economic structure of an enemy that were essential to his war making power."[3] The quick, simple solution offered by precision bombardment appealed to American proclivities:

> Precision bombing...promised victory independent of the other branches of the armed forces, with minimal demands on and risks for Americans, by employing

the bomber as an instrument of surgical precision rather than indiscriminate horror, laying its high explosives (not gas or incendiaries) on its targets with pinpoint accuracy, incapacitating the enemy without slaughter.[4]

The problems of precision bombardment were seen in technical and analytic terms: The right targets had to be found; the right bomber had to be built and then fitted with the right equipment—a bombsight and guns for its self defense.

> The invincibility of the unescorted bomber formation was an article of faith; Flying Fortress was no idle choice of name for the B-17. In theory, bombing by daylight permitted the necessary precision, while the bomber's speed, thick skin, bristling armament, and high altitude provided the requisite defense.[5]

The airmen's faith in technological progress obscured the lessons in combat which even then were emerging:

> The swift pace of technological progress in the 1930s also minimized doubts; if the full potential of precision bombing was not immediately realizable, some imminent development would surely close the gap between dream and reality. And of course opportunities for reality-testing were few, and when they arose, air officers thought the uses of air power in Ethiopia, Spain, and China were too primitive in technology and tactics to tell them much.[6]

The moral superiority of precision bombing was not an explicit issue, but it served to wall off moral concerns until the heat of war further obscured the slippery slope to terror bombing.

> [F]or the airmen, a measure of moral validity adhered to methods of war that achieved quick victory and minimized prolonged suffering.... [T]he historical significance of the doctrine of precision bombing was not its repudiation of moral concerns but its role in quieting consciences anxious about the future of air war. Proponents of precision bombing believed that it would reap the long-standing promise of air power without inflicting unreasonable harm to humanity. Of course, the promise of air power had always inhered in its capacity to bring terror. Precision bombing did not entirely divorce the two, but it pushed terror so far into the background, placed so much distance between the act and the result, that it had much the same effect. Like the strategy of economic blockade practiced by both English and Germans in World War I, it proposed to attack the enemy population indirectly, by disrupting and starving it rather than by blasting and burning. But if no quick victory came and the enemy's will remained the objective, then airmen might have to strike at it through systematic rather than selective destruction, that is, by direct attacks on the civilian population.[8]

Where Were the Dissenting Views?

Perry McCoy Smith speculates on why the American airmen were not affected by contrary evidence and arguments about the primacy of the offense and self-defended bombers:

> Intraservice (as opposed to interservice) rivalry and debate, which were present within the army as a whole in the twenties and thirties and which served the useful purpose of questioning the doctrine of various service arms, were largely absent with the AAF. In the 1930s intraservice rivalry did bring into serious question the efficacy of coast artillery and horse-mounted cavalry and, in turn, inspired the Coast Artillery and the Cavalry to turn to weapons systems which they could more easily justify—the anti-aircraft artillery gun and the tank.
>
> In the twenties and thirties, the infantry questioned the efficacy of the horse, the air corps questioned the value of the coast artillery gun, and neither cavalry nor coast artillery modified their weapons systems until they felt threatened by outside forces within the Army.... As the Army Air Corps slowly developed separateness, it did not at the same time develop the intraservice debate that was to blossom in the period following formal autonomy. In this period of un-formalized autonomy, the only voices questioning the dominant AAF doctrine came from outside the Air Force.[9]

The narrowness of the focus—no longer so much on air power as on precision bombardment—tended to draw the debate onto means more than ends:

> [The Air Force doctrinal] focus both before and during World War II was narrow, so that only ideas and weaponry which favored the offensive role of aviation were given thorough consideration. The doctrine developed in the Air Corps Tactical School from 1926 through 1940 was not airpower doctrine in its broadest sense of the word "airpower." It was strategic, daylight, precision bombardment, a very important part, but only a part, of military aviation.[10]

The principal ends of the airmen—autonomy and the big bombers—had become entangled with the concept of precision bombardment. The effect would be to suppress ideas and capabilities which would eventually come to haunt the AAF in war.

> Air Corps leaders had reached a doctrinal decision by 1935 as to the efficacy of unescorted long-range strategic bombardment and were unwilling either to question that decision or even to observe technological advances that might cause them to modify this doctrine until 1943 when the whole concept of strategic bombardment was endangered by the horrendous losses over Germany. It is paradoxical that their total acceptance of the doctrine prevented them from

observing the technological advances that would have been the salvation of the very concept they were proclaiming. From 1931 until 1938 the bombardment advocates denied pursuit aviation any role other than the harassment of enemy bombers. The more radical even advocated the discontinuation of all pursuit procurement.[11]

To point out the vulnerabilities of strategic bombardment was to jeopardize the Air Corps case for autonomy, for if strategic bombardment was proved ineffective as the element of warfare which alone might prove to be decisive in battle, then its case would be seriously undermined. If flights of bombardment aircraft could be turned back or if the defensive fighters could inflict unacceptable losses upon the bombing formation, then the whole concept of strategic bombardment would be proved erroneous, and the Air Corps would then be expected to accomplish only close support, air superiority, and interdiction, none of which (nor all in combination) could justify complete autonomy....

The quest for autonomy led to the advocacy of strategic bombardment, which led, in turn, to the deprecation of not only defensive pursuit aircraft but all pursuit aircraft. Bombardment and autonomy were so inextricably bound together that the questioning of bombardment by an Air Corps officer was not only impolitic but unwise.[12]

The problem was embedded in doctrine, the most theoretical and emotional of domains for discourse among the pioneering military airmen:

But the conflict between Tactical School bomber and pursuit advocates was fundamentally doctrinal and consequently all the more extreme. The bomber theorists believed fervently that heavy bombers flying in formation could penetrate enemy defenses during daylight hours in order to bomb with precision, and do so at an acceptable cost. That error in judgment extracted an extremely high price in bomber losses during the early months of U.S. participation in World War II.[13]

It wasn't the lack of counter-evidence; to acknowledge such evidence was to undermine what the airmen had worked to achieve in developing the bomber which would provide their ticket to autonomy.

Air forces exposed to combat in the 1930s learned, as World War II showed more fully, that tactical aviation in support of surface forces "could often destroy the forces in the field before strategic bombers could have a paralyzing effect." But no doctrine except strategic air power satisfied the drive to achieve an independent air force that would bring personal status, power, and probably most important, professional respectability.[14]

With respect to the thesis of this analysis, the important point is not whether air power theory was right or wrong, but that the power of the theory dominated—even in the face of contrary evidence. The theory provided direction and energy to the airmen as they strove toward their cherished goal of autonomy.

> Above all, air had a mission distinct from ground support. Autonomy equaled legitimacy for the strategic bombing mission. It was long-range bombing of the enemy's vitals that set air apart....[15]

Camouflaging the Bombers

To get the big bombers they needed for precision bombardment, the airmen were forced to camouflage their purposes in the hostile bureaucratic environment they faced in the Army and the Navy. General Frank M. Andrews, the Air Corps' greatest advocate for the big bombers, must have had to lie through gritted teeth when he was forced to argue that the big bombers were intended solely for coastal defense purposes:

> Despite the creation in March 1935 of general Headquarters Air Force as an offensive striking force, the army still saw the arm's function as tactical support of ground forces. Obviously, the big bomber would play little part in such a role. In December 1936 Embick [of the Army's General Staff] flatly asked Andrews if the bombers were not intended for an offensive role. Andrews, just as flatly, denied such intention. The weapons under development were purely defensive: "It is utterly absurd to consider them as anything else and I think we should emphasize this point on all occasions.[16]

The excuses for the airplanes the airmen needed took them through some logical labyrinths:

> Coastal defense and overseas reinforcement were the only missions requiring long-range bombers left to the Air Corps by mid-1937. And the coastal defense mission was still in debate with the Navy.... Within the next year Hap Arnold again asked for a clearer delineation of responsibility for coastal defense. To justify larger aircraft, the Army had to have the coastal defense mission. If the Navy were to have the task, then the Army had no need for long-range aircraft as the Air Corps aviation mission would be limited to close support....

> Air Corps maneuvers in the North-East during the spring [of 1938] led to a direct confrontation between the Army and the Navy. The Air Corps was the loser. On 12 May, to prove the capabilities of long-range aircraft, a flight of three B-17s took off from Mitchel Field, New York, to intercept the Italian liner *Rex* at sea. Despite lack of information on the ship's location and heavy cloud cover, the three aircraft made the interception 725 miles out, dropped a note to the liner, and returned to base....[17] The Army Chief of Staff, Gen. Malin C. Craig, immediately telephoned General Andrews and ordered that the Air Corps henceforth limit its

activities to a zone within 100 miles of the coast. The strange thing about this order was that though it was common knowledge—and a standard operating procedure, thereafter—it was never put in writing.

The Air Corps then needed a new reason for developing and procuring long range bombers....[18]

The details of this episode reveal Andrews to be an unrelenting advocate for the B-17 bomber.

Since the political and military emphasis was on *defense*, it was not possible to speak in terms of *offense*. But a bomber like the B-17 with a cruising speed of 230 miles an hour, a service ceiling of 25,000 feet, and a range of 2,200 miles, was obviously a defensive-offensive weapon of great promise. And while Secretary of War Woodring was calling, in 1938, for a balanced air arm with a promised 2,320 planes by June 1940, based on the belief that two or three smaller planes could be bought for the price of one large one, Andrews concentrated on building a strategic air force around the power and promise of the B-17. What he hoped to do was convince Westover and the War Department that over the next three years ninety-eight of the Boeings should be purchased, enough to equip his Air Force with two groups.

He demonstrated the B-17's promise time and time again, in maneuvers and long-distance flights. For example, in August 1937, during war games with the Navy, the 2d Bomb Group's B-17s, operating under almost impossible ground rules, sought out and soaked the *USS Utah* with water bombs 285 miles off the California coast. The Navy insisted that the outcome of these games be kept from the public. It was not.

Matters dealing with the promise of aircraft came to a head in May 1938. Conducting the largest aerial maneuvers on record, Andrews sent three of his B-17s out to sea some 700 miles in very stormy weather to intercept the Italian liner Rex, which represented an attacking task force. The photograph of two of the B-17s flying past the *Rex*, taken by Capt. George W. Goddard in the third bomber, made the front page of newspapers around the world. It sent a message to friends and to potential adversaries alike. The message bounced off the War Department, and Craig, instead of praising Andrews for the performance, informed him that henceforth his planes were not to venture more than a hundred miles off the coasts. When Andrews passed this order to Colonel Robert Olds, Commander of the 2d Bomb Group, Olds informed his crew that from now on all practice missions over open water would remain within the hundred-mile limit but courses would be plotted north and south.[19]

Trading a Career for a Bomber

Frank Andrew's problems were not fences drawn on charts to keep the Army airmen out of the Navy's hair but instead were fiscal, given the enormity of his vision for the times:

The continuing effort by Andrews to augment the strength of his B-17s fell on deaf ears; cost and necessity were the principal barriers. When he let it be known that ultimately he wished to build his bomber strength to 244 B-17s, or one-quarter of his promised total while phasing out the inferior B-18s, opponents began to refer jokingly to the Boeing as "Andrews's folly."

In a letter to Hugh Knerr, who had been transferred to Fort Sam Houston, Andrews wrote: "The situation with reference to our strategic mission and the proper equipment with which to perform it, seems to be getting progressively worse, and we have no court of appeal that I can think of...." Then came the August 1938 meeting with Marshall. The War Plans Division Chief, upon returning from his nine days of air power indoctrination, found that, indeed, the airmen has no real representation on the General Staff. He was to become Andrews's court of appeal.[20]

George Marshall, even then, as Chief of the War Plans Division of the Army Staff, exhibited the broad and long range views that he would bring to bear on the nation over the next decade.

On October 18, 1938, Andrews sent Marshall congratulations on his becoming Deputy Chief of Staff. He enclosed a copy of a talk he had recently given at the War College, saying it expressed the views of practically the entire operating personnel of the Air Corps...[who] believe in a larger percentage of high performance, large capacity bombers.... In every test or exercise we have ever had...this plane stands out head and shoulders above any other type; yet for 1940 and 1941 our estimates do not include a single one. For the support of the Monroe Doctrine on the American Continent such a plane would be of inestimable value....

On September 21, 1938, Air Corps Chief General Westover was killed in a crash at Burbank. The next day Andrews was asked by Army Chief of Staff Malin Craig to report to him in Washington. He found himself in a meeting with Craig and all the assistant chiefs. Craig informed him they were prepared to recommend to the president that Andrews succeed Westover on the condition that he stop trying to promote the B-17. Andrews politely refused to accept the condition, and a few days later it was announced that General Hap Arnold was to be the new Air Corps Chief....[21]

Andrews had stood firm on the position that he had fought so hard for—getting the big strategic bombers the Army Air Corps needed to the fulfill the only mission that offered the Army airmen autonomy—and he had paid the price of the most coveted of airmen's commands.

In view of his position, Andrews knew that when his tour of duty as GHQ Air Force Commander was up on March 1, 1939, his tenure would not be extended. He hoped that he would be assigned to head the Training Command, and if not that, the Air Corps Tactical School. Instead, with no prior warning, he was given the Billy Mitchell treatment: reduction in rank to his permanent grade of colonel and exile to Fort Sam Houston as District Air Officer. There can be no doubt that Secretary of War Woodring approved the action whether he originated it or not. The last straw for Woodring had been a public declaration by Andrews at the National Aeronautic Association convention on January 16, 1939, that the U.S. was a sixth-rate air power. This made headlines across the country, just at the time Woodring was assuring the public of the nation's aerial strength.[22]

However George Marshall would come to Andrews rescue, albeit at the risk or cost to his relationships with his superiors:

On July 1, 1939, George Marshall became Acting Chief of Staff of the U.S. Army. His first move was a formidable one. He appointed as his new Assistant Chief of Staff for Training and Operations (G-3), Frank M. Andrews, promoting him to a brigadier general of the line. Later Marshall was to say that when he submitted his choice to Woodring, Assistant Secretary of War Louis Johnson, and outgoing Chief of Staff Malin Craig, he knew he had a fight on his hands. He added it was probably the only time in the trio's association they had ever been in full agreement on anything. Nevertheless, Marshall prevailed and the appointment was announced. It was the first time in U.S. military history that an airman had been appointed one of the four assistant chiefs of staff on the Army General Staff.[23]

Breakthrough

In the anti-war climate of America in the 1930s, the big bombers would only be accepted if they were needed for defensive purposes. Offensive purposes wouldn't do. If the bombers weren't for coastal defense, maybe they could be for hemisphere defense. This turned out not to be the door, but the key that opened the door. Robert Futrell describes how the bombers were used to gain a broader horizon for their missions:

First recognition of the new need for defense of Latin America had been brought to the War Department by the Department of State. Alarmed by the increasing Nazi and fascist activity in South America, the State Department had convened a conference with the War and Navy Departments on 10 January 1938 to discuss means of combating German and Italian incursions....

Among the other measures adopted, the conferees agreed that more frequent visits of naval vessels and demonstration flights of military aircraft to South America would impress both the inhabitants and the Axis with the U.S. ability to react in defense of that area. Obviously, the visit of the [relatively short ranged] B-18s to the southern continent would impress no one as they would have to sneak in the back door in short hops from U.S. bases in the Canal Zone. Therefore, the War Department directed the 2nd Bombardment Group to send out its B-17s on a 6000-mile "good-will" trip to Buenos Aires, Argentina. Six of the long-range bombers left Langley Field, Virginia on 16 February 1938 for

Miami, Florida. The flight next flew 2695 miles non-stop to Lima, Peru; then, because of weather, proceeded toward Santiago, Chile, rather than directly to Buenos Aires. By the time the aircraft reached Santiago, the weather had cleared, and they went on to Buenos Aires rather than landing at Santiago....

Just three days later [after their return], seven B-17s took off from Langley for another "good will" mission, this time to Rio de Janiero—[for] another 12,000-mile flight.

The good will flights, combined with the new recognition of hemispheric threat and the continuing Air Corps desire for more of the big bombers led Brig. Gen. Arnold, then Assistant Chief of the Air Corps, to undertake a new approach in an attempt to establish a definite mission requiring long-range bombers.

Roosevelt, shortly after the order lifting the Air Corps operations to within 100 miles of the coast, had announced that the Air Corps would be responsible not only for preventing enemy landings on the North American continent, but also in South America.[24]

It was Arnold who saw the way to open the door with the key provided by the goodwill flights, aided by the war clouds then ominously gathering on the horizon.

Meanwhile, General Arnold, the assistant chief of the Air Corps, expressed doubts that the roles and missions of the Air Corps could be justified on an abstract basis. Early in June [1939], Arnold expressed concern that the forces of aggression building up in Europe could well threaten the Western Hemisphere. He, therefore, saw the need to study the employment of the Air Corps in support of national policy as represented by the Monroe Doctrine....

[T]he Air Corps Board had never before addressed a specific situation that so clearly demanded long-range bombers and quasi-independent air actions as did the requirement for air defense of the hemisphere under the Monroe Doctrine. After an analysis of the potential military requirements for support of the Monroe Doctrine, [Major Orvil A.] Anderson, who drew up the logistical requirements for the study, was able to demonstrate the inherent efficiency of long range aircraft in terms of planes, personnel, and bases required to defend the North American continent and the South American continent down to the 36th parallel against seaborne threat or invasion....[25]

Victory for the bomber advocates soon followed:

Several factors combined to end the restrictions on Air Corps operations over the oceans. Congress had approved the acquisition of the long-range bombers in April 1939. The chief executive, and the other nations of the Americas, recognized the Air Corps mission of hemispheric defense; and, finally, on 1 July 1939, George C. Marshall became Acting Chief of Staff of the Army. Marshall, since he replaced Embick, had given a sympathetic ear to the Air Corps. He then gave the aviation arm an even more prominent role. With the permission of the

War Department, the Air Corps on 24 August, 1939, issued a circular which permitted air operations over the sea to the maximum range of multi engine aircraft.

The long-range aircraft advocates had won. They had a mission and, on procurement, the aircraft that could perform it. The victory, after 14 years, recognized the strategic offensive role of the air force....

The major argument of Air Corps leaders for developing and procuring long-range bombers during the 1930s had grown out of the Army's coastal defense mission. However, the introduction of hemispheric defense and the good neighbor policy were the deciding factor. Where coastal defense had gained the grudging support of the General Staff, hemispheric defense brought the full support for the President for development of larger long-range aircraft which could be used not only for bombardment but also for reconnaissance, surveillance, and reinforcement of friendly nations and overseas U.S. possessions....[26]

The Gathering Clouds of War

The challenge now changed from getting the *right kind* of bomber to getting *enough* of them. The doctrinal war would be replaced by logistical war.

The Air Corps was left to build a new air force with hemisphere defense and aid to Britain and France as its only clearly sanctioned strategic missions.

Not surprisingly, therefore, airmen largely kept their own counsel in 1939 when they speculated on their strategic mission, working outside the formal structure of strategic planning. Tactical school instructors, still the fountainhead of more radical air doctrine, acknowledged the immediate priority of hemispheric defense but continued to emphasize that selective attacks on an enemy's economic structure remained the ideal employment of air power.[27]

The rationale for the build-up of forces, then as now, took on the tone of deterrence to avoid rather than wage war:

Major General Frank Andrews, commander of GHQ Air Force, gave a...guarded accounting of Munich's lessons in a well publicized speech on January 16, 1939. Andrews...couched much of his address in the familiar terms of hemisphere defense. But he stretched this concept beyond the breaking point. "Our country should be the first to span the oceans both ways nonstop" by building bombers with "a tactical range of 10,000 miles." Most American strategists were planning to intercept any German penetration into Latin America once it began. Andrews, citing Munich, proposed something else: "to stop the aggressor nation from even planning the attack, through fear of retaliation." Air power should be seen not simply as a war-fighting instrument but "as an instrument of national policy," one capable, as Munich showed, of "toppling the diplomatic balance" and perhaps eventually creating mutual deterrence through terror between two nations both "capable of powerful air action."

Officers like…Andrews were trying to link the aerial weapon to national policy, that is, to justify its potential not only for winning wars but for sustaining peacetime policies. They almost, but not quite, made the link.[28]

But the build-up of air power for the coming war could not provide for capabilities which the theory had neglected and even suppressed.

Though the airmen spent much time between wars theorizing and experimenting with employment of air power, combat would disclose tactical shortcomings. For instance, a great deal more experimentation would be needed in actual operations to find the best way for executing a raid using hundreds of bombers, and for protecting them from destruction by enemy planes. Further, war revealed that the airmen of the 1930s, obsessed with strategic bombardment, had neglected tactical air power, the air support of ground forces that would be vital to the campaigns of American and Allied armies in North Africa and Europe.[29]

However, the theory was an argument, not a fact. It was an argument toward ends, and the road toward the ends of the argument was finally being straightened and paved: "While the developments of the twenties and thirties did not prepare the Army's air arm for the war it would fight, they laid a foundation upon which to build the Army Air Forces of World War II."[30] And, the AAF of World War II was positioned to realize the military airmen's dream—independence and aircraft of astonishing capabilities in mind-boggling numbers.

Notes

1. Stephanides, *Dædalus and Icarus*, 18, 19.

2. Sherry, *The Rise of American Airpower*, 51.

3. Hurley, *Billy Mitchell*, 128.

4. Sherry, *The Rise of American Airpower*, 53.

5. Ibid., 55.

6. Ibid., 56.

7. Indeed, it was that promise that set the British on the course to deterrence through the threat of city bombing, precisely because of the terror they had experienced from zeppelins bombing their cities during World War I.

8. Sherry, *The Rise of American Airpower*, 58.

9. Perry McCoy Smith, *The Air Force Plans for Peace 1943–1945* (Baltimore: Johns Hopkins Press, 1970), 22, 23.

10. Ibid., 29, 30.

11. Ibid., 31.

12. Ibid., 34.

13. Paul F. Henry, "All the Way to Berlin," in *Makers of the United States Air Force*, ed. John L. Frisbee (Washington, D.C.: Office of Air Force History, 1987), 161.

14. Sherry, *The Rise of American Airpower*, 50, with the quotations referenced to Walter Millis, *Arms and Men: A Study in American Military History*, New York, 1956.

15. Herman S. Wolk, "Men Who Made the Air Force," *Air University Review*, vol. 23 (Sep–Oct 1972): 10.

16. James N. Eastman, Jr., "The Development of the Big Bombers," *Aerospace Historian,* vol. 25(4), (Winter, December 1978): 215.

17. LeMay was the navigator of the lead bomber. See Nick Kotz, *Wild Blue Yonder: Money, Politics, and the B-1 Bomber* (New York: Pantheon Books, 1988), 39.

18. Eastman, "The Development of Big Bombers," 215.

19. DeWitt S. Copp, "Frank M. Andrews: Marshall's Airman," in *Makers of the United States Air Force,* ed. John L. Frisbee (Washington, D.C.: Office of Air Force History, 1987), 57, 58.

20. Ibid., 58.

21. Ibid., 58, 59.

22. Ibid., 59.

23. Ibid., 60.

24. Eastman, "The Development of Big Bombers," 216, 217.

25. Futrell, *Ideas, Concepts, Doctrine*, 89, 90.

26. Eastman, "The Development of Big Bombers," 218.

27. Sherry, *The Rise of American Airpower*, 90.

28. Ibid., 88, 89.

29. Maurer, *Aviation in the U.S. Army*, 445.

30. Ibid., 446.

9

Founding the Church

Icarus was delighted with his new wings and swooped and soared as he flew. Harmless games enough they seemed, but Dædalus was worried, and cried out:

"Steady there, Icarus!"

"Don't worry, father," the boy shouted back, "there's no danger."

"There is, my boy, there is. Be careful. We're on a journey, not playing games!"

But unfortunately, Icarus thought he knew everything, and would not listen to his father's advice. That is how Phaethon came to a sad end, and that is how Icarus, too, was destined to die. So it has been for thousands of years, and so it will always be. Yet mankind needs courage, and youth cannot be blamed if it has more daring than its elders.

And Icarus was nothing if not daring. The higher he went, the more his spirits rose. The sun drew him like a magnet, and his father's warning flew right out of his mind.[1]

Every institution has its legendary leaders, and the Air Force is certainly no exception. The contributions of Mitchell, Andrews, Arnold, Eaker, Spaatz, Doolittle, Kenney, LeMay, Vandenberg, and many others have become legendary. Without diminishing the stature of any, Arnold must be considered the single giant among giants from the perspective of this analysis.

Before I undertook this analysis, Andrews was my Air Force hero, not Arnold or Mitchell. I saw Arnold as a skilled politician and bureaucrat,

Mitchell as a flaming evangelist; but I associated Andrews with that now-famous photograph of B-17s making their formation pass over the Italian liner *REX*, climaxing their daring search far out to sea in bad weather. There was a man who knew how to prove his point! No politician or evangelist there!

But as my colleagues combed through the historical literature for snippets that might shed light on the thesis of this manuscript, Arnold came up again and again. Yes, he was a politician and bureaucrat, but so much more. He was an extraordinary organizer of air power in *both* world wars. He was a visionary of extraordinary breadth and depth. He cared deeply about people; he was an egalitarian, not an elitist about pilots. And, most importantly for the Air Force as an institution, he was utterly devoted—above all things, even his own life—to the building of an institution committed to ideals, to a vision, and to the theory of air power.

Because of Arnold's stature on these important aspects, I think it appropriate to pause in this historical development of the Air Force and air power theory to examine Arnold and his thinking as a separate historical subject. As you read about Arnold's deeds and words, I would ask you to think about what he might say and do under the present circumstances. He might have been a leader for this season as well as his own.

Father of the Air Force

Edgar Puryear eloquently summarizes the Arnold that I have come to respect as the threads of this analysis were being pulled through the historical evolutions of air power theory and the institutional Air Force:

> If the Air Force were a church, Arnold would be its founder, its Saint Paul. If it were a country, Arnold would be its father, its George Washington or Simon Bolivar. None of the other giants of the Air Force did so much over such a long period as Arnold in building the Air Force as an institution. General of the Air Force Henry H. "Hap" Arnold was the embodiment and personification of the U.S. Air Force. He was there for its birth, and he grew up with it. His career covered the entire gamut of Air Force History. He commanded it as the Air Service during World War I, devoted his life to its arduous and difficult development between the wars, and commanded it through the challenging years of World War II.[2]

Organizing and building an Air Force was hardly new to Arnold:

> Arnold was responsible for supervising the extraordinary expansion of an Air Force that in April 1917 had only 35 pilots to a force of 10,000 pilots when the

Armistice was signed on November 11, 1918! There were only two airfields in April 1917; there were thirty at the war's end.[3]

Arnold had learned early, from the Mitchell debacle, that the institutional goals—at that time, independence and the big bombers—would not be gained by brashness.

Hap Arnold, as Assistant Chief of the Air Corps in 1936, and two years later as Chief when Gen. Oscar Westover was killed in a plane crash, was cast as a compromiser and obstructionist by Andrews and Knerr. That view was shared by many of their contemporaries who believed that air power independence was essential immediately for national security. But Arnold had learned his own lesson in military politics in the decade following the Mitchell court martial. He had been exiled to a cavalry post at Fort Riley, Kansas, and served his penance. Now, as Assistant Chief, he counseled a gradual approach in the matter of procuring B-17s and of seeking a separate air force.[4]

Compromise for the sake of institutional goals became his hallmark and, for some, his scarlet letter.

In his new position, Arnold walked a tightrope. With the possible exception of Spaatz, Eaker, and his immediate office staff, a large majority of "early bird" fliers was unenthusiastic about the Army Air Forces. Most supported—and many worshipped—Andrews as the Moses who would lead them out of the War Department wilderness. All along, Andrews had been senior rank to Arnold. More important, Andrews had held key combat-type command jobs for the past decade. Arnold, on the other hand, had achieved his reputation through a masterful public and congressional relations job at March Field, California. His monthly air shows attracted Hollywood stars by the dozen. His quick response to aid victims of the 1933 earthquake that shook nearby Long Beach, his handling of the Civilian Conservation Corps in the state, along with his command of the Western Air Mail Zone and the Alaskan flight—all these activities had garnered favorable attention. More important, his astute management had won for him the patronage of Malin Craig, IX Army Corps Area Commander at the Presidio in San Francisco, who succeeded Douglas MacArthur as Army Chief of Staff late in 1935. It was Craig who brought Arnold to Washington in January 1936 as Assistant Chief of the Air Corps.

When General Westover was killed, Arnold, with a major assist from General Craig, won the reluctant favor of President Roosevelt to be named Chief of the Air Corps.[5]

Arnold's political connections repeatedly paid off in furthering the institution's goals:

Significantly, Arnold had several long conversations with Roosevelt's closest adviser, Harry Hopkins prior to Munich. After 12 September [1938], Roosevelt secretly sent Hopkins to the West Coast to inspect the aircraft industry and its ability to increase production quickly. At this time, Hopkins says, "The President was sure we were going to get into a war and he believed air power would win it."

On 5 October, the Army again had told the Chief of the Air Corps that his continued arguments for long-range aircraft had been unsuccessful. The Woodring Air Corps program approved in March would be the guide for forthcoming expenditures and "4-engine bombers will not be included in the estimates for FYs 1940 and 1941."[6]

The big bombers had been turned down because they cost more than the twin-engined bombers of the day, such as the Douglas B-18 (derived from the DC-3). Since the mission was defense of the nation and the measure of defense was the number of planes purchased, the big bombers were easy losers in the Army Air Corps aircraft program.

The break came when the aircraft program moved onto President Roosevelt's desk:

On 14 November Roosevelt called a meeting in his office. Present were the Secretaries of the Navy, Army, and Treasury, the Army Chief of Staff, the Chief of Naval Operations, the Assistant Secretary of War for Air, and Arnold. To the surprise of everyone, except Hopkins and Arnold, Roosevelt dealt solely with the expansion of air power. Expansion of ground forces, he said, would not impress Hitler. Recognizing the important role which the Luftwaffe was playing in the appeasement at Munich, Roosevelt believed only airplanes would influence Hitler. He suggested an immediate increase in the production capability of the U.S. aircraft industry to 10,000 planes per year. Arnold would later convince him that the build-up should be based on quality rather than quantity but agreed that this number could be doubled with proper preparation.

The Chief of the Air Corps was most happy with one point which Roosevelt stressed:

[Roosevelt] stated "long range bombing is now the duty of the Army" and it was up to the Air Corps to keep anyone from landing in North or South America. The United States must be prepared to resist attack on all the Western Hemisphere and to deter landing in either North or South America. We must not be caught napping again as in 1917.

Arnold left the meeting with Roosevelt elated. He later said that he had "...the feeling that the Air Corps had finally achieved its Magna Carta." For the first time, the air arm had a program and could shoot toward a definite goal of planes and men. Arnold believed that the battle won at that time in the White House led to all the later victories in combat.[7]

Arnold's Air Force

The scale of Arnold's task in building the World War II Army Air Forces is evident from the statistics:

At the time Arnold was appointed Chief of Staff of the Air Corps in 1938 by President Franklin D. Roosevelt, the entire Air Corps consisted of 3,900 airplanes, most of them obsolete, and 22,000 officers and men in the combined services of the Army, Navy, and Marine Corps. At the end of World War II, there were two and one-half million people and 80,000 aircraft in the Army Air Forces alone.[8]

More impressive, however, were his views about the *kind* of air force he was trying to build. Early in the war, with Eaker, he laid out his thoughts about who airmen were and what they were about to a general audience. He began with praise for the airmen, in a style reminiscent of Mitchell talking about the new class of people who were taking to the air:

Military airmen are the chosen human instruments.... They fight and they fly; they strike a blow for country while dashing through the skies, man's last geographical frontier. The military airman is, therefore, most favored of all uniformed men. He must realize his great responsibility and the tremendous implications which flow from an acknowledgment of these facts.

The world is now engaged in the first armed conflict where air fighting is likely to play a predominant role. The military airmen even now winning their silver wings will shortly bow before the world footlights as the prime actors in the fiercest drama ever enacted above the five continents and the seven seas.[9]

Arnold then "banked" the claims of the air power advocates:

Some military men, outstanding among whom were General Mitchell and Admiral Sims, made claims for the power of air weapons so revolutionary as to be called fantastic by the Doubting Thomases upon whose ears they fell. The day to day deeds of military flying men today are making the wildest claims of those men of great vision seem conservative.

Military airmen today need not be thus restless and critical. The deeds and accomplishments of military airmen in all the air forces of the world have taken care of that. No sane man doubts any longer the power of the air weapon.[10]

This claim allowed him to close the book on the air power crusade and lay out the challenge which now lay ahead, not just for pilots and air crews, but for all those needed to contribute to winning the war in the air.

The end of one era and the opening of another could not have been much clearer:

> The task of the military airman now departs from the crusading role. It becomes a task of organization on a tremendous scale. No longer do we require flaming leaders with fanatic zeal to sell a cause; we need sound, even-tempered minds of great resource and depth to perfect the plans and build the structure of an air force larger than the armies and navies of old.
>
> No longer does the pilot monopolize the air-fighter role. He now knows that the navigator, the engineer, the gunner, the bombardier and many another important combat crew member play equally vital roles. The new size of the air army makes it impossible and even undesirable that every key artisan be a pilot. Many of them, as we now know, need not even be flyers at all.[11]

Arnold could then close his circle—having gone from praise to admonishment—advising that the era of strident advocacy for air power was and should be over:

> It is no longer necessary for the airman to claim that he can win wars alone. His arm has reached an acknowledged importance and a recognized value and size so that there is no longer need for hyperbole in describing its vital role. The simple facts now coming from the world's battlefields speak more loudly of the power of air forces than the strongest language the earlier prophets were able to paint by epithet or eulogy.[12]

Arnold's qualities and his vision of the Air Force reflect both harmony and contrast with those who preceded and followed him in air power leadership. During World War II, Arnold laid out ten principles for Air Force operations, provided below. His 1st, 2nd, and 5th principles are completely faithful to air power theory and doctrine. But the 6th, 7th, and 8th were antithetical to the tenets of air power as originally developed by its prophets and apostles. His 4th, 9th, and 10th principles are Arnold's hallmarks—deep and abiding concerns for the importance of all Air Force people—on the ground as well as in the air—and for the key role that technology would play in the institution's future.

> Throughout the war, I tried to have the Air Force operate under certain fundamental principles:
>
> > 1. The main job of the Air Force is bombardment; large formations of bombardment planes must hit the enemy before the enemy hits us. In short, the best defense is attack.

2. Our planes must be able to function under all climatic conditions from the North Pole to the South Pole.

3. Daylight operations, including daylight bombing, are essential to success, for it is the only way to get precision bombing. We must operate with a precision bombsight—and by daylight— realizing full well that we will have to come to a decisive combat with the enemy Air Force.

4. We must have highly developed, highly trained crews working together as a team—on the ground for maintenance and in the air for combat.

5. In order to bring the war home to Germany and Japan, and deprive them of the things that are essential for their war operations, we must carry out strategic precision bombing to key targets, deep in the enemy territory, such as airplane factories, oil refineries, steel mills, aluminum plants, submarine pens, navy yards, etc.

6. In addition to our strategic bombing, we must carry out tactical operations in cooperation with ground troops. For that purpose we must have fighters, dive bombers, and light bombers for attacking enemy airfields, communication centers, motor convoys, and troops.

7. All types of bombing operations must be protected by fighter airplanes. This was proved to be essential in the Battle of Britain, and prior to that our own exercises with bombers and fighters indicated that bombers alone could not elude modern pursuit, no matter how fast the bombers traveled.

8. Our Air Force must be ready for combined operations with ground forces, and with the Navy.

9. We must maintain our research and development programs in order to have the latest equipment it was possible to get, as soon as it was possible to get it.

10. Air power is not made up of airplanes alone. Air power is a composite of airplanes, air crews, maintenance crews, air bases, air supply, and sufficient replacements in both planes and crews to maintain a constant fighting strength, regardless of what losses may be inflicted by the enemy. In addition to that, we must have the backing of a large aircraft industry in the United States to provide all kinds of equipment, and a large training establishment that can furnish the personnel when called upon.[13]

Arnold's equitable respect for all who served in the Air Force—in contrast to the persistent tendencies toward pilot elitism within the institution—caused him problems:

The over-all program for the Army Air Forces required an overwhelming air superiority over our enemies in the shortest possible time. Our global field of operations required men from all walks of life. Each had a part to play, whether he was a hotel clerk, a railroad man, a shipping man, a barber, an auto mechanic, or a painter. We had need for all of them, each one fitting into his proper place— square pegs in square holes and round pegs in round holes....

During those early days, a great many Air Corps officers had the idea that everybody in the Air Force should be a pilot, regardless of whether he was running a hotel, a bus line, taking charge of motor transportation, or planning a hydroponics garden for the Pacific.

As in several other cases, so in this instance I immediately ran into old-fashioned opposition—indeed, a regular sit-down strike....[14]

We can only guess how both Arnold and the institution would react if they could, somehow, be brought back together again, 40 or more years later.

A Vision for the Future

Arnold spoke comfortably about his vision, not just of air power, but of the Air Force as an institution:

[I]t is worth noting that Arnold and Lt. Gen. Ira C. Eaker, Deputy Commander, AAF, and other air leaders, possessed a firm vision of the future. "We believe," observed Eaker in June 1947, "that the Air Force stands at the threshold of a new era. Whereas in the past it has been largely a corps of flying men, in the future, certainly, ten to fifteen years from now, it will be more nearly a corps of technicians and scientists."[15]

He recognized that a part of that *constant* institutional vision had to be a *dynamism* in its doctrines: "[A]ny Air Force which does not keep its doctrines ahead of its equipment, and its visions far into the future, can only delude the nation into a false sense of security."[16]

His faith in technology as a guarantor of national security and the Air Force's institutional future was evident early on: "General Arnold believed...that as long as the United States maintained its technological lead in aviation, in general, and in strategic bombardment, in particular, there would be little to fear from any potential aggressor."[17] Arnold realized that the demands for national security were changing as a result of technology, that a mobilization base was no longer sufficient and that the nation would need a substantial standing air force.

Even before the war ended, [he] was convinced that a force in-being was necessary because no longer would there be sufficient time to mobilize. The era of come-from-behind victories was over—World War II was the last of its kind.[18]

In that judgment, he may have been far more prophetic than even he could hope to be.

Notes

1. Stephanides, *Dædalus and Icarus*, 19, 20.

2. Puryear, *Stars in Flight*, 3.

3. Ibid., 11.

4. Green, "Hugh J. Knerr: The Pen and the Sword," 101.

5. Ibid., 112, 113.

6. Ibid.

7. Eastman, "The Development of Big Bombers," 217. A similar assessment is provided by Futrell in, *Ideas, Concepts, Doctrine*, 91.

8. Puryear, *Stars in Flight*, 29.

9. H. H. Arnold and Ira C. Eaker, *The Army Flyer* (New York: Harper & Brothers, 1942), 3, 4.

10. Ibid., 5.

11. Ibid., 6.

12. Ibid., 7.

13. Ibid., 290, 291.

14. Ibid., 292.

15. Herman S. Wolk, "Planning and Organizing the Air Force," *Aerospace Historian* (Fall, September 1987): 174.

16. H. H. Arnold, as quoted in Wolk, "Planning and Organizing the Air Force," 174.

17. Smith, *The Air Force Plans for Peace*, 106.

18. Wolk, "Men Who Made the Air Force," 10.

10

The Test of Fire

When Dædalus next turned his head to check that all was well with Icarus, there was no sign of the boy. Close to panic, he scanned the skies from horizon to horizon, till finally he made out a tiny dot, rapidly approaching the sun's bright disc.

"Icarus!" he shouted despairingly. "Icarus, come back!" But in spite of the urgency of Dædalus' voice, his words were lost in the boundless expanses of the sky and never reached his son's ears.

And soon the very thing happened which Dædalus had feared. The sun melted the wax and the feathers were scattered in the air. Soon there was not a single feather left, and Icarus fell like a stone from the heights. Dædalus made a desperate effort to catch him, but it was all in vain, and the daring young man found a watery grave in the arms of the blue sea far below.

On laboring wings Dædalus carried the body of his son to the nearest island, and there he buried him. Ever since, the island has been called Icaria and the sea around it, the Icarian sea, and all over the world the name of Icarus is remembered whenever men wish to honour those who gave their lives to make the dream of flight come true.[1]

The Anglo-American Divergence

Even though both the British and Americans had embraced the same principal elements of air power theory—the primacy of offense, air superiority, and independent control for decisive use—their motivations toward the theory had been quite different since World War I. Those differences soon became apparent in the opening phases of World War II.

The idea of *deterrence* through evident capabilities for strategic aerial bombardment took root in Britain 40 years before its transplantation to the United States. In World War I, Britain's loss of a generation of young men in stalemated trench warfare had been compounded by the terrifying aerial bombardment of its cities by German zeppelins and aircraft. Although the extravagant estimates of civilian casualties and panic that might result from future aerial bombardment were subsequently proven wrong in World War II, the interwar thinking about the future of warfare in Britain was dominated by those two disasters. The Spanish Civil War only reinforced the bleak impression of the aerial bombardment of cities:

> After the indiscriminate bombing of civilians at Guernica during the Spanish civil war, it was widely believed that aerial warfare would be so terrible that future wars would be over in a few weeks.[2]

Trenchard and then Harris offered a solution through long-range bombing aircraft: The threat of aerial bombardment might deter war and, if not, the execution of that threat could circumvent the stalemate of trench warfare.[3] The war, if it came, might very well be resolved in a test of civilian morale when cities inevitably came under aerial attack.

The American concept of strategic bombardment focused on the enemy's war-making potentials and infrastructures, not on breaking civilian morale, even though that might suffer as the enemy's industry and transportation were systematically destroyed. Americans saw strategic bombardment as a more *efficient* way to wage war decisively and quickly.

Although the concept of strategic bombardment was recognized elsewhere in the world, it flourished as a major military effort only in Britain and America during World War II. The German Luftwaffe had been conceived to support the army in the pursuit of its objectives, not as an independent means for defeating an enemy. "The Luftwaffe's creators had envisioned it as an adjunct to the German Army, primarily providing offensive support for ground troops."[4]

The wide-scale bombing of cities during World War II was more deliberately undertaken by the British (and eventually by the Americans) than by their German and Japanese enemies or even by their Russian ally.[5] Although Germany bombed London before Britain bombed Berlin, Germany stumbled its way into the bombing of London, whereas Britain had been preparing for just such an exchange for years. Deterrence had failed, the British executed their deterrent threat, and the bombing of cities on both sides rapidly escalated thereafter:

> On 24 August [1940] two German aircraft, hopelessly lost after failing to find their intended objective in the Midlands, scattered their bombs at random over [London], inadvertently breaching Goering's order that it was not to be attacked. Churchill ordered Bomber Command to attack Berlin as a reprisal, which in turn provoked Hitler to order that London should now become his air force's main target.[6]

But the details of those events reveal the British predisposition toward the aerial bombardment of cities:

> The two lost aircraft were part of a planned German raid on the Thames-side cities of Rochester and Kingston and the huge oil-tank storage installations at Thameshaven, some 15 miles downriver from London. The lead planes, which were flying on radio beams, were followed by others that were not so equipped. On the run-in to the targets, two of these planes lost visual touch with their radio-equipped pathfinders and strayed on beyond the main attack pattern. A fountain of flak rose to meet them and the antiaircraft barrage became thicker as they flew on, clinging together. At last, realizing they were lost, the two pilots decided that there was only one thing to do. They jettisoned their bombs, turned east, and raced for home.

> As it happened, they were over London itself when they unloaded their bombs. Two of them fell on the heart of the city, razing the ancient church of St. Giles in Cripplegate and ripping John Milton's statue off its pedestal in a nearby square. The rest of the bombs crashed down in the northern and eastern London boroughs of Islington, Finchley, Stepney, Tottenham, and Bethnal Green among others, killing customers as they came out of the pubs at closing time and audiences on their way home from movie houses.[7]

If the German bombing was a ghastly mistake, the British response was premeditated and sustained:

> There was little doubt, even at the time, that the [German] bombing [of London] was unintentional.... But Churchill was delighted to believe otherwise—and to act accordingly. [And he instructed] the RAF [to] keep hitting Berlin until the Germans reacted.[8]

The Americans entered the fray with a concept of decisive, strategic, precision, daylight bombardment of military and industrial targets; but they eventually learned what the British had concluded with some reluctance—their instrument was crude, costly, and could most effectively be employed in attacks directly against cities. As it turned out, neither the British nor the American proponents were able to prove their theories about the effectiveness or efficiency of aerial bombardment during the war; but in the end, the atomic bomb finally provided means so destructive that few could any longer doubt it.

Offensive Forever

As the war unfolded, the "blitzkrieg, the Battle of Britain, and the German submarine campaign seemed to teach the AAF planners nothing; their faith in the effectiveness of defensive action [only] on the ground and on the sea and of the absolute supremacy of the offensive in the air, the doctrine of the Air Corps Tactical School in the thirties, was not questioned."[9] The doctrine took explicit form as America's entry into the war loomed in mid-1941:

> On July 9 [President Roosevelt] sent the war and navy secretaries his request for an estimate of "overall production requirements required to defeat our potential enemies." Logistical needs were Roosevelt's primary concerns, but they could not be determined without making strategic assumptions, as FDR knew. For the AAF, Roosevelt's request was the opportunity to expound its vision of air war. Rather than pool its planning effort with that of the Army general staff, Arnold pressed hard for permission for his new Air War Plans Division...to do its own planning.[10] The general staff, perhaps itself overwhelmed by the magnitude of FDR's request, granted permission, acceding surprising autonomy to the AAF. Heavily staffed with bomber advocates like Haywood Hansell and [Laurence] Kuter from the tactical school, the AWPD wrote into basic war plans the long-standing faith in precision bombing.

> [AWPD-1], as the result was called, concentrated on Germany's defeat. The air planners believed that bombing alone might achieve that objective but hedged their bets because they still needed to make their plans acceptable to the general staff. Bombing would proceed with complementary objectives: to defeat Germany alone if possible, to prepare for invasion if not. Since the air force could go into action before an invasion force could be trained, a choice between those objectives seemed unnecessary for the moment anyway. A preliminary effort to subdue the German air force would be necessary, but the ultimate priority for bombing was the German economy, "presumably drawn taut," as Hansell later put it, by the massive demands of war. Scheduled to begin twenty-one months after American entry into the war, the main assault by an American force of four thousand bombers would "in six months bring much of her [Germany's] vital industry to ruin." The principal targets would be Germany's electric power system, its transportation network, and its petroleum industry.[11]

Once the war began, doctrinal debate largely disappeared:

War...attenuated the spectrum of debate on air power. Where once alternatives (however arbitrary) had been offered in the clash between prophets and skeptics, now public argument was largely confined to disagreement over the techniques and proportions of the air war.[12]

The Americans persisted in pursuing their distinctive concept of strategic bombardment—precision, daylight bombing against industrial targets—despite the prior, contrary experience of their British allies:

A master of strategic planning, Spaatz directed the decisive phase of the American bombing offensive against Germany.... Churchill had argued that destruction of Germany's industry would not be sufficient to bring victory, and the RAF Bomber Command under Air Chief Marshal Arthur Harris pursued general area bombing without wavering. But Spaatz proved adept at singling out the enemy's vulnerable industries and destroying them....[13]

To persist against rising losses and the lessons of the British experience in strategic bombing required extraordinary determination and courage from the AAF leadership: "When the determination of others flagged, [Hap Arnold's] conviction that the bombing offensive eventually would be decisive spelled the difference...."[14]

Command of the Air Revisited

Even before America's entry into the war, some surprising losses of bombers made AAF leaders uneasy about the soundness of their doctrine which called for self-defended bombers to penetrate to their targets.

General Arnold was far from happy. On November 14, 1939, he said the widely held Air Corps belief that large bombardment formations could defend themselves against fighters was open to question. General Arnold blamed acceptance of bomber invulnerability on teachings of the Air Corps Tactical School, and called on Maj. Gen. Delos Emmons, Commander of the Air Combat Command (successor to the GHQ Air Force) to submit a study of the bomber- versus-fighter problem.[15]

General Emmons called upon Harold L. George to testify since he had been one of the architects of strategic bombardment concepts at the Air Corps Tactical School (1931–1937) and was serving, at that time, with the only bombardment group equipped with the new B-17 bombers.

Harold George...told General Emmons: "There is no question in my mind but that American bombardment units could not today defend themselves against

American pursuit units." That forthright statement must have tried him sorely; it ran counter to all he wanted to believe. But it was a courageous and honest assessment that produced favorable results. The Air Combat Command found that "aerial operations of the present European conflict confirm the results of World War I: that is that the present bombardment airplane cannot defend itself adequately against pursuit attack."[16]

Nevertheless,

> Until the spring of 1943 the assumption that B-17 and B-24 aircraft in formation could defend themselves against fighters made the doctrine of the Tactical School seem valid. Then the "battleplane" did not work out as a defensive weapon and the need for very long range escort fighters was admitted, the only substantial modification of doctrine was the incorporation of the escort fighter within the strategic mission. During the 1943–45 planning period no appreciation of the possible defensive use of guided missiles was recognized, and all comment on guided missiles reflected a belief that in the future they would contribute to the supremacy of the offensive in airpower.[17]

The planning failure was not an inability to recognize the problem; it was myopia about possible solutions:

> It is unfair to say that…Air Force leaders completely ignored the vulnerability of long-range bombardment aircraft to defensive fighter attack, or that they were totally unaware of the lessons of the Battle of Britain regarding the technological advances in pursuit aviation. What was ignored or overlooked was the possibility of building a long-range escort fighter which would be essentially a pursuit aircraft and not a heavily armed bomber. While the Air Force leaders understood the value of the four-engine bomber…these same leaders almost totally ignored the advances being made in pursuit aviation—advances that were even greater than those made in bombardment aviation…. The neglect by the Air Corps leaders of technological developments in pursuit aviation, from 1935 to 1943, provides an interesting case study of the relationship between doctrine and force structure.[18]

The roots of the myopia went back to the 1930s birth of air power doctrine in the U.S. Army Air Corps:

> Ironically, the Air Corps Tactical School arguments of the 1930s about pursuit versus bomber employment had persisted, and now (in 1942) the bomber people still were very much in the doctrinal driver's seat. Bomber preeminence had not been materially affected even by the air lessons of Spain's civil war and the Battle of Britain, which clearly showed the limited effect of strategic bombing on civilian morale and the essentiality of fighter escort to keep bomber losses at an acceptable level.[19]

The American strategic bombing campaign over Germany soon turned into a campaign for air superiority:

> In these complex and shifting aerial campaigns carried on from February through June [1944], means and ends in Allied air strategy had been neatly reversed from those posited in original plans. Where once defeat of the enemy in the skies had been seen as a preliminary to the bombing of his factories—at that, a preliminary American airmen had hoped to reduce through their bombers' formidable defensive capability—now the bombing was a prod to engage the Luftwaffe, the bombers themselves bait to lure it into combat. The air force's historians acknowledged this shift but concluded that "in terms of final results it matters little whether...the German planes were destroyed in the factories, on the ground, or in the skies." In fact it mattered a great deal, for it greatly altered the costs and nature of victory as well as the doctrine on which the air force rested its claim to supremacy and virtue. If precision attacks did not paralyze the enemy's war economy, then victory could not come until his forces were defeated in battle and his territory occupied, precisely the traditional method of war the air prophets had hoped to avoid. And if victory came in the traditional way, the air force served fundamentally to complement traditional strategies, succeeding by a grinding attrition whose toll for both friends and enemies mocked earlier claims about the merciful speed of strategic air power.[20]

Day or Night; Factory or City?

The AAF battle for air superiority over Germany had to be fought at the same time as several bureaucratic battles:

> ...General Eaker was not just leading the American air attack against Germany; he was also waging several other campaigns crucial to Air Force success. One of these was with top figures in the Royal Air Force who sought to switch the American effort to nighttime bombing of cities. Another was the U.S. Navy, which sought to switch Army Air's effort to anti-submarine attacks, either in coastal patrol or on the U-boat pens on the French coast. A third battle was with American public opinion, which had yet to be convinced that daylight, precision bombing of strategic targets would really work.[21]

Apart from the arguments about the most efficient use of war resources, the American airmen were simply not prepared to consider alternatives to the approach they had designed and followed for more than a decade.

> Both British and German bombing had already shown how strategic air war might degenerate into futile barbarism. Supremely confident in their day bombers, the American air planners did not address this danger or the possibility that even successful precision strikes might fail to paralyze the German economy. True, they did not rule out "heavy and sustained bombing of cities" as

a kind of coup de grâce climaxing the success of economic attacks or decisive German setback in ground fighting. But throughout the 1930s their strategic arguments had rested on the moral assumption that precision bombing would bring swift, economical, and humane victory. The justification for strategic bombing was the alternative it offered to the carnage of ground warfare. In 1941 the air strategists saw no reason to challenge that assumption. Brushing aside the English and German experiences in 1940 and 1941, they felt no need to review the moral issue.

Their pressing concerns were neither strategic nor moral but political and economic. Their attention flowed to threading AWPD/1 [the AAF war plan] through the channels of the conservative general staff and to mobilizing industry for the war. To the air planners' relief, Marshall gave AWPD/1 his approval, steered it around the Joint Board, and set it on to a sympathetic Stimson. The general staff still believed that destruction of the enemy's ground armies was the only sure path to victory. But doubts about the survival of Britain and Russia ran large in the War Department, making a land invasion of the Continent seem remote at best: hence even conservative officers acknowledged the imperative of first weakening Germany by bombing. Strategy, then, along with Roosevelt's wishes about how to fight the war, made the War Department amenable to a vision of air war that would have seemed repugnant and fanciful a few years earlier.[22]

The British move to shift the American bombing campaign from precision daylight bombing of industry to night bombing of cities came at the Casablanca conference.

By the time Roosevelt and Churchill met at Casablanca on January 14, 1943, Arnold had heard of Churchill's intentions [to shift the AAF into night bombing alongside the RAF].... Arnold rushed Eaker from England to defend daylight strategic operations. Eaker personally took his case to Churchill, assembling the arguments for the daylight bomber, principally the economy of force achievable through greater precision. Eaker's position was tricky, for he had little new to say to the British, and he had to defend the Eighth Air Force without appearing to derogate the RAF's contribution. As before, the best tack was to deny conflict; British and American operations would be complementary, not competitive, the British destroying urban areas, the Americans hitting bottleneck targets or marking them by fire for British attack at night. Together they would engage the German air force and cause German war weariness by round-the-clock bombing. Twenty-four hour operations would also head off the hopeless congestion in Britain's airfields and air space sure to result if both British and American bombers were squeezed into the same schedule. Arguing from operational necessity just as the British had in defending their switch to night bombing, Eaker also asserted that his bombers had to strike by day because they were built to do so and the crews were trained only in that method; to switch to the dark would halt the AAF's offensive altogether for months. Too, only the daylight bomber could engage the German fighter force, depleting it so as to facilitate further bombing as well as ground operations.

There was troublesome logic here. Arguments from operational necessity allowed means to dictate ends—bombing forces, British or American, did what they could do best, not necessarily what it was best to do. Shooting down German fighters became a major achievement of the American bombers, but the initial intention had been to destroy the German air force in its factories and on its airfields. If now it was to be done substantially through the attrition of combat, the task could be grim indeed, especially without long-range fighter escort.[23]

Although the British may have had their doubts about the effectiveness of the American precision daylight raids, Joseph Goebbels, who was in a better position to judge, did not:

[T]he day raids on Bremen by American bombers...were very hard indeed. The Americans drop their bombs with extraordinary precision from an altitude of eight to nine thousand meters. The population has the paralyzing feeling that there really is no protection against such daylight attacks.[24]

The American daylight raiders were apparently doing precisely what the British had been trying to do with their night attacks—paralyzing the population.

By 1944, the two air forces were positioned to cross paths. The RAF was developing techniques that gave the night bombers a precision approaching that of the AAF's Fortresses and Liberators, while the Americans were beginning to loosen their definitions of precision bombing.[25]

Even retrospectively, the AAF leaders saw no inconsistencies between the theory and realities, or between the British and American bombing campaigns over Europe.

After the war, Spaatz was asked, "Do you feel that the faith of the Army Air Force in daylight strategic bombing was justified by the results?" He responded, "Why, certainly. We might have won the war in Europe without it, but I doubt it very much. I think it was the combination of the two bombings, the night bombing of the RAF and daylight bombing, that was largely responsible for successful conclusion of the war there. Everyone thought a year or two before the invasion that to invade the continent of Europe was an impossible undertaking, that the German air forces would smother it as they did at that first operation at Dieppe by Mountbatten. But actually, the result of the, and I say primarily, of the daylight bombing, which forced the German air force back to defend Germany, prevented any large German air force [from appearing] at the invasion. I think that there were only two or three German planes that appeared during the whole landing in Normandy."[26]

The Anglo-American Convergence[27]

By the end of the war, the American implementation of strategic bombardment had come full circle and coincided with the British ideas that the Americans had so vigorously resisted. Daylight precision bombing of military targets from self-defended bomber formations over Japan had finally been fully transformed to nighttime saturation bombing of cities from undefended bombers streaming independently on their missions. The transformation came at the hands of the civilian operations analysts who supported General Curtis LeMay in the conduct of his bombing campaign against Japan.[28]

The initial results with the new B-29 bombers operating from the Marianas Islands were disappointing. Compared to the size of the effort being mounted, the number of targets destroyed was embarrassingly small. The operational problems included long over-water flights, modest bomb loads, aircraft and engine unreliabilities, high winds, and a new and cranky airplane flown by uneasy crews.

But LeMay's bosses also faced an institutional problem: The AAF had fought hard in its battles with the Navy and the rest of the Army over the allocation of the available war resources and won its case for the B-29 bomber program. But the B-29 program had turned out to be much more difficult and costly than expected; its costs even exceeded those of the secret Manhattan Project to develop the first atomic bombs.[29] With such a large and contended investment riding on the AAF claims for the decisiveness of strategic bombing and the B-29, LeMay had to deliver what his institution had so publicly promised.

True to its strategic bombardment theories of the time, the AAF sought the heavy bomber it had always wanted in the B-29 program: a long-range airplane specifically designed for high-altitude, daylight, precision bombardment with high-explosive bombs dropped from self-defended formations. Of course, that is precisely how AAF initially used the airplane over Japan. The bombers formed up over the Marianas and then flew in formation to Japan where they bombed from high altitude in daylight. The Japanese defenses against such attacks were much less effective than the German defenses over Europe, partly because of the state of Japanese defensive resources at that point in the war, and partly because of the high altitude from which the attacks were made. However, the results of the bombing were disappointing too, partly because of weather (on navigation and bombing accuracy), but mostly because the bomb loads in the airplanes were being sacrificed to accommodate the weight of the fuel required to fly in formation and at high altitudes and to the weight of the bomber's defensive armament (automated gun turrets)—the very things that were designed to ensure its penetration of the Japanese defenses.

After finally succeeding in acquiring the airplane that could penetrate Japanese air defenses in daylight with acceptable losses, the AAF found that it was not very effective at accomplishing its purpose: destroying Japan's capacity and will to fight. LeMay posed the problem to his small staff of operations analysts; their answers turned the B-29 bombing campaign over Japan inside out. They recommended area or carpet bombing of Japanese cities with incendiaries instead of precision bombing of the Japanese aircraft industry with high explosive bombs.[30] They recommended flying the bombers independently at medium altitudes and stripping the planes of their guns instead of sacrificing bomb-carrying capacity for high-altitude and formation flying and for defensive armaments. They recommended flying at night in order to reduce the effectiveness of the Japanese air defenses.[31]

The flight crews considered the analysts' proposal that they simply "straggle" in over the target at night to be suicidal. They envisaged many of their airplanes colliding in the dark with hundreds of airplanes going to and from a single target. The analysts calmly demonstrated, with irrefutable mathematics, that the crews' chances of a collision were significantly less than their odds of landing in the "drink" because of multiple mechanical failures of their airplane's engines. The crews could appreciate this statistic, since engine failures on the long over-water flights were one of their several concerns with the new B-29 and something they had to confront daily.

LeMay adopted all the analysts' recommendations. Careful definition and analysis of the operational problem had overturned almost every design precept of the B-29 program and the AAF theory of strategic bombardment. The analysts' recommendations were counter to the intuition and doctrine of those they served, and it is unlikely that the AAF would have slowly come around to such a drastic approach to their operations. It is certainly to LeMay's credit that he had confidence in his analysts and the courage to fly in the face of AAF doctrine.

The B-29 bombing campaign proceeded to become so highly effective in accomplishing its realigned purposes, that LeMay, when asked when the war would be over, simply counted up the remaining unburned cities and estimated the time for his airplanes to carpet them with incendiaries. In retrospect, whatever the military or legal merits of that bombing campaign, it was important to the AAF aspirations for institutional independence, then within sight. LeMay and his operations analysts, although mostly concerned with making the new bombers more effective, may have prevented a failure involving costs and expectations that could have undone the Air Force's postwar bid for institutional independence.

The Slippery Slope

LeMay's bombing of Japan in 1945 was no longer distinguishable in either its means or ends from that of "Bomber" (or "Butcher") Harris' bombing of German cities. Freeman Dyson describes his personal journey on the slippery slope to city bombing and faults the flawed, but persistent, doctrine of strategic bombing:

> The last spring of the war was the most desolate. Even after Dresden, through March and April of 1945, the bombing of cities continued.... I began to look backward and to ask myself how it had happened that I let myself become involved in this crazy game of murder. Since the beginning of the war, I had been retreating step by step from one moral position to another, until at the end I had no moral position at all. At the beginning of the war, I believed fiercely in the brotherhood of man...and was morally opposed to all violence. After a year of war, I retreated, and said, Unfortunately, nonviolent resistance against Hitler is impracticable, but I am still morally opposed to bombing. A couple of years later, I said, Unfortunately, it seems that bombing is necessary in order to win the war, and so I am willing to go to work for Bomber Command, but I am still morally opposed to bombing cities indiscriminately. After I arrived at Bomber Command, I said, Unfortunately, it turns out that we are, after all, bombing cities indiscriminately, but this is morally justified, as it is helping to win the war. A year later, I said, Unfortunately, it seems that our bombing is not really helping to win the war, but at least I am morally justified in working to save the lives of the bomber crews. In the last spring of the war, I could no longer find any excuses.... I had surrendered one moral principle after another, and in the end it was all for nothing....

> ...The root of the evil was the doctrine of strategic bombing, which had guided the evolution of Bomber Command from its beginning, in 1936. The doctrine of strategic bombing declared that the only way to win wars or to prevent wars was to rain down death and destruction upon enemy countries from the sky. This doctrine was attractive to political and military leaders in the nineteen-thirties, for two reasons. First, it promised them escape from their worst nightmare—a

repetition of the frightful trench warfare of the First World War, through which they had all lived. Second, it offered them a hope that war could be avoided altogether, by the operation of the principle that later came to be known as deterrence. The doctrine held that all governments would be deterred from starting wars if they knew that the certain consequences would be ruinous bombardment. As far as the war against Germany was concerned, history proved the theory wrong on both counts. Strategic bombing neither deterred the war nor won it. There has never yet been a war that strategic bombing by itself won. In spite of the clear evidence of history, the strategic-bombing doctrine flourished in Bomber Command throughout the Second World War. And it flourishes still, in bigger countries, with bigger bombs.[32]

Not all would agree with Dyson's assessment of the validity of the theory. Fifty years after the RAF mounted its first 1,000-plane raid of the war (targeted against the heart of Cologne) the British still aren't sure:

Historians are sharply divided about the effect of the British bombing campaign. At this distance from the event, they are never going to agree. It reduced the cities of Germany to rubble and killed some 600,000 Germans, almost all of them civilians, 100,000 of them children under 14. Only by the last year of the war did it begin to reduce Germany's war production. The effect on morale is incalculable. The Germans continued to fight fiercely for three years after the destruction of Cologne.[33]

The British seem much more sure about the effect of German bombing on British morale:

In the event, the London blitz did not destroy civilian morale so much as increase hatred and a desire for revenge. The only time that British morale appears to have wobbled more than briefly was under the unpredictable new terrors of the V-1 flying bomb and the V-2 rocket.[34]

Yet, on the same day, on the same page of the same newspaper, Sir Bernard Lovell, one of the British scientists who developed radar bombing techniques for Bomber Command, cites a postwar interview with Albert Speer (Hitler's minister for armaments and war production) concerning the effectiveness of the British bombing campaign. With respect to the bombing of Hamburg in the summer of 1943, Speer said:

We were of the opinion that a rapid repetition of this type of attack upon another six German towns would inevitably cripple the will to sustain armaments manufacture and war production. It was I who first verbally reported to the Führer at that time that a continuation of these attacks might bring about a rapid end to the war.[35]

Were the airmen that close to a positive proof of their theory? Or were they caught up in an escalating cycle of carnage—not in the trenches which they had promised to avoid, but in the cities which they could not?

Notes

1. Stephanides, *Dædalus and Icarus*, 20.

2. Editorial, "Remembering Them All," *The Times*, London, May 30, 1992, 15.

3. Trenchard "had commanded the Army's Flying Corps in France and had also led bombing raids on Germany in retaliation for the attacks on England. His experiences had convinced him that the appalling casualties of trench warfare could be avoided through proper use of air power. He believed that the bomber—with only a little help from the Army and Navy—could win wars." Ronald H. Bailey, "The Air War in Europe," *World War II* (Alexandria, Virginia: Time-Life Books, 1979), 26.

4. Leonard Mosley, "The Battle of Britain," *World War II*, Alexandria, Virginia: Time-Life Books, 1977, 47.

5. This analysis of the path to city bombing during World War II is derived from Carl H. Builder, *The Future of Nuclear Deterrence*, RAND P-7702 (Santa Monica, Calif.: RAND, February 1991).

6. Norman Longmate, "London's Burning," *The Daily Telegraph*, London, editorial supplement, June 18, 1990, iii.

7. Mosley, *The Battle of Britain*, 118.

8. Ibid., 118, 119.

9. Smith, *The Air Force Plans for Peace*, 61.

10. The advocate behind Arnold's initiative was Lt. Col. Harold L. George, then chief of the Air War Plans Division. See Col. Ed Crowder, "Pointblank: A Study in Strategic and National Security Decision Making," *Airpower Journal*, vol. 6, no. 1 (Spring 1992): 58.

11. Sherry, *The Rise of American Airpower*, 99.

12. Ibid., 129.

13. Wolk, "Men Who Made the Air Force," 11.

14. Ibid., 12.

15. Hansell, "Harold L. George: Apostle of Air Power," 82.

16. Ibid.

17. Smith, *The Air Force Plans for Peace*, 61.

18. Ibid., 30, 31.

19. Henry, "William E. Kepner: All the Way to Berlin," 163.

20. Sherry, *The Rise of American Airpower*, 164, 165.

21. James Parton, "Lt. Gen. Ira C. Eaker, USAF (Ret.), An Aide's Memoir," *Aerospace Historian* (Winter, December 1987), 230.

22. Sherry, *The Rise of American Airpower*, 99, 100.

23. Ibid., 148, 149.

24. Louis P. Lochner, ed., *The Goebbels Diaries (1942–1943)* (New York: Doubleday, 1948), 354.

25. Sherry, *The Rise of American Airpower*, 162.

26. Puryear, *Stars in Flight*, 88. The quote is referenced to an interview by Alfred Goldberg with Gen. Carl A. Spaatz, May 19, 1965, USAF Oral History Program, K239.0512-755.

27. Much of the following is derived from my *The Masks of War*, 96–98.

28. The role of the civilian operations analysts is drawn from several conversations in the late 1950s with Professor Alex Boldyreff of the University of California at Los Angeles who served as an operations analyst for General LeMay during World War II. My memory of the details of those conversations 30 years ago may not be completely reliable, but the point of the example is almost certainly consistent with that was presented by Professor Boldyreff.

29. One of my colleagues expressed astonishment that the B-29 program was a more expensive undertaking than the Manhattan Project to make the first atomic bombs; and he suggested that I provide citations. The cost of the Manhattan Project was widely quoted at two billion dollars. That figure is given by Richard Rhodes in *The Making of the Atomic Bomb* (New York: Simon & Schuster, 1986), 605, and by Keith Wheeler in "The Fall of Japan," *World War II*, Alexandria, Virginia: Time-Life Books, 1983, 62. The B-29 program is described in several sources as "the three-billion-dollar gamble," once by Edward Jablonski in *AIRWAR: Wings of Fire* (Garden City: Doubleday & Company, 1971), 127, and twice by Keith Wheeler in "Bombers Over Japan," *World War II*, Alexandria, Virginia: Time-Life Books, 1982, 24, and again on 27. The three-billion-dollar figure was probably not a macabre exaggeration, for it can easily be approximated with separate estimates of the cost of each B-29 and the numbers produced. Keith Wheeler estimates that the B-29s "would ultimately cost about $600,000 per plane (in "Bombers Over Japan," 21). Lee Kennett observed: "Only the Americans could afford to offer themselves a bomber like the B-29, which cost over $800,000—a staggering sum for the era...." (in *A History of Strategic Bombing*, New York: Charles Scribner's Sons, 1982), 181. The numbers of B-29s produced (not including its post-war derivative, the B-50) was 3905, according to Elke C. Weal, *et.al.*, in *Combat Aircraft of World War Two* (New York: Macmillian Publishing Co., 1977), 191. According to these numbers, the B-29 program could have cost from $2.3B to $3.1B. The numbers get even larger if one takes into account that an additional 5092 B-29s were on order at the war's end, according to Bill Gunston in *The Encyclopedia of the World's Combat Aircraft*, (New York: Chartwell Books, 1976), 26. If those plans had been carried out, the B-29 program might have cost somewhere between $5.4B and $7.2B (assuming that the unit costs remained constant).

30. The rationale given at the time for this indiscriminate form of city bombardment was that the Japanese war industry had, after three years of war, become a cottage industry—almost any home could be involved in the making of aircraft engine components. The validity of that rationale seems dubious today; but at the time it seemed plausible to many; and some such rationale was necessary if the bombing was not to be a violation of the Geneva Conventions, which prohibit indiscriminate attacks upon civilians.

31. The Japanese radar capabilities were correctly judged to be insufficient for accurate direction of anti-aircraft artillery or night-fighter aircraft.

32. Freeman Dyson, *Disturbing the Universe* (New York: Harper & Row, 1979), 30, 31. (Also published in "The World of the Scientist," *The New Yorker*, August 6, 1979, 56.)

33. Editorial, "Remembering Them All."

34. Ibid.

35. Sir Benard Lovell, in a letter to the editor, *The Times*, London, May 30, 1992, 15, with the quotation of Albert Speer taken from an interview on July 18, 1945, and referenced to Charles Webster and Noble Frankland, *The Strategic Air Offensive Against Germany 1939–1945*, vol 4.

11

The Practitioners

There's only one hope of shortening this war— daylight precision bombing. *If we fold, daylight bombing is done with. I don't know, maybe it means the whole show.*[1]

A third day like this might kill precision bombardment.... I've spent 20 years working for bombardment; the Chief 25.[2]

Air power theory had finally been reduced to practice by Andrews, Arnold, Harris, Spaatz, Eaker, and LeMay. These were not the people who created or sold the theory, but who used it as the vehicle to do something—to build up air power at the beginning of World War II and then to use it in combat. In the application of air power during World War II, they were constantly mindful that they were testing the theory which had served as the foundation for the development of military aviation and especially the institutional independence they sought—and that all rested on how well they did.

Air power theory was now in the hands of practical, pragmatic operators who had to convert that theory into practice if they were to realize their diverse ambitions. Their individual challenges were the conversion of theory into tactics, doctrine, organization, equipment, training, and commitment in battle. Air power theory was the thread that tied all of these disparate but interdependent activities together. The new breed of operators wanted to prove the theory in all of its elements, but most especially the need for independence of application. Their opportunity had come in victory—in war and in the battle of ideas—and they wouldn't get another.

Independence Postponed

The combination of the urgencies of war and Arnold's astute institutional leadership resulted in the postponement of the airmen's persistent agenda for independence.

> ...Arnold [had] gained General Marshall's support for the post of Chief and subsequently Commanding General, AAF, in part, because he was willing to live with Marshall's strongly-held belief, expressed at the American Legion Convention in 1941, that a separate air force—"a great error"—would disrupt the War Department's "splendid organization." Marshall added "that nothing has developed as a result of the present war which indicates that a change should be made in the present setup."[3]

Arnold's adroitness in political navigation for the benefit of the institutional future of the Air Force is evident in the bargains he struck throughout the war:

> Arnold, ever an astute politician, had established a close friendship with Harry Hopkins in the White House and with Marshall. A powerful new player at the policy level appeared on the scene late in 1940 in the person of Robert A. Lovett in the reconstituted position of Assistant Secretary of War for Air. A brilliant Wall Street investment banker, Lovett had been a Navy flier in World War I and was a logistics expert who greatly reinforced President Roosevelt's and Secretary of War Stimson's growing stress on a huge build-up of American air strength. Out of this small group a tacit arrangement evolved as America entered World War II. Though the Air Corps was structurally a part of the Army, Marshall gave Arnold and the Air Corps equal status with the Army and Navy at the meetings of the Joint Chiefs of Staff. In return Arnold agreed that he and the Air Corps would desist from pushing for an independent air force until the war was over. The politic, lucid rationale for this marriage of expedience was well expressed in Arnold's and Eaker's second book, *Winged Warfare*, published in 1941
>
>> Many feel that eventually the defensive air components of the nation will be given a status coordinate and commensurate with that of the Army and Navy.... We shall be fortunate if our time for that reorganization comes in the relative time of peace or at the worst in the preparatory and not in the fighting stage....
>>
>> The separate air force idea is not something to be rushed at pell mell or hell bent for leather. It must not be approached with the state of mind that everything now in existence, or which has been done, is wrong. The Army and Navy, the older services, deserve great credit for the tremendous strides they have made in the development of

military and naval aviation.There are many essential services which the older and established bureaus, departments, or subdivisions of the Army and Navy now perform for the air arm. These include supply, ordnance—arms and ammunition—signal equipment, food, shelter, clothing, and the protection of air bases....

It may well be that eventually air forces of all countries will be separated from land and sea forces for the same reasons that sea and land forces were separated more than a century ago. There is as much diversity in equipment, strategy, technique and leadership between the air and land or sea operations as between land and sea fighting. It requires a different type of fighting man operating in a different type of vessel, differently equipped, differently trained over a long period of time, and instilled with different ideas of technique, tactics and strategy. This long step should be taken, if it is taken at all, only after careful planning and mature thought and not with a zest for radical reform. There should be a stage of gradual evolution as against an overnight cutting of binding ties....[4]

A House Divided

If what unified Army aviators was their desire for autonomy, what divided them was their affection for different kinds of flying and aircraft—bombers or fighters. Although air power theory provided a rationale for their independence, it also emphasized the primacy of the bomber, and the fighter pilots were ultimately left torn between their love of means and ends. That tension would remain unresolved for the fighter pilots until the 1960s when air power theory was neglected by SAC and partially subverted by TAC. Perry McCoy Smith described the dilemma in this way:

The AAF, being a separate service without formal autonomy, presented its leaders with a dilemma: Should intraservice rivalry among various Army Air Corps factions (bombardment, pursuit, attack) be permitted and encouraged to avoid neglecting any airpower technological breakthrough, or should intraservice rivalry be suppressed in the interest of presenting a united front for autonomy? The habits and the rationale of the 1930's continued throughout the war; that is, the fighter enthusiast was isolated by being placed firmly under the control of a bombardment leader, by being sent to an insignificant (or less significant) theater of operations, or by tacit bribery through the encouragement of long-range fighter development. The fighter enthusiasts' dilemma was the conflicting desire for autonomy and fighter development. At times, the fighter leaders would place autonomy ahead of fighter development; at other times, they would use alliances with ground commanders to push fighter development to the possible detriment of autonomy. Bombardment and autonomy were natural partners, but fighters were antithetical to both except when fighters were used to support the strategic mission.[5]

A significant degree of *operational* autonomy was achieved by the fighter or "tactical" pilots during World War II, but it was not the kind of autonomy that would lay the foundations for *institutional autonomy* from the ground campaign or the Army.

> Though Arnold always gave priority in his thinking about the European war to the strategic use of air power, "the ground arm" of course continued to regard "air support" as Army Air's primary responsibility—a view held not only by Eisenhower, but also by Montgomery The latter, however, was responsible in large measure for a further refinement in the evolution of air command. In the long Desert War campaign against Rommel across North Africa, the RAF's Air Vice Marshall Arthur "Maori" Coningham convinced Monty that air support of ground forces worked better when directed by one airman than by the traditional, scattered, on-call commands from units of foot soldiers. Spaatz quickly convinced Eisenhower likewise, and new AAF regulations were drawn up early in 1943 designating all U.S. air forces as either strategic or tactical. The 8th, for example, still commanded by Eaker, was designated "strategic" that summer and its air support command was set aside as the nucleus of a new air force to be solely tactical and to support the Normandy invasion the following year.[6]

Those divisions blurred as the war progressed and the realities of combat overrode the assumptions of theory.

> ...there were many occasions throughout 1943 when the tidy distinction between tactical and strategic became blurred, the most obvious being the invasions of Sicily and then Italy itself, when all air forces available were used on the same objective. After SEXTANT, where Arnold was able to persuade the Combined Chiefs of Staff to set up USSTAF in spite of the strong objections of the RAF, the American Joint Chiefs sought to protect the traditional "air support" priority by ruling that "Should a strategic or tactical emergency arise requiring such action, the Theater Commanders may, at their discretion, utilize the Strategic Air Forces...for purposes other than their primary mission." In the case of Normandy, the CCS promised Eisenhower as Supreme Commander complete authority over all air forces, strategic and tactical, British and American, after 1 April 1944. That was the date when the Combined Bomber Offensive was supposed to have achieved its strategic objectives. In the case of the Americans, that objective was the command of the air, always regarded as a prerequisite for the Normandy invasion.[7]

It wasn't until 1944 that the American fighter pilots in Europe saw their first opportunity to break out from under the domination of the bomber pilots. General Jimmy Doolittle, then commanding the Eighth Air Force in England gave his permission for the fighters escorting his bombers "to range away from the bomber formations and seek out the enemy."

Doolittle's decision also reflected the offensive spirit of General Arnold's New Year (1944) message to his commanders: "Destroy the enemy Air Force wherever you find them, in the air, on the ground and in the factories." [William] Kepner was quick to see that new opportunities to exploit fighter flexibility were on the horizon. On January 17, 1944, he issued a prophetic message to the pilots of his command:

> A fighter pilot must be able to use his versatile weapon in whatever way will do the greatest damage to the enemy...high or low, near or far, protecting bombers, destroying enemy fighters, preparing the way for our advancing ground troops, cutting the supply lines, strafing airdromes and other necessary missions.... Be ready. Today we are flying high altitude escort for heavy bombers. Tomorrow...?

That offensive philosophy suited the fighter pilot temperament. And, as the message had forecast, VIII Fighter Command's turn to the offensive did not stop with bomber escort.

> Col. Glen Duncan, Commander of the 353d Fighter Group, started something new early in 1944. He led his flight in a strafing attack on a German airfield as they were returning from what had been an uneventful escort mission. One pilot described this armed buzzing as "roaring down at terrific speeds on a chosen object, zooming over it with inches to spare—and the closer the better—add the hazards of flak and ground fire and you have a sport that is practically irresistible." Duncan's experiment soon grew to be a major (and unauthorized) tactic in VIII Fighter Command.[8]

In the Pacific theater of operations, the balance between strategic and tactical air operations was almost exactly reversed. George Kenney's tactical operations dominated the theater until the build-up of the B-29 strategic bombardment operations in 1944. If the Japanese had recognized the futility of continuing the war a year earlier—as well they might have under the strangulation of the American submarine campaign—the role of strategic bombardment in the Pacific would have been largely eclipsed.

In any event, the supporters of fighter aviation would not be stilled:

> Col. S. F. Giffin, who prior to the war had been an instructor in the Department of Economics, Government and History at the United States Military Academy, in a lengthy memorandum entitled "Future Trends in Air Fighting" attempted to point out the postwar requirement for tactical aviation. Colonel Giffin thought it unhealthy that there was no voice in the Air Force for fighter aviation. He attempted to fill that gap by arguing that the great unlearned lessons of World War II were the offensive and great range capability of the fighter aircraft, its ability to destroy enemy aviation in the air and on the ground, and its effectiveness

as an offensive weapon against tactical and strategic targets. He argued that the postwar Air Force should have at least twice as many fighter groups as bomber groups since fighters were needed for escort (on a one-to-one basis with bombers), for air defense, for close support of ground troops, and for strategic sweeps. In Giffin's words: "I believe it to be an unhealthy thing that within the Air Force itself there is presently so little difference of opinion as regards the future course of air warfare and the line which we must take in creating the future Air Force. We are committed to the big bomber and the bomber offensive as surely for the future as we have been throughout this war, and with scarcely a dissenting voice."

[Laurence] Kuter [then on Arnold's staff] rejected Giffin's analysis in the following manner:

> I feel that Col. Giffin's points are well taken with reference to the next year or two but do not go along with him on the longer range consideration. I feel sure that the fighter will go into the strategic air offensive in Europe and in Japan, but that a weapon much more similar to our present VHB [Very Heavy Bomber, the new B-29] than to our present fighter is the longer time backbone of air power.

Giffin's rather prophetic ideas were dismissed easily for two reasons. First, Kuter realized that strategic bombardment doctrine was so firmly established within the leadership of the AAF that Giffin's comments could be rejected without concern that a high-ranking Air Corps officer might use his arguments to modify the planned postwar Air Force structure. Also, Giffin was a Coast Artillery officer who had only recently transferred to the Air Corps—he was not a pilot and had not attended the Air Corps Tactical School at Maxwell AFB; he could be and was ignored since he lacked the qualifications to make his voice heard as an aviation expert. Had he solicited the support of a high-ranking Air Corps officer who was not firmly committed to the doctrine of strategic bombardment, his idea might have received more than the summary dismissal they got. In Washington, during the entire war, there were no high-ranking Air Corps officers who questioned strategic bombardment, and it would have been difficult for Giffin or any other critic of AAF doctrine to use a combat commander with a commitment to tactical aviation, such as Generals Kenney, Quesada, Griswold, or Saville, since their influence on postwar planning was minimal.[9]

The fighter pilots were caught between their desires for an independent Air Force and their convictions about the importance of tactical aviation.

If intraservice competition had existed in the 1930's, it probably would have continued into the 1940's, and a voice like that of Colonel Giffin might have been heard. Such competition was essentially non-existent in the interwar period largely because the Army Air Corps leadership did not consider the Army Air Corps a separate service. Those who might have defended pursuit aviation and pointed out the vulnerabilities of bombardment aircraft as well as the deficiencies of daylight precision bombing theory were silent for two reasons. They had no platform and they did not wish to sabotage the greater goal—autonomy.[10]

In the European theater of World War II, General Elwood R. Quesada worked most closely with the Army ground forces to use fighter aircraft as fighter-bombers. As commander of the Ninth Tactical Air Command, Quesada went out of his way to build communications and confidence between the ground and air forces. Not surprisingly:

> Quesada's intimate working relationship with the Army, however, was not without its price. He was criticized by some airmen who felt that his support of the infantry was abetting those who thought the Army should have its own air force.[11]

A New Breed

The war developed a new breed of airmen who were organizers and operators more than advocates or theorists. Certainly Arnold fit that pattern. LeMay may have been the quintessential example of the new leadership. Michael Sherry has described the two as follows:

> [What LeMay] prized most was his leadership in getting men ready for war. He excelled at fashioning reliable crews out of green trainees, ill-prepared for the smoke and confusion of battle. Always willing to experiment, he toyed with different bomber formations and bombing patterns and jerry-rigged new methods of maintenance and repair in order to increase the force available.... Operational challenges preoccupied LeMay, and for him joy lay in command itself—less for the power it bestowed or the victory it promised than for the creative skill it demanded.

> LeMay had little time or interest to explore the strategy or politics of air power. Before the war his rank had been too junior to place him in the service schools and the planning offices where these matters arose. The strategic issues raised by the failure of Germany's blitz against England, the RAF's shift to nighttime attacks against Germany, and the relationship between ground invasion and strategic bombing—these were beyond his providence as middle-level operational commander, and he was too busy anyway to worry about them. "The only thing I was thinking about was living for the next twenty-four hours and...trying to keep my outfit alive and the airplanes flying.... We weren't thinking about strategy at the time.... We had to have an air force before we could do anything."...LeMay's job was to fashion the machinery of war, not to worry about its purposes.

> To a surprising degree, Arnold shared that mentality despite his much loftier perch. Though a veteran of battles over air power and a defender of the AAF's interests, he was never an articulate or visionary exponent of air power on a doctrinal level. Almost everyone close to Arnold saw him as "in no sense a thoughtful, precise thinker but a doer." Had he been a visionary, he might never have become the air force's commanding general, and those who were mostly had fallen from the ranks. Arnold had the doctrinal flexibility to adjust to the

shifting strategies of the war. He owed his preeminence not to strategic imagination but to the energy with which he prepared his organization for war and lashed it into operation.

In this regard, Arnold and LeMay resembled the outstanding American military figures of the war, General George C. Marshall and General Dwight Eisenhower, whose greatest talents lay in organization and diplomacy. The airmen differed from the army generals in one important way, however. Marshall and Eisenhower knew history, and by virtue of long association with military and political leaders, they understood politics. They preferred, as the deepest traditions of American civil-military relations taught them, to ground their decisions in arguments from military utility; but they comprehended Clausewitz's precepts about war as an extension of politics, and they willingly responded when civil authority altered strategy to fit political needs.

Arnold and LeMay rarely thought to invoke Clausewitz—or Grant and Sherman. They had defined their service and their careers against military tradition, both doctrinal and ritualistic, and were contemptuous of standard operating procedure. LeMay disdained the conventions of military dress, acknowledgment of superiors, and close-order drill and delighted in the air force's "reputation for sloppy uniforms, slatternly salutes, and general shoddiness," practices which indeed had official sanction in air force policy. Disinterest in military tradition and in strategic doctrine went hand in hand. When LeMay and Arnold wrote their memoirs, neither said much about strategy; their memoirs faithfully reflected the focus of their wartime experience.[12]

While neither Arnold nor LeMay were theorists, Sherry's description omits the role that theory played in orienting their devotion to getting things done—politically and operationally. Arnold did not invent air power theory, but he exploited it exquisitely in building the Air Force as an institution. LeMay was not a visionary, but he ably executed air power theory as he adapted both his means and ends within the boundaries laid down by Trenchard, Douhet, and Mitchell.

Identifying the Enemy

Throughout their long quest for autonomy and, ultimately, independence, the airmen saw their adversary as the Army, of which they were a restive and unwilling part. For the airmen, the mainstream Army was wedded to weapons and a mode of warfare that the airmen hoped to make obsolete. As World War II drew to a close and AAF planners could once again turn to thoughts of an independent postwar air force, it was natural for them to think in terms of their prewar jousting against Army parochialism. "Perhaps all parochialism in the military is based on that perceived in others. The records show that despite the tendencies of certain Army officers, the Army generals demonstrated less parochialism during the war than did the Air Force or Navy officers."[13] Indeed, the AAF planners had their sights on the wrong adversary.

> In large measure, Army parochialism was an illusion of Kuter—Arnold's closest advisor in Washington from 1943 to 1945. Kuter identified the wrong adversary, for it was the Navy that caused the Air Force its greatest postwar problems. This false identification led the Air Force to tilt at windmills, while the Navy was able to organize its forces effectively to battle the AAF on the question of unification.[14]

If the airmen's prewar claims had disturbed the Army as fancifully preposterous, their postwar claims absolutely terrified the Navy as threatening its future existence.

> Certainly Colonel William Mitchell had claimed that airpower was the first line of defense and offense, but the Air Corps leaders of the 1920's and 1930's had been much more subtle in their arguments for autonomy. As World War II drew to a close, subtlety had largely disappeared and the obsolescence of navies and armies was pointed out by key AAF commanders such as Lieutenant General James Doolittle and General George Kenney. They claimed that they wanted equality with the Army and Navy, but in making their case before Congress and the press their arguments were such that they could justify not equality but supremacy of the Air Force.[15]

In the intense intramural battles that would attend the reorganization of the American military services over the first five postwar years, the Air Force would find its fiercest adversary in the Navy, not the Army. The Army would become an advocate for service unification; whereas the Navy would end up fighting against both unification and an independent air force—the first because it would encroach upon the Navy's traditional independence and the second because the Air Force was clearly bent on demonstrating that navies had become irrelevant.

Notes

1. From a scene in the 1949 film, *Twelve O'Clock High*, where General Pritchard (Millard Mitchell, a good look-alike for General Ira Eaker) tells Brig. Gen. Frank Savage (Gregory Peck) how it is with the first American bombardment groups in England at the end of 1942.

2. From two scenes in the 1948 film, *Command Decision*, where Maj. Gen. Kane (Walter Pidgeon) warns Brig. Gen. Dennis (Clark Gable) that the continued high losses of his bombers over Germany could risk all that they had worked for and, later, reminds his audience of the stake the Air Corps leadership has in their theory of bombardment.

3. Green, "Hugh J. Knerr: The Pen and the Sword," 112, 113.

4. Parton, "The Thirty-One Year Gestation of the Independent USAF," 154.

5. Smith, *The Army Plans for Peace*, 25.

6. Parton, "The Thirty-One Year Gestation of the Independent USAF," 155, 156.

7. Ibid.

8. Henry, "William E. Kepner: All the Way to Berlin," 170.

9. Smith, *The Air Force Plans for Peace*, 23, 24.

10. Ibid., 26.

11. John Schlight, "Elwood R. Quesada: Tac Air Comes of Age," in *Makers of the United States Air Force*, ed. John L. Frisbee (Washington D.C.: Office of Air Force History, 1987), 170.

12. Sherry, *The Rise of American Airpower*, 178, 179.

13. Smith, *The Air Force Plans for Peace*, 9.

14. Ibid.

15. Ibid., 15.

12

Breaking Free

It is important to note that the airmen's drive for independence was played out against two conflicting currents. One was the explosive demobilization of America's armed forces; between V-J Day and April 1946, AAF strength dropped from 2,253,000 to 485,000. The postwar nadir of about 304,000 was reached in May 1947. On the other hand, the Cold War heated up with Soviet moves in eastern Europe causing grave concern in Washington. It was in this atmosphere that a Gallup poll showed that the American public thought that defense funds were best spent on the air forces.[1]

The bureaucratic story of the birth of the Air Force as an independent institution is well documented[2] and need not be retold here. What is pertinent, however, is how air power theory was exploited and altered in that process—how it served as both a means to institutional independence and an end for the structural design of the institution. In dealing with tactical aviation, the means and ends became orthogonal, if not directly opposed.

Accommodating the Atomic Bomb

Whether or not the air power theory had been proven by the strategic bombing campaigns of World War II at the very end, the theory was accepted as validated beyond question because of the atomic bomb. "The atomic bomb did not change war, it enhanced its totality; and it ratified a shaky vision of strategic bombardment."[3] The validated theory could now be exploited to achieve institutional independence for the Air Force.

First, however, the Air Force had to assimilate the potential implications of this new, validating weapon. Had the atomic bomb vindicated the airmen's claim of the decisiveness of aerial bombardment, or would the atomic bomb diminish the need for the fleets of bombers the airmen cherished? The atomic bomb would be the first in a series of technical developments that would both enthrall and bedevil the military aviators by furthering the ends of air power theory while at the same time undermining its means.

> After the war, the Army Air Forces faced the immense challenge of developing a realistic program for its future. Among its most important problems was the assimilation of the war's most advanced technology into a vastly reduced and still unorganized Air Force. Although all the new technologies, from radar to jet engines and rockets, were significant, none was more important or represented a potentially more disturbing influence than the atomic bomb. The full implications of a weapon of such tremendous power, cost, and complexity were difficult to comprehend in the uncertain postwar situation. How the Air Force initially responded to the atomic bomb would be crucial not only to its future but to the nation's as well.[4]

Given the importance of the atomic bomb to the Air Force—to the claims of air power theory, to air forces as the delivery agents and future trustees of this decisive weapon, to the impetus it gave for an independent air force—the airmen found themselves remarkably ignorant about the bomb.

> Although the Air Force's 509th Composite Bomb Group (Very Heavy) had dropped the atomic bombs on Hiroshima and Nagasaki, the AAF itself had at best a peripheral involvement in the bomb's development. It had modified the B-29s and trained air and ground personnel of the 509th, but by the war's end, fewer than 20 of the AAF's top officers had even a rudimentary knowledge of the atomic bomb. The terrible damage inflicted on the two Japanese cities forced American air leaders to assess the impact of this powerful new weapon upon warfare in general and the Air Force in particular.[5]

From the outset, the implications for the needed size of the bomber force were troubling. Jeffrey Record has theorized that:

> General Curtis LeMay and other top Air Force leaders were less than enthusiastic about the use of the atomic bomb against Japan in 1945 and subsequently pooh-poohed its decisiveness in compelling the Japanese to sue for peace, (a conclusion shared, incidentally, by the U.S. Strategic Bombing Survey). One of the reasons for this attitude was fear that atomic weapons, because of their vastly

greater efficiency than conventional bombs, would jeopardize USAF postwar plans for retaining a huge bomber force.[6]

The writings of the time, particularly the report of the Spaatz Board (discussed below), indicate more subtle considerations. There was great uncertainty about how many of these new bombs would be available and when and how they should be used. If anything, LeMay seems to have been very positive about the importance of the atomic bomb and expansive about Air Force preparations for its assimilation and use:

> On 30 August [1945], Maj. Gen. Curtis E. LeMay, Chief of Staff of the U.S. Army Strategic Air Forces in the Pacific (USASTAF) and former commander of the XX and XXI Bomber Commands in the 20th Air Force, submitted a detailed and far-sighted plan for the AAF's postwar atomic program to Lt. Gen. Ira C. Eaker, the AAF's Deputy Commanding General. He stressed three things in his message: (1) that the efficacy of the bomb was clearly established; (2) that it was essential to U.S. national security to retain leadership in atomic energy; and (3) that the bomb was primarily an air weapon, which meant the AAF had to cooperate fully to insure U.S. leadership. To maintain its lead in atomic weapons, LeMay recommended top postwar priority for an expanded AAF program using the 509th Bomb Group as its nucleus. Among the most pressing requirements was "A comprehensive plan for an atomic bombardment organization, probably a wing...capable of immediate independent operation in any part of the world." LeMay cautioned against "post-war planning for this project on too small a scale." [7]

A fortnight later, only six weeks after the dropping of the atomic bombs on Japan, Eaker had commissioned the postwar planning the Air Force needed to adapt itself to a revolution in destructive power.

> On 14 September [1945], Ira Eaker formally designated Spaatz, Vandenberg, and Lauris Norstad, former Chief of Staff to Arnold as Commanding General, 20th Air Force, to determine at the earliest date the effect of the atomic bomb on the size, organization, composition, and employment of the Air Forces. He informed the members of what came to be called the "Spaatz Board" that the study and findings were urgent because of the "possible effect of this study upon appropriations and legislation which must be requested on Congress at an early date ...."[8]

But Eaker's planning group had little more to begin with than the air power theory and World War II doctrine which had brought them to this decisive juncture. Even so, the theory and doctrine sustained them surprisingly well.

Spaatz, Vandenberg, and Norstad attempted to foresee the atomic bomb's implications for the next 10 years with little concrete information to guide them. Because of this, the report that emerged was cautious in tone and conclusions. The views may now seem shortsighted or naive, but they... must be viewed in the context of their creation—frenetic demobilization, hastily devised and often-changed plans for the occupation Air Forces, increasingly virulent discussions between the War and Navy Departments on unification and independence for the AAF, and an uncertain postwar future for the AAF.

The Board argued that production and delivery were the most important factors to be considered in any assessment of the atomic bomb. The limited amounts of fissionable, weapons-grade material likely to be available and the great costs associated with facilities and bomb production, which itself was a meticulous and time-consuming process, indicated that the number of bombs on hand for any future conflict would be small. For some time to come, the bombs were expected to remain experimental "special weapons" of great cost and complexity, difficult to build and transport, and of limited availability.

Due to the bomb's shape, weight, and peculiar handling requirements, only the few SILVERPLATE B-29s modified during the war for the Manhattan Project could carry the bomb then or for the next several years because appreciable size and weight reductions were not foreseen. The Superfortress' range with this 10,000 pound load meant that strategically located oversea bases would be required for staging until the planned intercontinental B-36s began operating from the U.S. Plans for such "peripheral basing" were already a firm part of American postwar planning.[9]

Significantly, the experiences of the battle for air superiority over Europe, but not Japan, figured heavily in the deliberations of the Spaatz Board.

The AAF had learned during the war that air superiority and suppression of hostile air defenses were crucial for strategic bombing operations to proceed without unacceptable losses. In any future conflict such losses could not be risked with the few atomic bombs, modified B-29s, and trained crews that would be available. As in World War II, the full range of air forces would thus be required to gain and hold the air supremacy necessary to permit effective delivery of the atomic bombs. In the recently ended war, this air supremacy was acquired only after more than two years of steady build-up and bloody attritional aerial fighting; in the future, such time would not be available to the United States.[10]

This reasoning allowed the Spaatz Board to return to the traditional concepts of strategic bombardment, with large fleets of bombers with conventional bombs despite the advent of the atomic bomb.

The production and tactical limitations of the atomic bomb meant a continued reliance on conventional bombers and ordnance. By seeding the atomic bomb carriers among the conventional B-29s, they could be protected during daylight raids, thus lessening the probability of their loss while increasing target identification and bomb delivery.

The Spaatz Board saw that the unmodified B-29s had a much more important role to play than simply flying cover or diversions for the atomic bombing aircraft— they would be the backbone for any future strategic air offensive. The many uncertainties surrounding the bomb's employment meant that conventional bombing would remain the AAF's principal weapon of strategic warfare for some years to come.

The burden of any future strategic air offensive would fall to the conventional bombers because the relatively few and very expensive atomic bombs had to be saved for large targets where accuracy was not as critical as destructiveness and psychological impact. The best solution, it appeared to the Spaatz Board, was to select targets that were easily identified, visually or on radar, and most vulnerable to the blast, thermal, and radiation effects of the air-burst atomic bomb. Such targets were large urban and industrial areas, not military point targets. The characteristics and limited numbers of the earliest atomic bombs, the small size of the bomber force in the initial stages of any future conflict, tactical requirements, and lack of detailed target information for many parts of the world pushed the airmen even farther from their previous concept of precision attacks against an enemy's war-making capability and toward a doctrine of massive destruction of large population centers. The Spaatz Board tried to meld its recent strategic experience with the new weapon, concluding that the atomic bomb did not change the basic concept of strategic air war but merely added a weapon to the arsenal.[11]

But atomic bombs would eventually become a two-edged sword. The Air Force would not only have to be concerned with delivering these weapons but would also have to prevent their delivery on the United States by an enemy.

In stressing the crucial importance of establishing an adequate air defense at home, the Board echoed Arnold's view that the war's major scientific advances had enhanced the deadliness of air attack. With atomic bombs a terrible reality, air attack became the primary threat to the United States in the future. Thus, both Arnold and the [Spaatz] Board believed that the Air Force was now the nation's first line of defense as well as the main deterrent to any aggressor.[12]

Given its timing and background, the Spaatz Board was remarkably prescient about the future, including the demands of the yet-to-emerge Cold War. In its final report, the board offered seven conclusions:

1. The atomic bomb does not at this time warrant a material change in our present conception of the employment, size, organization, and composition of the postwar Air Force.

2. The atomic bomb has not altered our basic concept of the strategic air offensive but has given us an additional weapon.

3. Forces using non-atomic bombs will be required for use against targets which cannot be effectively or economically attacked with the atomic bomb.

4. An adequate system of outlying strategic bases must be established and maintained.

5. A system of national defense to provide for maximum adaptability to new weapons must be established. It should be maintained at maximum effectiveness and should be capable of immediate expansion.

6. An intelligence organization that will know at all times the strategic vulnerability, capabilities, and probable intentions of any potential enemy is essential.

7. A large scale scientific research and development program with the development of new weapons is mandatory to insure our national security.[13]

Clearly, the implications of the atomic bomb on the size of the bomber force needed were at the forefront of Air Force concerns in those first few months after the war. The atomic bomb could be a bane as well as a boon to the postwar Air Force.

On 3 December 1945, Ira Eaker cautioned the entire Air Staff about designating any atomic bomb striking force or a separate wing for atomic bombing. He thought it far better to designate the entire long range bombing force as atomic.

It strikes me we are very likely to find the attitude of the War Department and of Congress to be that the atomic bombing force is the only strategic air force we will require. If one wing will do the job, then one wing will be the size of the strategic force.[14]

The concept of an alert force of nuclear-armed bombers as a deterrent had emerged within four months of the dropping of the first atomic bomb.

Two days later [5 December 1945], the former secretary of the Spaatz Board, Col. William P. Fisher…outlined plans for building an atomic bombing force. Equipment and personnel then available would be used to set up a force "sufficient in size to fully exploit the expected availability and effectiveness of the atomic bomb." Outfitted with the latest aircraft and equipment, manned by the most competent personnel, and organized around the 509th, this force would be maintained in the United States in a state of constant war readiness and would be capable of immediate deployment to augment conventional bombing operations. These concepts of constant war readiness of a strategic air force-in-being and rapid deployment for immediate operations were a distinct departure from previous War Department thinking. They did, however, reflect the Spaatz Board report and Air Staff thinking about atomic matters and were integral to AAF postwar planning. In so many ways these views challenged the War Department's traditional mobilization concepts and post-war planning based on...a year's warning of war. Deterrence of aggression and immediate retaliation were very clearly coalescing in the Air Force's strategic thinking about the need for a strategic atomic air force in a constant state of war readiness.[15]

The establishment of that nuclear deterrent force as an independent command separate from the theater commander came only a year later.

> ...Arnold had created 20th Air Force in 1944 with himself as the JCS executive agent and Commanding General to make sure strategic air operations were conducted in conformity with air strategy rather than theater strategy and requirements. The AAF soon adopted the position, which became national defense policy in December 1946 (JCS 1259/27, 12 December 1946), that the "air-atomic" strategic air force should only come under the orders of the JCS because of the overriding importance of its strategic mission to national security.[16]

Hence, the outlines of the Strategic Air Command emerged barely more than a year after World War II, even before the Air Force had achieved its impending independence from the Army. *Air power theory in America had begun its 15-year transmogrification into deterrence theory.*

Where to Put Tactical Air Power?

Although the Air Force would seek a single combat command centered on its strategic bomber force, the Army's concern for continued support from tactical aviation had extracted an important concession:

> With the surrender of Germany accomplished and the defeat of Japan assured, AAF leaders resumed their prewar campaign for a separate air force. Newly elected President Harry Truman was known to favor a reorganization of the military structure.... After Japan capitulated later in the year, [Gen. Elwood] Quesada became part of an informal group including Spaatz, Eaker, Fred Anderson, Lauris Norstad, and Hoyt Vandenberg, which set out to sell the idea of a separate air force. While negotiations with the Navy took place at the Secretary's level, this group worked to persuade senators and the Army of the soundness of a separate air force. Quesada's role was to convince the Army,

specifically Eisenhower and Bradley, and Senator Leverett Saltonstall, the Chairman of the Armed Services Committee, that the Army did not need its own tactical Air Force. Principally through his wartime relationship with them, Quesada persuaded the Army generals that the air force knew better how to use its airplanes and that the flexibility air power had demonstrated so successfully in the war would be maintained by a separate air force. At one point, with Quesada present, Spaatz promised Eisenhower that if Eisenhower supported separation, the Air Force would always meets its commitment to the Army by providing permanent and strong tactical air forces. In part as a result of this promise, Eisenhower and Bradley were won over.[17]

This was a promise that Quesada knew he could keep because of his outstanding cooperation with the Army ground forces in Europe.

> Quesada approached his new job [as head of the Tactical Air Command] with the conviction that the best way to keep the tactical air mission from falling back under the Army was to provide such outstanding support that the Army would be totally satisfied and forget about having its own air force.[18]

In his bid for institutional independence, Spaatz had made promises that were antithetical to air power theory. He was obliged to adopt bureaucratic command arrangements that could not long endure alongside the intellectual foundations for independence provided through air power theory.

> Although he knew well the crucial importance that the strategic function would play, Spaatz found that Eisenhower's support had been purchased at the price of establishing a tactical command in the postwar air organization.... So, with the reorganization of March 1946, instead of a single combat command, three functional commands were established—strategic, tactical, and air-defense.[19]

But the concessions were short-lived:

> While Quesada battled with elements in both the newly created Air Force, and the Army, which wanted to create its own tactical air arm, worldwide developments were conspiring against his efforts. Since he took over the command in May 1947, the Cold War had set in. That very month Hungary had installed a Communist government, followed in June by the announcement of the Marshall Plan. Early in 1948, Czechoslovakia followed Hungary, and in the summer the Soviets tried to cut off Berlin from the Allies. In June, Hoyt Vandenberg replaced Spaatz as Air Force Chief of Staff. The emphasis on strategic preparedness and deterrence, which had been instrumental in creating the separate Air Force, assumed even greater significance. In the fall of 1948, Quesada was called to Washington and informed by Vandenberg that he was going to reorganize the Air Force's operational commands. The Strategic Air Command would be strengthened

while the Tactical Air and Air Defense Commands would be reduced to headquarters and placed under a new Continental Air Command. Quesada objected, reminding the chief of the promise to Eisenhower that there would always be a tactical force to support the Army. Vandenberg, disagreeing with Quesada's philosophy that the best way to keep tactical air out of Army hands was to make it indispensable while under the Air Force, and viewing Quesada's attempts at cooperation as a pathway to Army domination, went ahead with the plan. Spaatz, now retired, was furious. Quesada, "personally offended" at what he considered a violation of trust, turned down an offer to head the new Continental Air Command.[20]

Jeffrey Record describes the dilemma which tactical air power posed for air power theory and, hence, for institutional independence for the Air Force.

The post-World War II rationale for an independent air force rested largely on two claims, one intellectual, the other bureaucratic. The intellectual claim was the proposition that air power, specifically strategic bombardment, afforded a quick and relatively cheap means of winning wars autonomously, i.e., independently of the actions of surface forces. The theory had two corollaries: (1) that the functioning of the modern industrial state could be brought to a halt via the aerial destruction of carefully selected elements of its economic infrastructure, and (2) that there was no truly effective defense, direct or indirect, against aerial bombardment. By deliberate omission, the theory more or less ignored the role and value of tactical air power, which because it was tied to combined operations involving surface forces, provided no firm foundation for independence; until well into the 1960s official USAF doctrine cast the value of tactical fighter aircraft at first largely in terms of their ability to provide long-range escorts for strategic bombardment campaigns to be carried out as subcomponents of Massive Retaliation.[21]

Air Power Theory Sustained

The AAF leadership came out of the Second World War with the air power theory intact, despite considerable evidence that it was flawed and incomplete. It was as though World War II had never occurred and the specter of World War I still haunted its survivors:

Spaatz's views on strategic air followed the historical development of the Trenchard-Mitchell-Arnold school: *Prolonged ground wars of attrition must be avoided at all costs.* "Attritional war," said Spaatz shortly after succeeding Arnold, "might last years...would cost wealth that centuries alone could repay and...would take untold millions of lives." The lessons of World War II were writ clear:

Strategic bombing is thus the first war instrument of history capable of stopping the heart mechanism of a great industrialized

enemy. It paralyzes his military power at the core. It has a strategy
and tactic of mobility and flexibility which are peculiar to its own
medium, *the third dimension.*[22]

Those words could have been written 15 years earlier at the Air Corps
Tactical School and without the benefit of the experiences of World War
II. Perry McCoy Smith provides a clue as to why the lessons went unseen
when he describes the euphoria that enveloped the Army airmen at the
end of World War II.

The coincidence of opinion within the Air Corps on the supreme importance of
autonomy can be explained by years of frustrated efforts, the common bond of
the joy of aviation, and the crusading attitude of these men. At last the tenuous
theoretical arguments of Douhet and Mitchell had been justified in the eyes of
the Air Corps leaders and the years of frustration were over. The great joy and
overstatement in the period immediately following the successful explosion of
the two atomic bombs was well recorded in the press and in the congressional
hearings of 1945 and 1946. Airpower would defend this nation; airpower would
guarantee the success of a new international security organization; airpower
would punish aggression wherever it might manifest itself; airpower would save
the world. Salvation had come; all America and the world needed to do was to
maintain and support a strong United States Air Force—a simple, reliable
formula. The airplane was not considered just another weapon; it was the
ultimate weapon for universal peacekeeping.[23]

The optimism of the airmen's postwar planning was sufficient to
overcome any concerns about the dominance of the offense, despite the
brutal lessons of 1943 in the battle for air superiority over Europe.

Just as Air Corps leaders in the late 1930's were unwilling to observe technological
developments in pursuit aircraft and just as Air Corps leaders in the early 1940's
refused to recognize that development in German defensive tactics and technology
might proceed at a faster pace than offensive tactics and technology, the postwar
planners seemed unable even to contemplate the possibility that air defense
might ever gain an ascendancy over air offense.[24]

But this was consistent with the tenacity of air power theory and
doctrine because they were means to institutional ends, not just the ends
of war.

A long-time student of airpower, Professor William R. Emerson, has observed:
"Making all due allowances for the difficulties and the genuine accomplishments
of our strategists, it should, nevertheless, be perfectly clear that every salient
belief of prewar American air doctrine was either overthrown or drastically
modified by the experience of war.[25]

Perry McCoy Smith explains why the paradox could persist:

> Instead of making the common mistake of planning to fight the next war with weapons and techniques that had been effective in the last, the Air Corps planners were laying plans to conduct the next war using weapons and techniques that had been proven largely ineffective in [World War II]. The reason is quite obvious: the planners were not making detailed plans for fighting the next war but rather were planning for a force that could provide the justification for autonomy. The doctrinal dedication to strategic bombardment at the expense of close air support and interdiction led to difficulties, among them lack of adequate support of ground forces during the Korean conflict, deemphasis of tactical training, and lack of development of tactical weapons systems and tactical munitions (much of the development in these areas was done by the Navy in the two decades following World War II).[26]

The planners of today, of course, are not "planning for a force that could provide the justification for autonomy" but one that will justify retaining the airplanes, particularly the combat aircraft and most particularly now, the fighters.

Notes

1. Wolk, "Planning and Organizing the Air Force," 169.

2. See, for example, Parton, "The Thirty-One Year Gestation of the Independent USAF," and Smith, *The Air Force Plans for Peace.*

3. Michael Vlahos, "The Next Competition," in Patrick M. Cronin, editor, "Perspectives on Policy and Strategy," *Strategic Review* (Winter 1993): 83.

4. John T. Greenwood, "The Atomic Bomb—Early Air Force Thinking and the Strategic Air Force, August 1945–March 1946," *Aerospace Historian* (Fall, September 1987): 158.

5. Ibid., 158, 159.

6. Jeffrey Record, *The Future of the Air Force*, The Hudson Institute, unpublished draft, April 1990, 23, with a reference to Leon V. Sigal, *Fighting to a Finish, The Politics of War Termination in the United States and Japan, 1945* (Ithaca: Cornell University Press, 1988), 178.

7. Greenwood, "The Atomic Bomb," 159.

8. Ibid.

9. Ibid., 160.

10. Ibid.

11. Ibid., 160, 161.

12. Ibid., 161.

13. Ibid.

14. Ibid., 162.

15. Ibid.

16. Ibid., 165.

17. Schlight, "Elwood R. Quesada: Tac Air Comes of Age," 198, 199.

18. Ibid., 199.

19. Wolk, "Men Who Made the Air Force," 14.

20. Schlight, "Elwood R. Quesada: Tac Air Comes of Age," 202.

21. Record, *The Future of the Air Force*, 13, 14.

22. Wolk, "Men Who Made the Air Force," 15. The quotations are taken from General Carl A. Spaatz, "Strategic Air Power," *Foreign Affairs*, April 1946, 385, 388, 389.

23. Smith, *The Air Force Plans for Peace*, 18.

24. Ibid., 25, 26.

25. Ibid., 27.

26. Ibid., 28.

13

Realization

Flying in the Golden Age...1949–1954: Man, we were at the center of the world...if you loved to fly. The old air force was being scrapped, and a new air force was being born right on our doorstep. Prop planes were obsolete, and the thousands of B-29s and Mustangs that had won World War II were being cut up for scrap, replaced by an air fleet of jet and rocket-propelled supersonic fighters and bombers.[1]

The Golden Age of Air Power

With an independent Air Force and the American public's widespread acceptance of deterrence through air power as the basis for national security in the Cold War, air power theory could finally be translated into adequate forces in being. The triumph of the concept was manifested in the forging of SAC under General Curtis LeMay (1948–1957). Because of the temporary conjunction of world politics, technology, and LeMay as one of air power's most able operators, air power theory emerged in its ultimate form—a monument to Armageddon—composed from weapons of mind-boggling destructiveness, carried by giant, globe-girdling airplanes, crewed and supported by an elite cadre of airmen, with chillingly explicit purpose by deterrence theory. The exploitation of air power theory had reached its zenith, its institutional ends, and would subside thereafter. Henceforth, operations and efficiency, not theory would dominate; and if theory were needed, it would be supplied by deterrence theory.

LeMay was a strong operational leader, devoted to professionalism. He was probably less driven by air power theory than he was the mission he

145

had been given based on his track record as an operator.[2] Whether or not the mission (massive retaliation or assured destruction) conformed to air power theory was probably less important to LeMay than the clarity of the mission and his freedom to build a professional force to fulfill it.

At the same time, the leadership of the Air Force was steadily shifting to the more numerous aviators who were not so much air power theorists as they were World War II fliers and operators. These were people who had come into the war as aviation enthusiasts and for whom air power theory was accepted as proven background, not to be questioned and without any need for development. Fighter pilots might chafe under the dominance of the Air Force by bomber pilots; but that was the way things had always been since the bomber advocates had found the keys to the kingdom of independence at the Air Corps Tactical School.

During this period, alternatives to the airplane began to emerge as means for fulfilling the ends of air power theory. Both cruise and ballistic missiles, in the forms of the V-1 and V-2 missiles, had appeared at the end of World War II. The Army and Navy had acquired both models of these captured German missiles for experimentation after the war. The Navy went so far as to fire a V-2 ballistic missile from the deck of one of its new large aircraft carriers. But the Air Force, preoccupied with the development of a fleet of jet aircraft, largely ignored these new missiles, perhaps in an unconscious unwillingness to pursue what they saw as potentially competitive means to airplanes and their pilots. But some of those who had originally been attracted to air power theory for its ends rather than its means found themselves attracted to missiles as more effective means than airplanes to the ends of air power.

This was a period of fermentation in Cold War strategy and in guided missiles, rockets, and jets. All of the services were involved in experimentation; but the Strategic Air Command (SAC) was being forged into a complex of forces, culture, plans, bases, and doctrine that would dominate the Air Force and strategic thinking for almost two decades, worldwide. LeMay's SAC would own the Air Force; SAC *was* the Air Force; and SAC was the world's most awesome and respected military force.

Even as the Air Force was enjoying this "golden age" of air power theory—consolidating, even exaggerating, its realization through the airplane—the world and other institutions were beginning to explore and develop alternatives to the means, if not the ends, of the theory. The theory, in its original form, would soon face competition; but the theorists had been replaced by operators who had more important, more tangible things to do.

The Vandenberg Legacy

As the Cold War unfolded, revealing its ugly dimensions in the blockade of Berlin (1948) and the Korean War (1950–53), the new and independent Air Force's greatest problem was logistical—similar to the problem Arnold had faced in the run-up to World War II. This time, Hoyt Vandenberg would lead the expansion.

> Few leaders have had as difficult a challenge as Vandenberg did as Chief of Staff. When he took command, the Air Force had just gone through rapid, total demobilization of aircraft, materiel, and personnel. His job was to build it up again. At the height of World War II, there were 80,000 aircraft and 2.5 million officers and men. When Vandenberg took over from Spaatz, there were only 375,000 officers and men—on paper, 55 wings, most of them with obsolete planes. At his retirement, Air Force personnel had grown to 960,000 officers and men, 137 wings, all of them combat ready. It was a remarkable achievement, the result of brilliant leadership.[3]

In rebuilding the Air Force structure to meet the Cold War challenges, Vandenberg saw both the limits and strengths of American air power. At the height of the Korean War, he said,

> Air power doesn't guarantee America's security, but it exploits the nation's greatest asset—our technological skill. We cannot hope to match enemy nations in manpower but we can, as in the last war, produce more and better airplanes than any other country. And we have young men with the mechanical facility for flying all the airplanes we build. Training can quickly give them efficiency.[4]

This was the American formula for victory in World War II: substitute equipment for people, exploit the mechanical facility of its people, and give reign to its penchant for logistical efficiency.

Air power theory did not fare well in the Korean war. As in the early days of World War II in the Pacific, the heart of the enemy was not accessible to air attack for decisive strikes. However, this time it was not because of the range of airplanes but the political limitations imposed by the threat of an expanded war in a world of atomic bombs. The strategic bombing campaign in Korea, with conventional bombs, quickly exhausted the worthy strategic targets; but the airmen pointed to targets in China and the Soviet Union as the true heart of the enemy. Within the political limits imposed, the principal roles available to military aviation in the war were tactical, not strategic. The reaction of the airmen was not to question the theory, but the war itself:

> The opponents of the air theory said the Korean experience "proved" that strategic bombers were overrated. The heavy bomber supporters said that this was not so; Korea was the wrong war, in the wrong place, at the wrong time. And nearly everybody missed the point. The strategic bombers were then, as they are now, fully able to do their job. The only hitch was that the assumptions did not coincide with reality. The Korean War was real enough; it was the assumptions that were not valid for that particular reality. Whether the reality—i.e., the Korean War—was "right" or "wrong" was irrelevant.[5]

So air power theory would no longer be held accountable in the only conflicts that the world would now choose to wage—in the world of constraints that nuclear deterrence had wrought, in conflicts less than all-out war. Indeed, it was now easier to associate air power theory with nuclear deterrence than with "police actions" or "brush fire wars"—the only kinds of shooting wars that would be waged during the Cold War. Air power would keep the peace, but not win the wars anyone cared to fight. Air power theory, as a theory for winning wars quickly and cheaply, was being abandoned for a fleet of nuclear bombers (a nuclear force structure). The soul of the new Air Force had been bought for airplanes.

The essence of air power theory—reliance upon the offense instead of defense, striking at the heart of the enemy with decisive effect—was clearly evident in Vandenberg's decision to rebuild the Air Force for the Cold War around SAC and strategic bombardment.

> One of the most important decisions Vandenberg made was to give primary emphasis to strategic air power as the essential force for the defense of the United States and the free world.…
>
> This emphasis on strategic bombing was not an easy decision to stand on. There was disagreement within the Air Force on such a heavy emphasis on SAC. After the Korean War began, some complained about the performance of the Air Force in supporting ground troops. Vandenberg's critics accused him of neglecting tactical aviation. SAC supporters dismissed these charges by pointing to Vandenberg's record before and during World War II as a member of the tactical air team. Actually, however, as Vandenberg explained, his concern was the defense of the United States, but he did not believe that air defense alone, in the narrow sense, could accomplish this. He cited the Battle of Britain and the experience of the Luftwaffe in World War II as proof that defending fighters can

stop only a relatively small percentage of attacking bombers. "When the enemy is carrying atomic bombs, every air attack can result in holocaust." Vandenberg felt that the way to counter the enemy's strategic air power was not only with interceptors but with our own strategic air power—by destroying the enemy's ability to strike at U.S. industry.[6]

By focusing the Air Force on strategic bombardment and, hence, deterrence of nuclear war, Vandenberg connected the Air Force mission directly to the security of the nation. This opened the door to the concept of the primacy of the Air Force to provide for national security and to compete for defense budgets.

Before Vandenberg became Chief of Staff, the defense money was apportioned among the services, and the idea of a "balanced force" was one in which equal sums of money were spent by the Army, the Navy, and the Air Force. Military leaders felt that if the respective services could not receive the necessary funds in order to accomplish the mission as they saw it, then the only thing to do was to divide what money was available equally among the three services.

In an unprecedented speech for the Air Force Association in Los Angeles in the fall of 1950, Vandenberg urged that the defense dollar should be distributed in accordance with the expected value to national security. Under his leadership there was a departure from the standard policy that each of the three military services received one-third of the budget for defense. The turning point came in 1951 with the approval for the forthcoming budget of 1953 allocating $22 billion to the Air Force, $14 billion to the Army, and $13 billion to the Navy. Vandenberg defended this new policy. "The Air Force recognizes that air superiority over enemy nations cannot alone win a war, though loss of air superiority could lose it. Total victory in modern war is a product of ground, air, and sea power. Nothing can be gained, everything will be lost, if one component is sacrificed to such a point that it is unable to contribute to the big objective. We are building the Air Force as rapidly as possible without sacrificing the integrity of our already existing forces...."[7]

As strategic bombardment dominated both the Air Force and the national strategy of deterrence for the next decade, the Air Force found itself at the head of the line for service budgets. The Faustian bargain was in its payoff phase. The bill would not be presented for another 30 years.

The New Look

For President Eisenhower, air power—now pumped up with the muscles of nuclear weapons—provided precisely the same bait that had attracted British politicians between the two world wars: Air power could provide cheap defense against the public's worst nightmares.

Eisenhower had first come to office in 1953 with a dramatically different perspective. His defense strategy waged the Cold War by threatening "massive retaliation" with nuclear weapons whenever and wherever American vital interests were threatened by communist aggression. The new Republican president backed up his threat by building a massive bomber force that indeed could destroy the Soviet Union or China with little danger of nuclear retaliation against the United States. In warfare, the president warned, nuclear weapons would now be used "just exactly as you would use a bullet."[8]

General Thomas D. White provided the institutional leadership as the Air Force tried to adapt to Eisenhower's "new look" and yet ensure its own future. It was a time of great change in the Air Force environment— guided missiles were challenging airplanes as competitors (ballistic, cruise, and standoff missiles) and as adversaries (surface-to-air and air-to-air missiles); space was rapidly opening as a new and competitive medium to the air (for reconnaissance and surveillance, perhaps even for bombardment). General White had to pick his way through a minefield of overlapping political, technical, and institutional issues:

> The Air Force needed a leader like General White, particularly at that point in its history. When the Korean War was over then, there was needed at the helm a man who understood how to work successfully in Washington within the executive branch and within Congress. General White was eminently well qualified to do that. In addition, the Air Force was sort of trying to find its way.... White's grasp of overall strategy and his ability to sort of look out beyond today's world and see what might be important in the future is what really set him apart. He believed in the space program, and he did more than most men of his time to assure that the Air Force had a special kind of mission.[9]

Unfortunately, General White may have been more what the Air Force wanted at the time as a leader than what the institution really needed at that point in its history. Giving the airmen the airplanes and missions they wanted may have been less important than moving the theoretical foundations of the institution onto firmer ground against the looming technological flood of missile and space systems capabilities.

The Quest for a New Bomber

With the primacy of the Air Force to national security and defense budgets established, the evolution of its principal means rose to the top of the institutional agenda.

> Each military service is of course dedicated to meeting the needs of national defense. But each has also zealously promoted the weapons that best advance its

own special interests—on which billions of dollars, thousands of jobs, and countless careers are staked. For the Air Force this has meant pursuit of the strategic bomber; for the Navy, a determination to build more super aircraft carriers; for the Army, a desire to have its own helicopters to carry its troops into battle and provide them with close air support.[10]

Throughout this checkered history, the Air Force and its allies in science, industry, labor, and politics have relentlessly pursued their goals—and other groups have opposed them. On both sides, the motives of patriotism, financial gain, career ambition, political aggrandizement, and loyalty to an institution or idea were often so mixed that it is hard to tell what was narrow self-interest and what was concern for the national good.[11]

After the Korean War, the Air Force began receiving deliveries of the B-52, the airplane that would become its mainstay heavy strategic bomber for the next four decades—although Air Force leaders would have been aghast to know that at the time. Even as the B-52 ranks were swelling, the Air Force was embarked on the development of the B-70, its triple-sonic successor.

Air Force officers began referring to the still-secret new airplane as their "manned missile." General Thomas S. Power, commander of the Strategic Air Command, called it "the Savior." These nicknames had a special significance. Both the Soviet Union and the United States were developing their first ICBMS. Missiles were the future, but the bomber represented the heart of the Air Force's guiding military doctrine, the overriding importance of strategic air power. General Power and his fellow officers hoped that the B-70 would "save" bombers from being made obsolete by the missile.[12]

Somewhere during this time, the institutional Air Force was shifting its compass from a *guiding* theory of air power to a devotion to the *symbols* or means of air power—to the airplanes themselves. We have this chilling description of General White pleading his case for the B-70 to President Eisenhower:

Like an attorney making his final emotional plea for a client facing the gallows, White asked the President for the B-70, based not on its military value but on its importance to the institution to which he had devoted his life. "There is a question," he implored, "of what is to be the future of the Air Force and of flying. This shift [to missiles] has a great impingement on morale. There is no follow-on aircraft to the fighter and no new opportunity for Air Force personnel."[13]

The golden age of air power theory had begun its slow decline.

Notes

1. Gen. Chuck Yeager and Leo Janus, *Yeager: An Autobiography* (New York: Bantam Books, 1985), 175.

2. My colleague, Duane Deal, reminds me that LeMay was more than an operator of *bombers*. As Commander in Chief of the USAFE (American Air Forces in Europe), LeMay directed the beginning and then the operational control of the Berlin Airlift in 1948.

3. Puryear, *Stars in Flight*, 136.

4. Ibid., with the quote taken from "Vandenberg Speaking: Our Air Might," *Newsweek*, February 19, 1951, 22–24.

5. J. C. Wylie, *Military Strategy: A General Theory of Power Control* (Westport, Conn.: Greenwood Press, 1967), 66.

6. Ibid., 120.

7. Ibid., 3, also with the quote referenced to "Vandenberg Speaking."

8. Kotz, *Wild Blue Yonder*, 27, 28.

9. From a personal interview with Lt. Gen. Royal B. Allison, July 6, 1977, by Puryear, as reported in *Stars in Flight*, 199.

10. Kotz, *Wild Blue Yonder*, 7.

11. Ibid., 8.

12. Ibid., 32.

13. Ibid., 35.

PART IV

EROSION

14

The Technology Janus

janus-faced or janus: looking in opposite directions; having two contrasting aspects...

januslike: looking or acting in opposite or contrasting ways...[1]

The Technology Altar

Most institutions revere some principles or ideals that, over time, become enshrined upon an institutional altar where they can be worshipped. The altars are repositories for the ideas or concepts that serve as institutional inspirations and aspirations. For the knights of old, the altar might have been the code of chivalry. For the hippies or "flower children" of the 1960s, it might be "love." Altars, when discovered, usually reveal something about how the worshipers see themselves and their values.[2]

The Air Force has long worshipped at the altar of technology—the benefactor of winged flight for man. The airplane has, from its inception, been an expression of the miracles of technology. The very knowledge of how to fly came from technical devices and experiments, and fliers have been the major instigators and beneficiaries of technological advances in everything from structural materials to microelectronics.

If human flight is a wondrous gift of technology, and if technology poses the only limits on the freedoms of that gift, then it is to be expected that the fountain of technology will be worshipped by military fliers and the Air Force. This is the catechism: If the Air Force is to have a future of expanding horizons, it will come only from understanding, nurturing, and applying technology. There is a circle of faith here: If the Air Force fosters technology, then that inexhaustible fountain of technology will ensure an open-ended future for flight; which, in turn, will ensure the future of the Air Force. The critical element, of course, is the continued expansion of flight-related technologies, which is at least arguable as the air and space technologies mature.

One evidence of a slowing in the expansion of the aeronautical technologies is the growing lifetimes of aircraft designs before their obsolescence. The most successful aircraft designs have always had useful lifetimes about equal to the time span between Kittyhawk (1903) and the year of their design. An airplane design ten years after the Wright Brother's original flyer might expect, at the best, a ten year life; but a good design today, might last for the better part of a century.

That rule of thumb can be applied across 90 years of aviation during which successful airplane designs have eventually succumbed to technological obsolescence, such as the Curtiss Jenny, Douglas DC-3, and the Boeing 707. The best military aircraft designs—such as the DeHaviland DH4, Chance Vought F4U Corsair, McDonnell F4 Phantom, and Boeing B-52 Stratofortress—have all had somewhat shorter useful lives, but have followed the same trend.

This continuing extension of useful lifetimes implies that technological obsolescence in aircraft is slowing. Although that might be welcomed by those paying the bills for aircraft, it is not by those devoted to designing and building new ones, for they have to search harder for reasons—the threat of competition or technology—to replace the existing aircraft. For the military airmen, with an expectation of the joys of a new machine rooted in a view of aviation's past, the future is likely to be more frustrating than rewarding.

The Air Force has occasionally argued for its needs in terms of the number of wings of bombers or fighters needed or desired.[3] But the Air Force's appetite for newer and more technologically advanced aircraft, with their accompanying higher cost, has tempered its demands when the choice came to more of the old or fewer of the new. For the Air Force, aerodynamic performance and technological quality of its aircraft have always been of higher priority than the number. Thus, in measuring the adequacy of its forces, the Air Force is likely to speak first of the kind or quality of its aircraft (speed, altitude, maneuverability, range, armament, or carrying capacity) before their quantity.

This emphasis on quality over quantity is easily observed: The Air Force does not lament the size of its bomber force so much as it does the age of its B-52s. It considers the necessity of fathers and sons' flying the same bomber as a national disgrace. The trade of larger quantities of arguably less capable F-16s for F-15s was never attractive to the Air Force. When confronted with having a mix of the new B-1 bomber and an even newer B-2, the Air Force favored more B-2s.[4]

The Air Force concern about the adequacy of its forces becomes acute only if their technical superiority is threatened. New aircraft developments by other nations are of much greater concern if they reflect new flight envelopes than if they are being produced in large quantities; to be outnumbered may be tolerable, but to be outflown is not. The way to command the American flier's attention is to confront him with a superior machine; that has not happened very often or for very long in the relatively short history of aviation.

Hap Arnold's Bug

The Air Force's love of technology is the result of the technological era that crested around 1950 and dominated the decades on each side of that peak.[5] It goes back to the beginning of military aviation; and it transcends manned aircraft—at least for some of the most far-sighted aviators. Hap Arnold provides the following description of his fascinating quest for unmanned aircraft as missiles. What makes it fascinating and worth reproducing here at length is how it reveals Arnold's love for technology and *his devotion to the ends of air power theory even over its traditional means of manned aircraft.* Arnold's recollection begins with the advent of the German V-1, a pulsejet powered cruise missile:

[E]xactly one week after Eisenhower's troops hit the Normandy beaches on D-Day, the world was horrified by the sudden appearance over London of the first V-1's, the gruesome pilotless buzz bombs. A number of people in this country, including Ket,[6] were not surprised, for he and our own Air Force had fathered, if not invented, this weapon back in 1917.

Early in the fall of that year, working with the Sperry Company, and with Ket's Delco firm, we had developed—not merely experimented with, but successfully tested—two pilotless planes. One was a full-sized airplane, but equipped with complete gyroscope controls, built at Sperry's Long Island plant. Further tests in the spring of 1918 showed that this flying bomb was sufficiently accurate to reach a point within a hundred yards of its target after a forty-mile run, but the necessary precision devices, man hours to be expended, and so on, made it too expensive to pursue in terms of quantity production. Under Ket's direction, we then devised a pilotless airplane—or bomb—which we called the Bug. It was a complete little airplane built of papier-mache and reinforced with wooden members, its smooth cardboard wing surfaces spreading less than twelve feet. Its fuselage held 300 pounds of explosives, and it weighed, unloaded, 300 pounds itself. It took off from a small four-wheeled carriage which rolled down a portable track, its own little two-cycle, 40 h.p. engine, built by Henry Ford, meeting the requirements for both pressure and vacuum necessary to operate the automatic controls. The actuating force for the controls was secured from bellows removed from player pianos. They rotated cranks, which in turn operated the elevators [and] the rudder. The direction of the flight was insured by a small gyro, elevation from a small supersensitive aneroid barometer, so sensitive that moving it from the top of the desk to the floor operated the controls. This kept the Bug at its proper altitude. At first we relied only on the dihedral of the wings for lateral stability, but later, more positive directional controls had to be installed with orthodox ailerons. Including the $50 gasoline engine built by Ford, the entire device cost about $400.

To launch the Bug, tracks were pointed toward the objective. The distance to the target, and wind direction and intensity, were figured out as accurately as possible. The number of revolutions of the engine required to take the Bug to the target was then figured, and a cam set. When the engine had turned exactly that proper number of revolutions, the cam fell into position, the two bolts holding on the wings were withdrawn, the wings folded up like a jack rabbit's ears, and the Bug plunged to earth as a bomb. (In 1944 the German V-1's flew to their objectives on similar principles, insofar as range was concerned.)

By mid-1918, the development of the Bug had proceeded so favorably that we decided to tell General Pershing and the Commanding General of the Air Service in France what we were doing. We were sure we would be ready to send some of the pilotless bombs overseas within a few months. A proposed Table of Organization was drawn up showing the number of officers and men that would be required in each Bug squadron, and an estimate was prepared showing the number of Bugs each squadron would be able to launch in twenty-four hours. It was planned to launch thousands every day against German strong points, concentration areas, munition plants, etc.—which would certainly have caused great consternation in the ranks of the German High Command at least.

The Bug was twenty-five years ahead of its time. For all practical purposes—as a nuisance weapon—it compared very favorably with the German V-1. It was cheap, easy to manufacture, and its portable launching track would have permitted its use anywhere. Considering the trends in air weapons today, and that the first German V-1 was not launched against Britain until the fifth year of World War II, it is interesting to think how this little Bug might have changed the whole face of history if it had been allowed to develop without interruption during the years between the two wars. It was not perfect in 1918, of course, and as new gadgets and scientific improvements came out they continued to be incorporated into the Bug until the economy wave of the mid-twenties caused it to be shelved....[7]

Arnold's experience with the development of the Bug was not simply a passing fancy. The idea of an unmanned bomber for strategic bombardment was revived as America entered World War II. But this time, it posed a doctrinal confrontation with what had become the central ideas of the American airmen: the big self-defended bomber and precision daylight bombardment. Arnold addressed the question fearlessly:

> As already stated, our whole fight for an Air Force had come to center more and more around bombardment, precision bombardment by daylight, all the things summed up by the great word "B-17." I now had to decide whether the four-engine bomber, and the whole bombardment program we had worked toward for so many years, should take second place in favor of something else. This time the problem was not pressed on us from outside the Air Force. We faced it ourselves, deliberately. The reason for it was not any lack of faith in our development of precision bombardment. There was the possibility that we now had something still more useful in our air power arsenal, when and if we entered the war against Germany. The "something" was nothing less than a highly improved version of that same little pilotless Bug which we had devised in 1917–18, and had kept on developing as well as the strict attention to "Economy in Government" permitted.

> Recently revived trials indicated that the Bug was now ready for operational use. Its flight-tested range, in December, 1941, was better than 200 miles, both this and its accuracy apparently being capable of rapid improvement. It might be necessary to change the original concept. It was now controlled by radio. We could employ one of the many other modern scientific devices that would insure it a direct-reckoning course to its objective. The pilotless Bug was, in any case, already a modern military weapon in being. It would cost, per unit, between $800 and $1000 as compared to $200,000 for a medium, or $400,000 for a single heavy bomber, and could be produced quickly in large numbers.[8]

The comparative analysis that Arnold then presented is remarkable—not for its pertinence, but for its forthright consideration of possibilities so threatening to the very heart of the institutional Air Force:

> For the price of one B-17 with a bomb load of 6000 pounds, we could send 500 of these little Bugs over enemy territory, each carrying about 800 pounds of explosive. Much more important than any monetary factor was the possible saving in human life. It has been mentioned that some time before this we had come to the decision that the loss rate for which we must be prepared in an all-out air war would probably be around 25 percent of our combat planes and combat personnel per month.

> C. F. Kettering, of General Motors, the real father of the Bug, not only had an intimate knowledge of its development from the start, but in the intervening years had worked on devices to perfect it. Elmer Sperry, who had made the first controls for the full-size pilotless plane, was dead, but his Sperry Gyroscope Company was still in full stride. Orville Wright, and some of the men in the Aeolian Company who had pioneered with us in the earlier experiments, were

still active. There was no doubt that the Bug could be put into large-scale production within a very short time.

I called a meeting at which only Kettering, Bill Knudsen [Lt. Gen. Knudsen, the USAAF production "czar"] and myself were present. We discussed the availability of bases; of targets; the cost; production; comparison of production between the Bugs and heavy bombers; raw materials needed for the two types of weapons. We finally came to the conclusion, unanimously, that even with the most improved type of Bug, the best we could do from England would be to hit Paris, or some of the other large cities in France, Belgium, or Holland. We could not get at the real heart of our enemy—interior Germany itself.[9]

The problem with the Bugs was not doctrinal, at least with Arnold, but the geographical asymmetries between the Allies and Germans:

Had we been in the position the Germans then were, and had the Germans instead of the English inhabited the British Isles, the story would have been very different. We could, and we would have concentrated the flight of thousands upon thousands of these Bugs on practically all the interior of southern and middle England, including the key industrial areas. We could probably have had this assault in full swing by late 1942, or early 1943, and have used the Bug by the thousands and tens of thousands. The Germans could have done little to stop it. As it was, the first pilotless bomb did not buzz across the English Channel from a German launching site until the night of the 12th of June, 1944, a week after our ground forces had landed in Normandy, and two and a half years after Kettering, Knudsen, and I held this discussion in my office.[10]

Arnold didn't dismiss the German V-1 "buzz" bombs as a mere nuisance weapon, even though he had used that term to describe them. Indeed, the Allied bombing effort directed at the V-1 launch sites suggests the level of concern engendered by their potential to bombard England and the forces building up for the Normandy invasion.

The Eighth Air Force...from August, 1943, until the summer of 1944, dropped approximately 100,000 tons of bombs on the [V-1 launch sites].... But apart from other failures to stop them, the USSBS [the U.S. Strategic Bombing Survey] estimates that these bombings by the Eighth, the R.A.F., and subsequently by both American and R.A.F. mediums, cost the German V-weapon program a loss of three to four months. The damage done to the sites once they started firing was not great. They had eventually to be captured by the infantry....

The bombs the Eighth Air Force sent down on the "No Ball" and "Cross Bow" targets between August, 1943, and the summer of 1944 amounted to 9 percent of the bombs they dropped against Germany in that period. Apart from the human desolation when the reduced robot bomb program was finally launched—2752 civilians dead, 8000 injured, Churchill announced, after only thirty-five days of the robots on London—it can be fairly claimed that the diversion of so many bombers to such a defensive purpose proves the V-1 to have been much more than a nuisance weapon. I agree—if they had been used rightly, and in time....

Anyway, I'm as glad as any Londoner that we did bomb these launching sites when we did. I happened to be there when the first V-1's came down on England, and regardless of larger strategic considerations there seemed to me to be quite enough of them.[11]

Technology as Threat

The Air Force pays a price for its love of technology: Technology shows no reverence for institutional doctrine or structure. In fostering technology, even for its cherished instruments, the Air Force is necessarily instigating new concepts and capabilities that challenge the form and preferences of its institution. Perry McCoy Smith explains why the Air Force has often looked at particular new technological developments with a blind eye:

Once a military doctrine is established it is difficult to change, especially if technological advancements in weaponry seriously bring into question a doctrine upon which a specific military service is based. Like policy, doctrine has a gyroscopic effect. And if service doctrine is questioned by members of that service, there is a tendency for the leadership to brand the critics heretics, especially if the doctrine is the basis upon which the primary goals of a service are constructed. In addition, the formulation and articulation of the doctrine is ordinarily designed to justify fully the service's attempt to obtain or maintain exclusive control over certain missions. Criticism usually results in an undermining of the case the service has so carefully made for certain roles and missions in national defense. Dissent is therefore discouraged, and breakthroughs in technology which might bring established doctrine into question are often ignored.[12]

Richard Hallion suggests that doctrine must be made as dynamic as technology if the Air Force is to fully benefit from its worship of technology:

[B]ecause the Air Force as a service is wedded (and rightly so) to technology, there is always the danger that technology will make one's doctrine obsolete, will replace doctrine as the determinant of the future course of the Air Force, and will become merely a convenient shibboleth endowed by advocates with greater significance than it really possesses.

We must recognize that both technology and doctrine are *dynamic* processes, always advancing or receding, and are necessarily adaptive to change lest they stagnate and lose relevance. Neither is independent of the other; rather, each generates a synergistic impulse that encourages and strengthens the other....[13]

Hallion provides some historical examples:

> Generally speaking, the technology tail has wagged the Air Force dog. This is not necessarily a bad thing, but it does require some clarification. Since technology and doctrine are inherently dynamic, the rapid expansion of technology should trigger an anticipatory, proactive impulse within the doctrine community so that doctrine can be established to guide the application of high technology for suitable Air Force missions. Too often this has not taken place. Tying technology too closely to existing doctrine and philosophy immediately after World War II led to the creation of classes of straight wing aircraft, ironically blending advanced turbojet propulsion with late-1930s aerodynamics. These were awkward vehicles rendered quickly obsolete by the swept-wing transonic designs of the late 1940s. On the other hand, when technology was freed from such doctrinal constraints but while doctrine itself did not keep pace with technological development, the result tended to be wildly fanciful ideas perhaps best typified by the atomic airplane program of the 1950s or the aerospace plane program of the 1960s.[14]

Technology not only directly threatens doctrine, but it can also indirectly threaten force structure.

> The only thing certain about the current pell-mell pace of technology in conventional air warfare is its spiraling costs, which are driving the price of individual aircraft up into the tens of millions of dollars. Since these cost increases must inevitably have the effect of reducing the numbers that will be made available, if not indeed the willingness to commit them to combat, some airmen—usually lonely renegades—have begun to call for a retreat to greater numbers of less capable aircraft....[15]

However, this retreat from quality in favor of quantity seems culturally remote. Norm Augustine, an aerospace executive of considerable renown and wit, observing the inexorable rise in military aircraft costs, has suggested,[16] only partly in jest, that, if the current trend lines continue, the Air Force will find itself limited to only one very costly airplane sometime in the 21st century. The trend lines seem so immutable that it is hard to see an escape from Augustine's conclusion. Could it be that Augustine is correct? By that time, few would care about how many airplanes the Air Force owned. By then, might the Air Force, itself, like coast artillery or calvary, become largely irrelevant?

David MacIsaac has a more likely answer, but one which would not make the military airmen any happier:

> One possible switch of emphasis would be from the weapons platform—that is, the aircraft—to the weapons themselves, in particular precision-guided munitions,

or PGMs. It is only natural that airmen have tended to concentrate on the platform itself, especially with regard to improvements in speed, range, agility, and other performance characteristics. It is similarly only natural that airmen have proved reluctant to foster rapid advances in the field of remotely piloted vehicles, or RPVs. However much the official spokesmen of the air services may deny it, RPVs are not considered an appropriate topic for discussion by most pilots, among whom it is an article of faith that a manned aircraft can perform any mission better than an unmanned aircraft.

This uneasy, love-hate relationship between technology and the Air Force helps to explain what happened when the Air Force and air power theory met the great challenges of the ballistic missile and space operations during the late 1950s and early 1960s. That encounter would be the turning point for air power theory and, eventually, for the Air Force as an institution.

Notes

1. *Webster's Third New International Dictionary* (Merriam-Webster, 1986), 1209.

2. The following relies on material from my *Masks of War*.

3. The Air Force sought 70 groups after World War II, when it was dominated by strategic bombing enthusiasts. See Paul R. Schratz, "The Admiral's Revolt," *Proceedings*, U.S. Naval Institute, vol. 112, no. 2 (February 1986): 70.

4. Air Force Colonel John Frisby argues that my explanation of the Air Force preference for quality over quantity is too shallow. He writes (in a letter to the author dated 11 March 1992), "From my observations, much thought, analysis of threat, mission requirements, and projected needs always went into the process. New systems and force structure decisions were always carefully thought through." I would readily yield to his protest if we had examples of the Air Force choosing quantity over quality in its airplanes. Analysis may not be a sufficient defense of the Air Force preference for quality over quantity, for analysis can be doggedly pursued until the "right" answer emerges (see my *Masks of War*, 98–101). If quality is *always* to be preferred over quantity in Air Force airplanes, despite much analysis, then my simpler explanation for that phenomenon may suffice.

5. For the rise (and fall) of the American society's love affair with technology, see Carl H. Builder, *Patterns in American Intellectual Frontiers*, RAND N-2917-A (Santa Monica, Calif.: RAND, August 1990).

6. Charles Kettering, of Delco, who was responsible for many technical contributions to the Air Force, including the development of the anti-knock properties so essential to high-performance aviation gasoline in aircraft engines.

7. H. H. Arnold, *Global Mission* (New York: Harper & Bros., 1949), 74–76.

8. Ibid., 259–260.

9. Ibid., 260–261.

10. Ibid., 261.

11. Ibid., 499.

12. Smith, *The Air Force Plans for Peace*, 30.

13. Dr. Richard P. Hallion, "Doctrine, Technology, and Air Warfare: A Late Twentieth-Century Perspective," *Airpower Journal*, vol. I, no. 2, (Fall, 1987): 16, 17.

14. Ibid., 23, 24.

15. MacIsaac, "Voices from the Central Blue," 646.

16. Norman R. Augustine, *Augustine's Laws Revised and Enlarged* (New York: American Institute of Aeronautics and Astronautics, 1983), 53–60

17. MacIsaac, "Voices from the Central Blue," 646.

15

New Dimensions

Although all the services had some factional interests in ballistic missiles, they were vested in minorities that had more in common with one another than they did with their parent services. None of the services evidenced great enthusiasm for major investments in ballistic missiles even as their factions noisily pursued research, experiments, and proposals. The mainstreams of the services were much more concerned with pursing their established interests in aircraft carriers or bombers or divisions.[1]

Although pilotless aircraft, rockets, and dreams of space flight found comfortable niches in the growing and confident Air Force of the 1950s, they were treated as harmless fringe elements that came with the scientists and engineers the Air Force needed for its exciting journey into the "jet" age. But in the late 1950s, air power theory was credibly threatened for the first time with alternative means to the airplane for its ends. The threat of alternative means did not come from some wild-eyed advocate advancing theories,[2] but from the most serious and dangerous enemy of the Cold War.

The Soviet developments in ballistic missiles and space in the late 1950s forced a dramatic change on the Air Force. What had been tolerated, sometimes even resisted, within the Air Force before now gained center stage for budgets, interservice competition, and national security. Unless the Air Force dominated missiles and space, the role of airplanes in the Air Force of the future could be threatened. It was much better for these new means to be in the hands of the Air Force than in the hands of those who might still challenge the legitimacy of the Air Force as a separate institution.

But there were many in the Air Force, such as the technologists attracted to the Air Force because it was at the cutting edge of technology, who found these new means even more attractive and technically demanding than airplanes. Missile and space enthusiasts appeared within the Air Force. Theories about control of space—the high ground— echoed the air power theorizing of 40 years earlier.[3] The leadership of the Air Force, however, remained firmly in the hands of the pilots and operators of World War II.

When the development of missiles reached the point where their efficacy could no longer be denied—when they emerged in the hands of potential enemies, and when the Army and Navy appeared prepared to champion these new means at the expense of the Air Force—the Air Force leadership was finally compelled to include them. But the admission of missile and then space advocates into the Air Force was not as full citizens. The aviators dominated the institution; and while they tolerated others pursuing their own interests in different means or specialties, they demonstrated in many ways that aviators and airplanes were the mainstream of the Air Force. This attitude was the beginning of an institutional divisiveness that would be even more destructive than the split between the fighter and bomber pilots. It was destructive because the exhibited discrimination was not in favor of an altruistic mission—striking quickly and decisively at the heart of an enemy—but in favor of an elite class: the pilots.

The Blind Eye

It was easy for the victorious aviators of World War II to be dismissive of the technical prospects for ballistic missiles. It was equally easy for them to be expansive about the prospects for jet aircraft:

A top level scientific survey commissioned by the Air Force Chief of Staff, General Henry Arnold, concluded just after the war that long-range ballistic rockets were feasible. It added, however, that such weapons were not likely to be available until the distant future. For the present, Air Force attention should be devoted to manned aircraft and particularly toward the almost equally new jet airplanes. If any effort were to be devoted to long-range missiles, it should proceed cautiously by way of slower, less revolutionary, air-breathing vehicles. This judgment led to emphasis upon the air-breathing Snark and Navaho—a priority that continued into the 1950s. A June 1947 Air Force report on missile development placed long-range, surface-to-surface missiles at the fourth level of priority and stressed missile types that could increase bomber and fighter capabilities. More important ...ballistic rockets were excluded from the already down-played long-range efforts. Air Force Research on long-distance ballistic missiles was cancelled in 1947, not to be revived until 1951 and then only at a minimal level and under the influence of Korea induced defense spending increases.[4]

Without someone like General Arnold to foster technological alternatives to manned aircraft, missile developments in the Air Force after World War II were relegated to those hobbyists who were willing to sacrifice their institutional careers in favor of their technological dreams.

For many years after World War II, intercontinental ballistic missiles were neglected and virtually ignored within the Air Force (and consequently more or less within the United States government). After the retirement of General Arnold in 1946, no powerful figure or group within the Air Force gave much consideration to long range ballistic missile potentials until 1953. No important command or agency saw its function as their promotion. On the contrary, the Air Force structure was geared to concentrate on manned aircraft. Furthermore, the research and development arm of the Air Force was, until 1951, subordinated within an airplane-oriented command and thus both naturally and by orders followed that lead. A major American redirection of effort to accelerate ballistic missile development did not occur until 1953–54, some seven years after the Soviet Union had initiated such a program.[5]

This neglect was not a deliberate conspiracy against ballistic missiles and for manned aircraft but was a myopia created by who the Air Force was and what it was about at the time. As Edmund Beard put it,

My opinion is that the United States could have developed an ICBM considerably earlier than it did but that such development was hindered by organizational structures and belief patterns that did not permit it.

In its simplest form, the proposition could be that the Air Force was committed to manned aircraft and particularly to manned bombers, and refused to change. Such a bald statement could not adequately describe the ICBM story, however, although in some ways it is quite true. Before the reversal and acceleration of 1954, the Air Force's stance toward ballistic missiles can best be characterized as neglect and indifference. This attitude was commonly associated with public judgments that the weapons were extremely unlikely if not impossible. Until late 1953, and despite the existence of contrary evidence and opinions, a general emphasis on manned bomber systems (or on missile types that did not threaten them) with a slow, conservative approach to ballistic missiles persisted within the Air Force. Contrary opinions were disregarded, contrary evidence dismissed. Men who had always flown and relied upon bombers found it hard, indeed almost impossible, to sense the revolutionary implications of ballistic missiles. Organizations that had been designed to advocate and maintain bombers continued to do so.

For much of the period there was no institutional lobby for the competing missiles; even though the Air Research and Development Command—an organization that perceived missiles as a major area of responsibility—had been created in 1951, that agency remained for some years weaker and less influential than its peers. In addition, the ARDC birth was accompanied by friction and bitterness from the parent Air Materiel Command, a problem that persisted for several years.[6]

Although aircraft and missile technologies were changing rapidly during the first decade after World War II, the Air Force priorities were not.

There is little that differs in the Air Force analysis in 1950 from its position in 1946–1947. The strategic bombardment function was still the most important within the Air Force. The chosen means to accomplish the mission remained the manned bomber fleet and would continue to be so with the future deployment of the B-52. Long range surface-to-surface missiles were not important within the relevant future of the Air Force. It was important, however, that other services not develop such weapons which would then compete with the Air Force responsibility and the chosen Air Force vehicles. Air Force distribution of responsibility agreements with the other services were designed to prevent such competition. By June 1950, the Air Force missile program was down to four projects from an immediate postwar high of twenty-six, and there was every indication that the program might be reduced further if budgetary restrictions continued to be imposed.[7]

If the attitudes and motivations in the Air Force about ballistic missiles in those early postwar years were speculative, the budgets were not:

By 1949 the Air Force was spending almost $3 billion annually for the development and procurement of manned airplanes; only $39 million supported their sundry missile projects. Those funds were directed exclusively to aerodynamic missiles, a preference which was perhaps related to the fact that such missiles resembled "their familiar aircraft, flew at comparable speeds, and could be controlled by guidance they understood." Aside from certain component development work, the only funds devoted to long-range ballistic rockets between 1947 and 1951 were those modest sums supplied by Convair Corporation out of their private investment budgets.[8]

If missile developments were cheap enough to keep the hobbyists in the Air Force entertained, missile production and deployment would have seriously encroached upon manned aircraft force structures. Thus, although several missiles were partially developed, budget pressure truncated their paths toward the mainstream of the Air Force.

During the late 1940s and early 1950s, Air Force interest in long-range surface-to-surface ballistic missiles, if persistent, had been quite sporadic. By 1953 a number of individual projects had been initiated and were reaching the stage where prototypes had to be constructed if further progress was to be made. Naturally this would entail significant increase in the level of development expenditures. At the same time their jet aircraft program was approaching a similar stage in the development cycle. But rather than being able to anticipate increases in defense spending, the outcome of the 1952 elections and the conclusion of the Korean War brought new pressures for economy. In this atmosphere of retrenchment the Air force chose to defend its embryonic jet combat units by reprogramming funds away from their sundry missile projects.[9]

The circumstances of the Snark cruise missile development bring Edmund Beard to suspect conspiracy:

[A]ir planners consistently predicted that surface-to-air antiaircraft missiles would become available during the early 1950s and that these weapons would be particularly effective against subsonic aircraft. These same planners agreed that ballistic missiles were, within any conceivable technology, unstoppable. Yet development of these vehicles was persistently delayed. Enormous efforts were put into developing the B-52 as a follow on to the B-36. In addition, during the 1950s the Air force strongly promoted the B-70, a supersonic long-range heavy bomber designed to follow the B-52.

[M]uch money was also invested in the Snark, the least efficient of the contemplated long-range missiles. The Snark and the B-52 were broadly comparable weapons, but the Snark always lacked accuracy and reliability and never developed operational capability. The suspicion remains that the Snark may have been supported in some quarters precisely because it did *not* constitute a real threat to the B-52 or any follow on bomber. During the same period, the Air Force hierarchy devoted significant efforts to standoff missiles, which were considered vital to the health and effectiveness of the manned bomber fleet. The cultural identification with manned airplanes and the cultural resistance to ballistic missiles seems obvious.[10]

Jeffrey Record argues that the prejudice against missiles was explicit:

As General Thomas D. White, Air Force Chief of Staff from 1957 to 1961, once candidly conceded, "To say there is not a deeply ingrained prejudice in favor of aircraft among flyers would be a stupid statement...."[11]

Whether the stakes did or did not motivate the actions, the actions reflected the stakes of those involved.

Robert L. Perry, a perceptive analyst and sympathetic critic of the Air Force, has succinctly stated the bomber-missile issue:

Without going deeply into the sociology or psychology of the phenomenon, it is plain that the people who had grown with manned bombers before and during World War II and who mostly stayed with them through the next decade developed an abiding affection for them, an affection based in some degree on what aircraft meant as a way of life, a symbol, a means of performing their military assignment. With minor exceptions, those who sought to bring on change had no such commitments; they were primarily engineers and scientists of one sort or another and only secondarily airplane commanders. It is not really important whether the opponents of change, or its supporters, consciously recognized the possibility that the adoption of the ballistic missile as a primary means of delivering nuclear weapons would cause the decline or even the disappearance of the strategic bomber. It is important, however, that they sometimes acted as if they foresaw that possibility.[12]

The blind eye most often took the form of reasonable skepticism:

The impossibility inference appears to have been present in the early history of the ICBM. Most Air Force personnel at the Air Staff level (and probably elsewhere) simply denied that an "accurate" long-range rocket was possible, at least in the foreseeable future. The ballistic rocket was at least implicitly a competitor to the manned strategic bomber. The bomber was...the central focus of identification within the Air Force. To conceive of a new weapon that might someday perform its primary task much more efficiently would require great restructuring of beliefs. The literature of cognitive psychology, as well as most people's everyday experience, makes it clear that such restructuring is a difficult, unpleasant task. The normal reaction is to reject the disturbing new element. The Air Force's behavior in the early days of the ICBM followed this pattern.... It is worth remembering that Air Force planners in 1947–48 did not expect even long-range supersonic bombers to be operationally available before 1957. Since the Air Force officers not only understood bombers and knew they worked but often equated their own personal usefulness and well-being with that weapon it is not surprising that long range supersonic missiles were placed even further into the future.[13]

Michael Terry suggests that the prejudice was not just from flyers towards their airplanes, but also from the institution towards its missions and newly won independence.

The "cultural identification" with manned aircraft and the organizational resistance to ballistic missiles was apparent. Without its independence anchored to a bedrock of uncompromising "roles and missions," the Air Force faced an unraveling of their newly established institution. Their resistance to changing their basic functions, or to sharing them with other defense organizations, could be understood. Military institutions are very conservative regarding their missions and attempt to maintain them; at stake is "their autonomy, organizational morale, [and] organizational essence."[14]

Jeffrey Record provides a nice summary of the "blind eye," including what the loss of Hap Arnold cost the Air Force in terms of breadth of perspective and objectivity.

> Indeed, during the period 1945 to 1954, an Air Force attitude of "neglect and indifference" toward the development of ICBMs permitted the Soviet Union to gain an early lead in long-range ballistic missile technologies. Until the Office of the Secretary of Defense and other civilian authorities, including President Eisenhower, intervened to impose an accelerated schedule and new management organizations and procedures that in effect removed the ICBM's development from normal USAF channels, "cultural resistance" within the Air Force to a new weapon that promised to displace the manned bomber restricted USAF interest in the ICBM largely to situations in which it "perceived a threat from...a sister service" to acquire them. Though General "Hap" Arnold exhibited great enthusiasm and prescient anticipation of ICBMs, for almost a decade the Air Force's postwar leadership consciously retarded ICBM development by withholding adequate funding and imposing nearly impossible performance requirements.[15]

Not All Were Blind

Was the "blind eye" an inevitable consequence of the Air Force's institutional circumstances? There is too much evidence that the Air Force had leaders who were willing to contemplate and embrace alternatives to manned aircraft.

> Gen. Carl A. Spaatz, one of the foremost military experts, wrote in 1945: "Lethal rockets will flash through the stratosphere scores of miles above the earth, carrying atomic weapons...."[16]

Arnold's clear perception of the world, which would unfold decades later is astonishing:

> In the fall of 1944, Arnold established von Karman as head of a new Scientific Advisory Group for the air force and ordered him to look far into the technological future. According to von Karman's dramatic account, the two rendezvoused at a remote corner of La Guardia airport, Arnold dismissed his chauffeur ("Not another car was in sight"), and the general disclosed his plans. As fleshed out by his staff, Arnold's rationale for a permanent alliance of officers and scientists was both political and strategic. The strategic danger to the United States lay largely in the unfolding technological revolution: the United States would face enemies and the possibility of "global war" waged by offensive weapons of great sophistication. But the American response would be shaped by considerations of domestic politics. The United States had to reverse "the mistakes of unpreparedness

prior to World War II," particularly the failure to harness civilian science to military needs. And technological development would respond to "a fundamental principle of democracy that personnel casualties are distasteful. We will continue to fight mechanical rather than manpower wars."

Arnold had a certain brutal foresight into the shape of wars to come, a vision of intercontinental aerial struggle extrapolated from the lessons of Pearl Harbor and wartime technology. But the politics and strategy of future conflicts interested him less than their technological basis. "I see a manless Air Force," he told von Karman: "I see no excuse for men in fighter planes to shoot down bombers. When you lose a bomber, it is a loss of seven thousand to forty thousand man-hours, but this crazy thing [V-2] they shoot over there takes only a thousand man-hours...." While other airmen might wax sentimentally about the manned bomber, Arnold asked von Karman to look into "manless remote controlled radar or television assisted precision military rockets" and imagined the day when such devices would "fly over enemy territory and look through the leaves of trees and see whether they're moving their equipment."[17]

Arnold was explicit about the need for dynamism considering internal and external forces on the military institutions:

We must stop "shoeing dead horses." We have been doing that far too long. We have, in the United States, been operating this Army station, or that Naval base, or that piece of equipment for years, because—well, because what? Well, any old reason. We did it because of Congressman or Senator "X"—we must have his support; he might lose votes, and so not support the Army, Navy, or Air Force Bill; or we have had this unit ever since the Revolution, and tradition is behind it, so we will keep it in being; or, some time or other there may be a use for this station, or that base, or some obsolete technique or pieces of equipment.

There is only one question that should be asked about these things: "Do they fit into the modern war picture?" Not the picture of 1919, nor of 1941, but of the war of the future. If they don't, we should be ruthless, and throw them out. For instance, who knows whether 70 groups of airplanes is the right or wrong number to prevent another war? Was not that number selected in relation to costs and expenditures, rather than with regard to the composition and strength necessary to our armed forces in the world picture? Do 70 groups have any relationship to our new foreign obligations? The proper number may be 47, 70, or even 170; but it should be based upon our foreign policy and the part we must take in the operations of the armed forces of the Alliance....

The principles of yesterday no longer apply. Air travel, air power, air transportation of troops and supplies have changed the whole picture. We must think in terms of tomorrow. We must bear in mind that air power itself can become obsolete.

Duplications, obsolete construction projects, obsolete techniques and policies, overlapping in the armed services' operations and organizations must go by the boards. There is no place for two air forces today any more than there is for two ground forces or two navies. Let us get smart, and, while we have a few years in which to reorganize, do it right. Let us give the people of the United States the best, the most efficient, the most modernly equipped armed forces possible, using as determining factors, our *foreign policy, and the capabilities and limitations of our probable enemies.*[18]

Although an operator more than a theorist or visionary, LeMay appears to have been much more comfortable with the prospects of guided missiles than his contemporaries. In a memo dated 20 September 1946 to General Spaatz,

> General LeMay concluded with several observations about the importance of missile and rocket development to the long-term future of what would soon be the independent Air Force.
>
> > The present situation with regard to guided missiles in Europe, with Russia, England and France all hiring German engineers and pressing development energetically, with the Russian reopening of Peenemunde and Nordhausen, with Russian missiles seen in Sweden, makes it absolutely imperative that the U.S. press guided missiles development with maximum energy.
> >
> > The long-range future of the AAF lies in the field of guided missiles. Atomic propulsion may not be usable in manned aircraft in the near future, nor can accurate placement of atomic warheads be done without sacrifice of the crews. In acceleration, temperature, endurance, multiplicity of functions, courage, and many other pilot requirements, we are reaching human limits. Machines have greater endurance, will stand more severe ambient conditions, will perform more functions accurately, will dive into targets without hesitation. The AAF *must* go to guided missiles for the initial heavy casualty phases of future wars.[19]

Playing Catch-Up

When the Air Force was pushed by outside events into the ballistic missile business, it did so in a partnership with the aircraft industry which dated back to the 1930s.

> Nevertheless, in 1954 in the face of the anticipated obsolescence of manned bombers, the Air Force and its industrial associates accepted the missile era as inevitable and made a major effort to capture the new market. At that time, the industry was in the unhappy state of a producer falling upon evil days, with but a single buyer—the Government—and facing competition from new sources— the Army, the Navy, and their industrial affiliates. The instinct to crush the competitor was compelling, and in the highly politicized atmosphere of defense supply, political methods were among those employed. If the Air Force was interested in excluding the Army from missile and space missions, the air frame

industry was equally desirous of eliminating competition from the automobile industry and liquidating the competition emanating at that time from the Redstone Arsenal missile engineering team. They also wished to discredit the concept of weapons development implicit in the Army's arsenal system.[20]

General White tried to find an acceptable path across the chasm that now yawned before the airmen with the advent of missiles: There would be a transition to missiles and thence to space, but airmen would participate at every stage and not be displaced.

On November 29, 1957, White announced at the National Press Club the decision to speed the United States readiness for combat use of long-range ballistic missiles, placing the missile program with the Strategic Air Command. The intermediate and intercontinental ballistic missiles were in the Air Research and Development Command. He emphasized that existing air power was not sufficient. The next step was for the Air Force to control space—the twenty miles of atmosphere encompassing the earth as well as the regions beyond. This was the essence of his thinking: "We are working into the future, and in the future I see integrated forces of manned and unmanned [aircraft] systems, for missiles are but one step in the evolution from aircraft to true spacecrafts." This comment was reported in the November 30 issue of the New York Times....

He could see beyond the glamor of what seemed to be the weapon of the future— the missile—to its lack of flexibility. The Air Force of the future would need both. A lesser man would have "hung on to manned planes," and a man more limited than White would have been content with missiles. As early as December 14, 1957, on the anniversary of the Wright brothers' flight at Kitty Hawk, North Carolina, White said in a speech to the embryonic Air Force Academy that the idea that manned aircraft would soon be a thing of the past was wrong, that the missiles of today "are but one step in the evolution from aircraft to piloted spacecraft. "When the B-52 finds its way to the museum, it will not be because man has been eliminated from flight. Rather," he said, "it will be because new equipment has been perfected to propel him higher, drive him faster, keep him in motion longer and enable him to do more tasks better." "It is quite obvious," he said, speaking before the National Press Club on December 6, 1957, "that we cannot control air up to twenty miles above the earth's surface and relinquish control of space above that altitude and still survive.... We airmen who have fought to assure that the United States has the capability to control the air are determined that the United States must win the capability to control space." He pledged he would lead the Air Force in the race for control of space.[21]

At the same time he was trying to placate the airmen, White also tried to warn them against adopting a siege mentality for the changes that would soon be imposed on the Air Force.

Even though White believed that "there is no question that SAC, as presently constituted, is the only thing between us and oblivion and will be for a long time to come," he also believed that the Air Force was late in realizing the potential of missiles and that "the top level of the Air Force does not know enough about missiles." Addressing an Air Force commanders conference on 30 September 1957, White warned: "The senior Air Force officer's dedication to the airplane is deeply ingrained and rightly so, but we must never permit this to result in a battleship attitude. We cannot afford to ignore the basic precept that all truths change with time."[22]

White's sugar coating on the bitter pill was that airmen would soon have their own manned space vehicles for fighting wars in space.

To General White "almost everything in space" fitted into the Air Force mission. "We foresee," he said, "that we are not only going to have manned bombers and missiles, but that eventually we will have manned space vehicles as combat weapons in the future."[23]

Michael Terry sums up the position of the Air Force leadership on the "missile crisis" they faced in the last half of the 1950s:

Throughout the period from 1955 to 1959, Air Force leadership, although endorsing a struggling missile program, was not committed to supplementing or augmenting the bomber force with ballistic missiles if it meant deemphasizing the status of an aerial bombardment strategy, if it undermined the superior position of the manned bomber, or if it denigrated the priority in development of any "follow-on" manned bomber. In addition, a technological parallel to the manned bomber was envisioned by airmen to operate in space and keep the institutional tradition at the forefront of Air Force thinking.[24]

Then, in the wake of the Soviet missile and space developments, the Air Force lost control of the pace of transition to a concerned American public and its administration:

In 1959, Eisenhower established the nation's highest defense priorities: development of the ICBM and launching the Vanguard satellite to compete in the space race. LeMay's quite different priorities were acquisition of more B-52 bombers, development of the B-70, and development of the nuclear-powered bomber. ICBMs ranked at the bottom of LeMay's list.[25]

The difference in the reactions of the American military services to the accelerated development of ballistic missiles is revealing:

Morton Halperin has observed that "most senior naval officers have tended to view the Polaris missile-firing submarines as a service to the nation extraneous to the Navy's 'essential' tasks." It should be noted, however, that neither the

Army nor the Navy suffered the internal strains and bitterness that beset the Air Force during the development and introduction of ballistic missiles. The most immediate explanation is simply that the missiles did not threaten any established Army or Navy weapon. Without harming the central purposes of either service, ballistic missiles offered the opportunity of broadening their roles. The Army, indeed, from their earliest days showed continuing although sporadic interest in the weapons and bitterly resisted the transfer of operational responsibility of the Jupiter IRBM to the Air Force.[26]

The unique Air Force institutional problem with ballistic missiles was its threat to the manned bomber—not to the fighter or transport—since it offered an alternative to the one means of air power theory cherished by the airmen. The ballistic missiles did not threaten the theory itself or its ends. Indeed, ballistic missiles would become the supreme means for underwriting air power theory as it applied to the Soviet Union during the Cold War.

> Yet, were another service to gain responsibility for development and operations of ballistic missiles, the Air Force's purpose, and indeed its independence, would be threatened. Neither the Army nor Navy suffered from the institutional paranoia paralyzing Air Force thinking during the development and introduction of ballistic missiles....
>
> In underfunding development and imposing unrealistic performance requirements on ballistic missile technology, Air Force leaders secured the role of the manned strategic bomber. Maintaining a priority of a bomber tradition over strategic missile technology neither necessitated a rearrangement of the institutional environment nor a "restructuring of belief patterns."[27]

If fulfilling air power theory was what the Air Force was really about as an independent institution, the ballistic missile was a boon, not a bane.

> Ironically, the Air Force's parochial views of strategic bombing handicapped their ability to realize the traditional concept concerning the decisiveness of air power.... In the dawn of the atomic age, the ability to deliver tremendous firepower on target could have been accomplished by ballistic missiles more efficiently than by manned bombers; ballistic missiles could have been the symbol of the "decisiveness of air power," but the Air Force preferred to advocate their manned bomber over new strategic missile technology....
>
> For the Air Force, 1955 to 1959 was a formative period, integrating improved missile technology into its role and concept of air power. Their myopic view against ballistic technology in the early 1950s gave way to "benign neglect" as the leaders of the Air Force modified their perspective on aerial warfare to include ballistic missiles....[28]

That modification of perspective was to trade-in air power theory for deterrence theory; and the owners of deterrence theory would be civilian academics more than military airmen.[29] Thereafter, air power theory would be given little more than lip service as the guiding basis for the institutional Air Force. Henceforth, the Air Force would be guided by:

- accommodating new technical means for the missions it already "owned;"

- preserving its roles, missions, and budget slice against the predations of its sister services; and

- insuring that its own factions or fiefdoms had their futures secured with the prospect of "follow-on" vehicles, whatever they might be.

The fractionation of the Air Force followed more quickly than the vehicles it sought.

Notes

1. Builder, *The Masks of War*, 201.

2. There were those who immediately grasped the significance of the guided missiles, both cruise and ballistic, and became ardent advocates; but they could be dismissed as dreamers by those experienced aviator heroes who had won the war.

3. In the earliest days of the American space program, in the late 1950s, Dandridge Cole of Martin (Denver), advanced what he called *A Panama Theory of Space*, a statement of space theory not unlike that of Douhet's for command of the air. This was long before space was dubbed the "high ground" or the "high frontier."

4. Edmund Beard, *Developing the ICBM: A Study in Bureaucratic Politics* (New York: Columbia University Press, 1976), 5, 6.

5. Ibid., 12.

6. Ibid., 8, 9.

7. Ibid., 105.

8. Michael H. Armacost, *The Politics of Weapons Innovation: The Thor-Jupiter Controversy* (New York: Columbia University Press, 1969), 26, with the quotation referenced to Paul Jacobs, "Pilots, Missilemen, and Robots," *The Reporter*, SVIII, 6 February 1958, 15.

9. Ibid., 56.

10. Beard, *Developing the ICBM*, 224.

11. Record, *The Future of the Air Force*, 122, with a reference to Futrell, *Ideas, Concepts, and Doctrine*, 253.

12. Beard, *Developing the ICBM*, 229, 230, with the quotation from Robert L. Perry, "The Ballistic Missile Decisions," a paper prepared for fourth annual meeting of American Institute of Aeronautics and Astronautics, October 1967.

13. Ibid., 237, 238.

14. Major Michael R. Terry, "Formulation of Aerospace Doctrine, 1955–59," *Air Power History*, vol. 38, no. 1, (Spring 1991): 48, with the last quotation attributed to I. B. Holley, Jr., *Ideas and Weapons: Exploitation of the Aerial Weapon by the United States During World War I: A Study in the Relationships of Technological Advance, Military Doctrine, and the Development of Weapons* (Washington: Government Printing Office, 1983), 14.

15. Record, *The Future of the Air Force*, 122, with references to Beard, *Developing the ICBM*, 8 and 222.

16. Col. Clarence E. "Bud" Anderson with Joseph P. Hamelin, *To Fly and Fight: Memoirs of a Triple Ace* (New York: Bantam Books, 1991), 312, excerpt from the author's thesis for the U.S. Army War College, dated 8 March 1963.

17. Sherry, *The Rise of American Airpower*, 186, 187.

18. Arnold, *Global Mission*, 614, 615.

19. As reported by Beard in *Developing the ICBM*, 39, (emphasis in original).

20. Armacost, *The Politics of Weapons Innovation*, 155.

21. Puryear, *Stars in Flight*, 199–201.

22. Futrell, *Ideas, Concepts, Doctrine*, 514.

23. Ibid., 551.

24. Terry, "Formulation of Aerospace Doctrine," 52.

25. Kotz, *Wild Blue Yonder*, 42.

26. Beard, *Developing the ICBM*, 230, 231.

27. Terry, "Formulation of Aerospace Doctrine," 48.

28. Ibid., 49, 50.

29. My colleague, Ted Warner, correctly points out that a substantial number of Air Force officers were also committed contributors to deterrence theory, particularly those at the Strategic Air Command who were responsible for planning and targeting American strategic forces, both bombers and missiles. In that sense, deterrence theory was not the exclusive property of civilian academics. I accept his point, but argue that most of those Air Force officers were converting the theory into *operations* and *procedures*—figuring out how to *implement* the theory—not developing or debating it in the same sense as their predecessors had with air power theory at the Air Force Tactical School 30 years earlier. The academic think tanks had replaced the Tactical School as the principal site of theoretical ferment about bombardment means and ends.

16

Slow Fall from Grace

The pride of association is with a machine, even before the institution. One could speculate that, if the machines were, somehow, moved en masse to another institution, the loyalty would be to the airplanes....[1]

False Idols

As an institution the Air Force started to fractionate once it shifted its devotion from the unifying ends or mission of air power to its separate (and unequally statured) means. Missiles and space were not the only areas accepted as different means and careers in the Air Force. If they could coexist alongside the aviators, then so too could the long-suppressed fighter (pursuit) pilots. Tactical air power as another independent means and career grew rapidly under the limited war theories of the 1960s. The Vietnam war brought TAC into full bloom and put TAC pilots into the senior leadership of the Air Force for the first time. SAC found itself challenged not only from within the Air Force, but from outside in the Navy's strategic encroachments.

In their devotion to means rather than ends, and their devotion to the symbols rather than the theory of air power, the aviators allowed all to pursue their interests and specialties, provided that airplanes and aviators came first in priorities and promotions. The fighter aviators, who had long been suppressed by the bomber aviators under the tenets of air power theory, were suddenly released to pursue their own interests and, as aviators who were more removed from air power theory than their bomber brethren, eventually came to dominate the Air Force leadership. Not only was air power theory neglected, the people who were now running the Air Force had no roots in the theory. Indeed, the fighter pilots were knights of the air who were prepared to battle for control of the air, but who had lesser interests in either supporting the ground war or striking at the heart of the enemy.

The purpose of the Air Force increasingly became one of continuing to acquire the systems of each faction—a new bomber, a new fighter, a new transport, and a new missile. Each of these acquisition efforts became a battle of monumental consequences for each faction of the Air Force because that is what each faction came to be about.

During periods of expanding resources and opportunities, the deleterious effects of this fractionation or "stovepiping" on the Air Force tended to be suppressed from view. There was an anesthetic quality to the growing budgets since each faction could pursue its pet programs. But the losses became apparent as budgets eroded and cuts had to be made everywhere including in people and in things.

With the ascendancy of TAC over SAC to the leadership of the Air Force, the application of the theory of air power to war came increasingly from the Army and its "AirLand" battle doctrine. Air power theory had now devolved into deterrence theory, AirLand battle doctrine, and the dictum of air supremacy. The first had to be shared with the civilian strategists and the Navy, the second yielded the initiative to the Army, and the third was of interest only to the aviators.

The Rise of Occupationalism

Without the commitment to mission provided by air power theory, the commitment of the airmen increasingly reverted back to what it had been before air power theory—a love of flying and flying machines, a narcissistic indulgence that enjoyed little constituency in the public which would have to support an increasingly expensive hobby.

In part because of the apparent carryover of their skills to civilian work, airmen could more easily look upon wartime service as part of a career or profession rather than as a duty in which fighting itself was the essence. They differed sharply from other servicemen in their higher sense of satisfaction with the particular jobs and tasks they performed. To a considerable degree, their mentality was occupational rather than military. They saw themselves more as technicians and professionals than as warriors, and the techniques learned in war promised social and economic mastery in peacetime.

It also provided a sense of mastery over self and nature, especially for pilots. Flying allowed fulfillment of a "child's dreams of omnipotence in the face of his toddling weakness." These dreams "are usually abandoned with fairy tales and toys," commented air force psychiatrists; but "this supertoy, this powerful, snorting, impatient but submissive machine, enables the man to escape the usual limitations of time and space." Flying created "a feeling of aggressive potency bordering on the unchallenged strength of a superman." When the author of *God is My Co-Pilot* flew over Mount Everest, "he felt that he had humbled this highest mountain and patronizingly saluted his fallen opponent." The airplane offered "the perfect prescription for those that are weak, hesitant or frustrated on earth. Give them wings, 2000 horses compressed into a radial engine, and what can stop them?"[2]

The cultural separation of the Air Force from the other American military services widened:

Sanctioned by the air force, the contractual perception of the airman's duty strengthened the disjunction between means and ends characteristic of the air war. Duty involved the performance of technical tasks. The ethic was not a military one bound to the achievement of victory as it was for most other servicemen, but a professional one, related of course to war but both more finite than the war and transcending it because so many of the rewards were to carry over into the peace. Other men in combat performed tasks—bayoneting an enemy soldier, operating a machine gun—which had little or no counterpart in civilian life, whose only utility lay in war itself. They were simply warriors. To a considerable degree, airmen were technicians and professionals who happened to be waging war.

This model of service in air combat, recognizable as still another expression of air war's inseparableness from a civilian context, placed airmen in the vanguard of a historical transformation in definitions of military service. Traditionally defined, such service was different and apart from the broader society, undertaken by men with a higher sense of duty, whose loyalty lay with the organization, whose objective was to win wars, and whose rewards could not be justified by the civilian marketplace. They had not merely a job but a calling if professionals, an obligation if conscripted. The status, rewards, and duties of combat airmen moved them toward an entrepreneurial or occupational model of service. Self-interest was defined as distinct from the warwinning purpose of the organization; rewards were defined by and carried over into the civilian marketplace; the rituals of military life were subordinated to the attainment of skills and status useful in a larger world. And because the distinction from the civilian world was eroding, civilians performed many tasks once assumed only by military men, and the language and methods of the civilian, particularly of the corporate world, entered military institutions. As volunteers for combat duty (even when initially conscripted), airmen were in a strong position to contract for terms of service. The air force's rotation policy, by limiting risks and establishing rewards validated in the civilian marketplace, looked forward to a practice commonplace in the American armed forces by the 1960s.[3]

The bond was now the profession of flying rather than the profession of arms:

> The goals defined for airmen accorded well with those held by civilians and generals serving the wartime air force. For all, there was a definition of goals and rewards distinct from a traditional military ethic of winning wars. Victory could not be forgotten; it had attractions of its own, and it was a vehicle for meeting other goals. But mastery of technique—bureaucratic, intellectual, scientific, mechanical—promised rewards apart from and beyond the objective of winning the war. The inventors, organizers and handlers of the technique of air war found a satisfaction in war that infantrymen or their commanders could not achieve. Concern with mastering technique was often what the leaders of the air force meant when they referred to the operational necessities that supposedly dictated strategy and tactics....

> Because the criteria governing air war did not relate wholly to war itself, bombing had a momentum apart from the conflict. Because men did not have to view bombing solely as an act of war but could also see it as the perfection of technique, they did not always look at its consequences in war or measure its virtues in terms of its impact on war....[4]

Overkill

The quest for means rather than ends led to insatiable appetites for "follow-on" vehicles:

> Meanwhile, Congress and the Air Force pushed for more ICBMs and for more B-52 bombers. Eisenhower reluctantly agreed to a hundred more planes, but observed, "If six hundred won't do the job, certainly seven hundred won't." Pressed still again for more B-52s, Eisenhower retorted: "I don't know how many times you can kill a man, but about three should be enough."

> In the fall of 1959, the Pentagon for the third consecutive year requested $10 billion in new arms. Eisenhower examined U.S. retaliatory capacity of the bombers, submarines, and ICBMs in production and concluded that it was more than adequate. In denying the funds, he questioned again, "How many times do we have to destroy the Soviet Union?"[5]

The quest was nowhere more exaggerated and frustrating than in the Air Force's efforts to acquire a follow-on bomber for the B-52:

> In the spring of 1960, [Senator Lyndon] Johnson held hearings that highlighted support for the B-70 Valkyrie by Congress and the military. Disputing President Eisenhower, General Twining urged construction of the B-70 to maintain a flexible "mixed force" of bombers and missiles. "What bombers would the United States have in 1967, if the B-70 is not built?" Twining was asked. "None," he replied—even though the Air Force was then engaged in manufacturing a total of 660 B-52s in addition to 140 B-58 bombers.

Twining based his dire prediction on the assumption that the technological revolution in the weapons of the space age would soon make the B-52 obsolete. The military thought it would take an endless succession of new weapons to stay ahead of the Soviets. No one accurately predicted the success and incredible longevity of the B-52, still a potent weapon almost thirty years later.[6]

The insatiable appetites for new means would soon be curbed by new theorists who were explicit about the ends:

> Air Force officers could not match the whiz kids at using their analytic techniques. When Enthoven testified before Congress, he overwhelmed the generals with charts and graphs showing that "the B-70 would add minimal extra firepower at huge cost." Still, the military rejected the notion that a computer-generated "truth" provided better answers than the judgment and experience of men who had actually fought a war.
>
> "I am profoundly apprehensive of the pipe-smoking, tree-full-of-owls type of so-called professional defense intellectuals," said General Thomas D. White, who had just retired as Air Force chief of staff. "I don't believe a lot of these often overconfident, sometimes arrogant young professors, mathematicians, and other theorists have sufficient worldliness or motivation to stand up to the kind of enemy we face."
>
> General LeMay shared White's contempt for the whiz kids and for McNamara. He believed the civilians had usurped the proper role and expertise of the military. In LeMay's analogy, McNamara was a reckless amateur who ran the Defense Department like "a hospital administrator who tried to practice brain surgery." Exasperated by McNamara's iron grip on Air Force programs, LeMay would ask friends: "Would things be much worse if Khrushchev were secretary of defense?"[7]

But much of the Air Force's frustration stemmed from the fact that they no longer argued their cause in terms of a theory with ends but from their love of traditional means. They had no countertheory to combat their antagonists as they had in the 1930s and 1940s. The ownership of theory had shifted to the whiz kids who called it deterrence theory, not air power or even aerospace power theory.

Focusing on Means

The bureaucratic battles for the Air Force now became defensive actions about means: how to get the next manned bomber and how to keep the missiles from taking over.

> In the late 1950s, it was Curtis LeMay, promoted to Air Force vice chief of staff under General Thomas White, who led the Air Force's fight for the new B-70

bomber, even over the objections of President Eisenhower. It was LeMay who determined that missiles would not displace bombers, and thus reduce the Air Force to being "the silent silo-sitters of the sixties."

LeMay was one of the small group of generals who emerged from World War II as genuine fighting heroes. Unlike such legendary figures as Eisenhower and General George Marshall, whose fame came from their managerial ability and leadership finesse, LeMay earned his stars in battle. His experience as a battle-tested bomber pilot shaped his vision of warfare. His entire career was inseparable from the concept of strategic air power. LeMay was both its embodiment and its spokesman.[8]

The search for rationales to defend the need for new bombers took some turns that reflected desperation more than credibility, directions that remain evident even today:

Taking another tack, General Twining, a former Air Force chief of staff, argued that the Air Force needed the B-70 to penetrate the Soviet Union to search out and destroy mobile ICBMs on railroad tracks. "If they [the Air Force] think this, they are crazy," replied Eisenhower. "We are not going to be searching out mobile bases for ICBMs; we are going to be hitting the big industrial and control centers."

Finally, General White presented the Air Force's case for the B-70: The nation could not rely wholly on missiles, none of which had ever been fired in combat. Missiles could not be recalled, as airplanes could. Bombers could lift off and remain airborne while awaiting orders, thus giving the president a range of options in a crisis. Bombers would complicate the enemy's problem, forcing it to defend against several different kinds of attack. Finally, bombers as a demonstration of military might had a powerful psychological effect on friend and foe alike. The Air Force would repeat White's arguments, with embellishments but few variations, for decades to come.

Eisenhower respected General White, both for his leadership in World War II and for his wide-ranging intellect. But the president also knew that White was pressing him as the official representative of a large bureaucratic institution with its own interests at stake. And the president did not accept White's military rationale for the B-70. He told the Air Force chief of staff that the bomber role was served adequately by the B-52, and by the time the B-70 was ready its role would be filled by missiles....

At the moment that General White lamented the decline of the Air Force, the service possessed 1,895 bombers, including 243 brand-new B-52s with several hundred more scheduled to be built. The Air Force had control of all three land-based ICBM systems. It was hardly about to go out of business. Tommy White's protests represented the Air Force's fear that strategic air power, the core of Air Force purpose, would vanish in the coming missile age. To keep the bomber alive and competitive against the missile, the Air Force thought it needed a much faster, more capable plane than the B-52.[9]

As in Vietnam, the Air Force won some tactical battles in this defensive war with DoD and Congress for retention of a bomber force. In the late 1960s, after the B-70 had been cancelled, the Air Force made another run at a follow-on to the B-52 in the form of the Advanced Manned Strategic Aircraft (AMSA).

John Ryan was one of a long line of SAC generals[10] who rose to head the Air Force. He stressed to [Deputy Secretary of Defense] Packard the bomber's vital role in strategic defense. A "mixed force," which included bombers as well as missiles, would complicate Soviet defenses and increase American safety. With the still-remarkable B-52 fleet aging (some of the older models were fighting in Vietnam), Ryan insisted a new, more capable bomber was needed. Packard agreed.[11]

As this quest for a "follow-on" bomber dragged on, the symbology of the new bomber grew more portentous:

This ideal bomber [the B-1] would be a flying temple to enshrine the Air Force ethos: the dominance of strategic air power. Air Force leaders had been fighting to build such a bomber for more than a decade. Their B-1 would silence those who believed that the bomber was an anachronism in the age of missiles.[12]

More and more, treasure and careers rode on the outcome:

Despite two costly experiences, the Air Force leaders were undeterred. Strategic Air Command generals dominated the Air Force. Most were pilots by background, with little knowledge of aeronautical engineering; they were awed by technology, having experienced the magical feats that man and machine can accomplish together in the sky. SAC bomber pilots, taunted...by the non-SAC fighter pilots flaunting their flashy supersonic planes, wanted to reach higher and faster into the wild blue yonder. And the Air Force as a whole felt driven to demolish all the criticisms that bombers were outmoded in the age of cheaper, faster intercontinental missiles....

The B-1 bomber's demanding requirements had been basically established in a six-month 1963 study by Colonel David C. Jones and Lieutenant Colonel James Allen. Neither of these bright Pentagon aides had any experience designing airplanes. They didn't approach their assignment from a technical or engineering viewpoint. As pilots, they thought more about how they wanted the plane to fly than about what might be the best way to accomplish the bomber mission. They had a mandate from Curtis LeMay, then Air Force chief of staff, who carried on his crusade to get a "manned missile" that could silence bomber critics like Robert McNamara.[13]

In the end, SAC and the Air Force got its "follow-on" bomber in the form of the B-1B, an airplane which may or may not have been technically satisfactory, but one which was clearly a political disappointment for both the Air Force and the American public. A battle had been won, but there was no theory for what constituted victory in war.

The focus on means meant that the Air Force now needed a different kind of officer and leader:

> The generals who led the Air Force before the 1970s rose to top command through combat in World War II. The new men came to leadership when the Air Force was already an established, independent institution. They were molded by different experiences; to rise to the top in a huge defense complex, the new leaders needed management skills, and they needed political savvy to defend the Air Force's institutional interests. The modern Air Force had little call for crusty, undiplomatic leaders like Curtis LeMay.

> But like SAC pioneers LeMay and Thomas Power, [MG Kelly] Burke and [Lt Gen Thomas] Stafford both understood how closely the penetrating bomber was linked to the identity of the Air Force. Unlike their predecessors, however, they accepted the fact that the ICBM had forever changed the nature of warfare. If the bomber were to survive, its advocates would have to formulate new reasons for its existence.[14]

TAC Takes Over

The most consequential effect of the fractionation of the Air Force after the abandonment of air power theory was the rise of the fighter pilots who were so long suppressed under that theory. Prior to Vietnam, TAC had sought to escape SAC domination by emulating SAC's global mission on a regional or theater basis:

> Strategic bombing is not mere doctrine to the United States Air Force; it is its lifeblood and provides its entire raison d'être. Strategic bombing is as central to the identity of the Air Force as the New Testament is to the Catholic Church. Without the Gospels, there would be no pope; and without strategic bombing, there would be no Air Force. Like the Church, the Air Force has its fundamentalists—for whom salvation came on the silver wings of B-29s—and its reformers, who might not question the faith but look to expand it beyond the literal interpretation of its basic tenets. From the earliest days of airpower, the proponents of tactical aviation have had to work with and around this orthodoxy, and the limits it sets have been the single most important determinant of tactical doctrine and capabilities.

> [This orthodoxy was subverted by a] gradual shift away from the traditional concept of "tactical" aviation toward a new concept of "theater" airpower. One of the earliest manifestations of this shift was the redesignation of tactical aircraft from "pursuit" (passive, subordinate) to "fighter" and "attack" (positive,

aggressive, independent). Among airmen, "tactical aviation" carried the rhetorical stigma of air-ground operations and conjured up unpleasant memories of organizational subordination. In a more concrete sense, what was tactical was not strategic; thus, resources devoted to tactical aviation directly depleted those available for USAF's strategic (read: "independent") missions. "Theater airpower" gave [the Tactical Air Command] the rhetorical flexibility necessary to create for itself a more "strategic" mission. In so doing, it hoped to become on a regional or theater level what SAC was on the global level: no longer a residual appendage...but an integral part of the independent, war-winning USAF.[15]

The war in Vietnam provided TAC the opportunity to apply its regional or theater air power in "strategic" missions. Unfortunately, it was under circumstances where the assumptions underlying strategic bombing doctrine did not apply to the new realities of limited war in the third world:

[D]octrine can become irrelevant if the assumptions that support it are not frequently reexamined for their continuing validity. The development of U.S. air power doctrine provides a pertinent example. Based on the ideas of Gen. William "Billy" Mitchell and further developed at the Air Corps Tactical School by Mitchell's proteges, the Army Air Forces went into World War II with a doctrine based on the belief that strategic bombing would (and should) be decisive in war. The World War II experience and the availability of nuclear weapons and long range aircraft in the postwar era further ingrained this notion. Military budgets, force structures, equipment procurement, and training were all based on the central doctrinal belief in the deterrent and warfighting decisiveness of strategic bombardment. Even the tactical air forces became ministrategic forces in the late 1950s and early 1960s. The crisis came in 1965 when the United States entered the Vietnam War and the bombing of North Vietnam began. American air power doctrine was found to be bankrupt in Vietnam because its underlying assumptions were untrue in that situation. Strategic bombing doctrine assumed that all U.S. wars would be unlimited wars fought to destroy the enemy and that America's enemies would be modern, industrialized states. Both assumptions were crucial to strategic bombing doctrine. They were reasonable and valid assumptions in the 1920s and 1930s, but invalid in the 1960s in the age of limited warfare in the third world. The results were frustration, ineffective bombing, wasted blood and treasure, and eventually the renaming of Saigon to Ho Chi Minh City.[16]

The deterrence theory that had replaced air power theory as the guiding light for SAC did little to help the fading core of the institutional Air Force.

Since the beginning of the nuclear age, the SAC-dominated Air Force had single-mindedly promoted the strategic bomber for one exclusive purpose—to penetrate and attack the Soviet Union in a nuclear conflict. During the Korean and Vietnam wars, the Air Force resented using its prized strategic bombers in traditional, nonnuclear combat, and more demeaning yet, in tactical roles supporting ground troops.[17]

The stage was now set for an overturning of the Air Force which had steadily evolved over four decades following World War I:

- The stature of the bomber pilots and SAC as the owners and core of the Air Force would decline.

- The fighter pilots would now take over the institutional leadership.

- The most prized capabilities of senior officers would shift from institution building to program management, particularly for the aircraft acquisition programs.

- The devotion of airmen would turn from their missions of institutional independence and the demonstration of air power to their own careers and aircraft.

The *impetus* within the Air Force for these changes was not new. The fighter pilots had been struggling since the 1930s for a greater role in the Air Force leadership. What had changed, however, was that such interests and incentives were *now no longer subordinated to a higher purpose*—the ends of air power theory.

Notes

1. Builder, *The Masks of War*, 23.

2. Sherry, *The Rise of American Airpower*, 215. The last quote is referenced to Roy R. Grinker and John P. Spiegel, *Men Under Stress* (Blakiston, Toronto, 1945), reprinted as *War Neuroses*, ed. Richard H. Kohn (Salem, NH: Ayer Co Pubs, 1979).

3. Ibid., 217.

4. Ibid., 218.

5. Kotz, *Wild Blue Yonder*, 33.

6. Ibid., 62.

7. Ibid., 70, 71.

8. Ibid., 38.

9. Ibid., 34, 35.

10. Jack Ryan was originally a World War II fighter pilot. In the post-World War II Air Force, spending time in the Strategic Air Command was an essential experience if one aspired to the highest leadership positions. Thus, for the first 40 years of USAF independence, all Air Force chiefs could be considered "SAC generals."

11. Kotz, *Wild Blue Yonder*, 92.

12. Ibid., 107, 108.

13. Ibid., 111. Colonel Jones went on to become Air Force chief of staff and then chairman of the Joint Chiefs of Staff. Colonel Allen went on to become commander in chief of the Military Airlift Command.

14. Ibid., 184.

15. Caroline F. Ziemke, *In the Shadow of the Giant: USAF Tactical Air Command in the Era of Strategic Bombing*, Ph.D. Thesis (Columbus: Ohio State University, 1989), 20, 21.

16. Col. Dennis M. Drew and Dr. Donald M. Snow, *Making Strategy: An Introduction to National Security Processes and Problems* (Air University Press, Maxwell AFB, 1988), 167. Col. John Frisby (in a letter to the author dated 11 March 1992), notes that Drew and Snow may overstate the connection between strategic bombing theory and results of the air war in Vietnam. He says, "[A]irpower was grossly misused during Vietnam (both tactical and strategic).... I believe that it's still a debatable point to argue the possibilities of what might have occurred had Airpower been employed against the north—as it finally was—earlier in the war.... Also, the Vietnam War can be used to illustrate that military force alone cannot, by itself, resolve that kind of conflict."

17. Kotz, *Wild Blue Yonder*, 189.

PART V

FAILURE ANALYSIS

17

Picking Up the Pieces

*Accident: Anything that happens without foresight
or expectation; an unusual event, which proceeds
from some unknown cause, or is an unusual effect
of a known cause....*[1]

The Search for Cause

When a plane crashes, investigators look for evidence of cause. I use the singular, cause, because that is the ultimate object of their search. Many factors may have contributed to the crash and will be examined for saliency, but they will look for that single human act—of omission or commission, in design, construction, maintenance, or operation—without which the crash would not have occurred. Sometimes, several potential causes will arise and the investigators must consider different theories for their relative roles in the crash.

In our increasingly litigious society, crash investigations these days may appear to the public as mostly a search for liability—a means for determining who shall pay the claims. But the history and purposes of crash investigations are longer and broader than this more recent civil phenomenon. Investigations are aimed most fundamentally towards a search for safety, for correctives—for ways to prevent a similar crash from occurring again.

> The fundamental purpose of investigating accidents under these Regulations shall be to determine the circumstances and causes of the accident with a view to the preservation of life and the avoidance of accidents in the future; *it is not the purpose to apportion blame or liability.*[2]

Is there something that needs to be changed to prevent a similar crash? Often, there is. We learn that an airplane should not be flown under certain weather conditions, that maintenance procedures should be changed, or that a certain part needs to be redesigned against failure.

Pilots frequently complain that too many crash investigations end up with the finger pointed at them. They think "pilot error" is too often an easy cause for crash investigators to hang on the hapless (and often deceased) pilot when the evidence for other potential causes is not readily apparent. They would urge the investigators to look harder and to consider more possibilities. Indeed, that is the dominant theme in the 1964 film, *Fate is the Hunter*.[3] The problem has also been explicitly addressed in the law

> to give some protection to airmen and their families against the...all too frequent findings of "pilot error" as the cause of an accident [which has] been abused in recent years...in the civil proceedings which follow aircraft accidents [by] persons who may tend to forget that it is not the purpose of accident investigation to apportion blame or liability.[4]

On the other hand, pilots bear such broad authority, responsibility, and risk for their aircraft and its safe flight that we should see it as remarkable that so many causes for crashes can be found elsewhere.

Crash investigations are also frequently—and perhaps negatively— labeled as demonstrations of the "20-20 vision of hindsight." Indeed, that is precisely what crash investigators seek—what could have been done by those who designed, constructed, maintained, and operated the airplane which might, given what has been learned from the crash, have prevented the crash from occurring. If crashes due to similar causes are to be prevented in the future, then 20-20 hindsight is to be prized, not denigrated. If something was done six minutes or six years before the crash that should have been done differently, we need to know it and learn from it. The discovery of that something can be disparaged as "finger-pointing with 20-20 hindsight," but knowledge, not blame, is the goal.

When crash investigators sift through the debris at a crash site, every broken piece and part, of course, is not immediately taken as a cause of the crash, but as a potential clue to *the* cause. The obvious point is that wreckage is not a cause, but a result of some failure. A broken wing at the crash site could have been broken upon impact with the ground, by collision with another object, by violent motion through or by the air, by structural failure of another part, or any number of other proximate causes. And each of these potential causes for the broken wing could be the consequence of an earlier or prior event. The investigators keep looking backward in time from the crash, through a chain of evidence and events, to that one act or event that can be properly blamed as the cause of the crash.

That single act or event may be surrounded by all sorts of contributing circumstances—such as bad weather or a radio malfunction—each of which by itself might not have caused the crash, but which compounded to narrow the margin of safety for dealing with some subsequent failure that resulted in the crash. It is the act or event, without which the crash would not have occurred, that is the object of the crash investigation. This distinction between the cause and other adverse circumstances attendant to a crash is illustrated by the crash of a United Airlines flight in 1969.

Cause and Circumstance

On January 18, 1969, United Airlines flight 226, using a Boeing 727, departed at 6:07 pm from Los Angeles enroute to Denver. Shortly after takeoff, the flight reported they "had a fire warning on number one engine [which] we shut down [and] we'd like to come back." Thereafter, there were no further communications and the aircraft was observed to lose altitude in the departure area over the Pacific. The plane crashed into the sea about 11 miles off the coast with the loss of all 32 passengers and six crew members on board. The wreckage of the aircraft was found on the sea bottom at a depth of about 1,000 feet and was partially recovered. Both the flight data recorder and the cockpit voice recorder were recovered with readable tapes. The report of the crash investigation was published 14 months later.[5] This is what the investigation revealed.

Each of the three engines of the Boeing 727 airplane has an electrical generator to supply the aircraft electrical power. Only one of those generators is sufficient to supply all of the normal electrical needs for safe operation of the aircraft in flight. Because of this redundancy—more than was available from contemporary two-engine aircraft—it was an acceptably safe practice to operate 727 aircraft temporarily with one generator out until it could be repaired during routine maintenance. If a second generator went out, the aircraft would have to be grounded for repairs even though one generator could provide adequate power through all phases of flight. Flight 226 was operating that night, as it had for the past

28 flights (41 flight hours), with the number three generator (on the right engine) out; and the crew was aware of that condition.

Standard procedures for operation with two (instead of three) generators required that the galley (kitchen) power be turned off and that no more than one of the two air conditioners be on during takeoff, approach, and landing. This ensured that the electrical power required during low-speed flight would not exceed the allowable loads for the two remaining generators. If, in flight, a second generator were to fail, then the galley power and *both* air conditioners would have to be turned off to ensure the availability of sufficient electrical power during low-speed flight.[6] It was assumed that the crew was operating according to the standard procedures for two-generator operation.

During the climb after takeoff, a fire warning came on for the number one engine, and it was shut down. Under normal conditions, the one remaining generator on the number two engine should have been sufficient for all flight operations, assuming that the procedure for one-generator operation was properly implemented. The cockpit voice recorder indicates that the crew was concerned about reducing the electrical load on the remaining generator; but about 45 seconds after the fire warning on the number one engine, the number two generator popped its circuit breaker.

Flight 226 had lost all generator power, even though two of its engines continued to provide adequate thrust for flight and hydraulic power for control. Backup battery power was available within the aircraft to power and illuminate the flight instruments and essential radios in just such an emergency; but it may have been inadvertently turned off in the hurried efforts to ensure that the power on the last generator was reduced. The battery switch was located right next to the galley power switch and while verifying that the galley power was off, the crew could have accidentally turned off the battery power. In any event, the flight recorders indicate that backup battery power was not provided for the cockpit instruments and lights. With no flight instruments and perhaps preoccupied with their futile efforts to restore electrical power from the number two generator or from the battery, the crew lost control of the aircraft and it crashed into the sea.

It is apparent that many circumstances were involved in the cause of this crash; but what was *the* cause? Was there a single act or event that ultimately doomed this flight? Or were there many independent causes, each of which, by itself, could have caused the crash? Flying the 727 with one generator out was considered safe practice, yet it narrowed the safety margin. So did darkness and poor weather which imposed instrument flying for attitude control of the aircraft during its departure. Although the crew may not have correctly implemented the routine procedures for two-generator operation or the emergency procedures for one-generator operation, such failures would not have doomed the aircraft. Losing a second generator was not a catastrophic failure, because there was still a third adequate for normal flight loads. Even the loss of the third generator, brought about by the two immediately prior failures, would not have been catastrophic, for there was battery power available to power and illuminate the instruments for safe, controlled flight.

Ultimately, one comes to the crew who either failed or were unable to control the flight of the airplane under circumstances which were specifically anticipated in the design of the airplane and its emergency procedures. If they had been able to provide battery power to their instruments and ensure control of the aircraft in flight, the crash could reasonably have been avoided. They may have been prevented from both of those things by their efforts to restore the power from the number two generator.[7] Indeed, in those efforts, they may have accidentally turned off the battery power. Their priorities should have been first to control the flight. To ensure that control, they needed battery power for their basic flight instruments. Restoring generator electrical power should have come third. Without those cockpit priorities in place, flight 226 was doomed with the loss of the last generator, but not because of it. There was a single cause of this crash, but there were many adverse circumstances that led up to it and increased its odds.

As a result of this accident, several corrective actions were undertaken by the Federal Aviation Administration. One was to provide for *automatic* switching to battery power for essential flight instruments. Another was to relocate and redesign switches so that the battery power could not be inadvertently turned off.

The Icarus Incident

To suggest that what has happened to the Air Force was an institutional crash is stretching the metaphor too far; however, the questions raised in the investigation of a crash are good ones to ask about the causes of institutional problems. And the search for a single cause that can account for all of the evidence is a way of getting at the roots rather than the manifestations of the problems.

What should the institutional "incident" investigators conclude about the Air Force? What would their incident report say? What was the single human act—of commission or omission—that "doomed" the institution to these problems? What were the adverse circumstances that attended the incident, but were not the ultimate cause? Here is what I think an incident investigation report should say at the end when it must summarize the cause:

The Air Force was adequately established and endowed as an independent institution by the visionaries that successfully sought to create it.[8] Those visionaries advocated air power as a better way to forge and use military power. After three decades of subordination to Army views of air power, those visionaries were convinced, as they had been almost from the beginning, that to be most effective air power had to be wielded *independently.* Toward the end of their long and uncertain struggle for independence, independence became almost an end in itself. As with many who find themselves in the urgency and passion of battle, means can become ends. Nevertheless, they were able to achieve that goal; and the institution they created was viable by any reasonable standards. The Air Force had a vision—a unique sense of identity and a shared sense of purpose—and broad support for that vision, inside and outside of the institution. The only significant skeptics were the new institution's older siblings—the Army and Navy—who had been roughly handled by the visionaries as they wrestled the Air Force free.

But even as the Air Force found its independence, two trends were developing which would prove to be adverse only in their combination:

1. Alternative means to the airplane—in the form of ballistic and cruise missiles—to fulfill the ends of air power had emerged from World War II in the form of Hitler's vengeance weapons, the V-1 and V-2.

2. The pilots and operators, who had forged and wielded air power during World War II, by their sheer numbers, were ascending into the leadership of the Air Force, replacing the visionaries who had created the institution on the theory and claims of air power.

It was the simultaneity of these two trends that presented adverse circumstances that attended the cause of the crash. If the visionaries had remained the leaders of the Air Force, their attitudes toward the alternative new means found in missiles would have been quite different from those of the pilots and operators who followed them. Once they had gained their intermediate goal of institutional independence, the visionaries could again embrace the ends of the air power theory. Missiles would have been an acceptable, even attractive alternative means to the ends of that theory as they saw it.

However, the pilots and operators entering the Air Force leadership were attached to air power theory more for (what they thought were) its only means, the airplane, than for its ends. The missiles were seen mostly as a threat to the airplane and, hence, to the institution.[9] While the Army and Navy were actively exploring the potentials of the V-1 and V-2 as prototypes for future missiles, the Air Force was just as actively ignoring them. Air power theory devolved to massive retaliation on a scale that would make the destruction of World War II modest.

Through the first decade of the new, independent Air Force, these two trends continued without any sign of impending danger. As pressures for missile and space developments increased during the 1950s, the Air Force kept itself in a competitive position with its sibling services, but not with the enthusiasm it had for new generations of supersonic fighters and bombers. The Air Force did not intend to be second to anyone in anything that might fly, and the airplane was clearly the most important thing that flew. Under deterrence theory (now eclipsing air power theory as the guiding compass of the thermonuclear age), the airplane still appeared to offer, by far, the most "bang for the buck."

The triggering event was the Soviet development of ballistic missiles, dramatically demonstrated by the launching of the first space satellite. The Air Force hand was forced; and the Soviets had done it. The future would, after all, include missiles and space systems; and the Air Force had to be the leader in these fields or relinquish to others a virulent competition with the airplane. Still, that imposed choice did not foreordain the crash which was to follow almost 30 years later.

It wasn't the fact of accepting missiles and space systems into the Air Force that caused the problem. It was that air power theory had already been transformed—its means into an institutional affection for airplanes and its ends into assured destruction. The missiles and space systems were accepted into the Air Force as additional *objects* for someone's affection (certainly not the pilots), not under any theory of *how* to project military power, but under deterrence theory, mostly about how much destruction was enough.

Once unified under a theory of air power, the Air Force had, in the space of little more than a decade, become a collection of object- and process-oriented factions under the management of the airplane pilots and operators. The time for fateful action—of commission or omission—had arrived. The fateful act was one of omission, sometime between the late 1950s and the early 1960s. The Air Force leadership had the opportunity then, at the very latest, to stop the fractionation of the Air Force by recasting its theory about air power into something much more comprehensive about both the means and ends of air and space (or aerospace) power. Indeed, there were some efforts to do just that; but they were little more than word changes because there was no concomitant change in the demonstrable preference of Air Force leadership for airplanes. The words weren't enough; and too many could see who ran the Air Force and what their interests and affections were really about. Discussion of air power theory was all but lost in the factional struggles over the primacy of strategic or tactical air power.

Who was in charge at this critical time in the late 1950s and early 1960s? The Air Force Chief of Staff (1957–1961) was General Thomas D. White. He was the one who had asked the President for the B-70, based if not on its military value, then at least on its importance to the institution.[10] And White's Vice Chief and successor (1961–1965) was Curtis LeMay. It was LeMay who expressed his determination to prevent the Air Force from becoming "the silent silo sitters of the sixties."[11] It was the operators, not the visionaries, who would now lead the Air Force through the heavy weather of a changing world.

Under the many challenges of their rapidly changing environment, the Air Force leadership may have become more focused on the preservation of flying and fliers than on the mission of the institution. As in the darkened cockpit of United flight 226, the Air Force leadership appears to have been preoccupied by a threat to means and, in their preoccupation, lost sight of the ends of the institution they were piloting.

Notes

1. *The Oxford English Dictionary* (Oxford: Clarendon Press, 1961).

2. Civil Aviation (Investigation of Air Accidents) regulations, 1989, United Kingdom, regulation 4, (emphasis added here).

3. The film was based more on the title than the content of Ernest K. Gann's original collection of aviation stories, *Fate is the Hunter* (New York: Simon and Schuster, 1961). However, the same point is made in one of those stories, "A Certain Embarrassment," (327–347) where Gann concludes:

> In both incidents the official verdict was "Pilot error," but…it seemed that fate was the hunter. As it had been and would be.

4. C. N. Shawcross and K. M. Beaumont, *Air Law*, (Sevenoaks, Kent: Butterworth, Borough Green, 1983), vi-46, fn. 1.

5. *National Transportation Safety Board Aircraft Accident Report: United Air Lines, Inc., Boeing 727–22C, N7434U, Near Los Angeles, California, January 18, 1969*, Report Number NTSB-AAR-70–6, SA-413, File No. 1–0004, Adopted: March 18, 1970.

6.The author is indebted to Sidney T. Kleiger, Captain, Delta Air Lines, for significantly clarifying several of the details of the Boeing 727 electrical system, particularly the relationships between the wing flaps and the air conditioners. The largest non-essential demands for electrical power came from the galley and the cooling fans for the two air conditioning "packs" or units. Like the thermostatically-controlled, electrically-driven radiator fans on many modern automobiles, the cooling fans kept the air conditioners from overheating whenever the forward speed of the aircraft was insufficient to provide adequate cooling air. This system was designed to operate automatically whenever the wing flaps were extended—i.e., at low speeds. Hence, the requirement to turn off one (or both) of the air conditioners during takeoff, approach, and landing to prevent the automatic air conditioner cooling fans from overloading the electrical system when one (or two) generators were out.

7. There is evidence from the flight recorders that the crew continued to work on restoring the generator electrical power and, too late, realized that the aircraft was out of control.

8. Aircraft accident report conclusions or summaries usually begin with some perfunctory statement about whether the aircraft or crew were properly licensed and documented.

9. Col. John Frisby, (in a letter to the author dated 11 March 1992), argues "that the pilots and operators, who grew up in the era when the visionaries were fighting for the very existence of the Air Force, were not likely to become visionaries themselves. Once independence [for the Air Force] had been attained, it became the supreme end to be defended at all costs.

10. See Chapter 13 for the context of this plea.

11. See Chapter 16 for the context of this vow.

18

Crash Analysis

*In ancient days two aviators procured to themselves
wings. Dædalus flew safely through the middle air
and was duly honoured on his landing. Icarus
soared upwards to the sun till the wax melted which
bound his wings and his flight ended in fiasco.... The
classical authorities tell us, of course, that he was
only 'doing a stunt'; but I prefer to think of him as
the man who brought to light a serious construction
defect in the flying machines of his day.*

*So, too, in science, Cautious Dædalus will apply his
theories where he feels confident they will safely go;
but by his excess of caution their hidden
weaknessess remain undiscovered. Icarus will
strain his theories to the breaking-point till the
weak joints gape. For the mere adventure? Perhaps
partly, that is human nature. But if he is destined
not yet to reach the sun and solve finally the riddle
of its construction, we may at least hope to learn
from his journey some hints to build a better
machine.[1]*

The thesis of this analysis is that many of the unique institutional
problems which now plague the Air Force have their roots in the Air
Force's abandonment of air power theory as its source of institutional
mission and vision. Major elements of the Army Air Forces had steadily
drifted away from air power theory during World War II as the actual
demands for military aviation expanded their missions well beyond those
originally conceived within air power theory. Although the bomber
commands continued to see air power mostly in terms of the theory—
striking decisively at the heart of the enemy—the fighter and air transport
commands found themselves deeply involved in supporting the needs of

Army ground forces—the very thing which the original air power theorists had seen as the squandering of air power when it was controlled by ground commanders.

General George Kenney's centralized control and use of air power in the Southwestern Pacific is regarded by many as *the* example of the tactical use of air power in effective support of MacArthur's theater campaign objectives. But he was guided by the military situation which confronted him, not by air power theory of the time. He did not have the means for striking decisively at the heart of the enemy and thus could only reach the outposts of the Japanese perimeter.

> In Europe, the mission of strategic bombers was to destroy Germany's war economy. In the Southwest Pacific there were no typical strategic targets other than a few oil refineries. Thus, in the Pacific the air mission was to interdict Japan's sea supply lines and enable the ground forces to conduct an island-hopping strategy.[2]

More pertinently, Kenney's application of air power would not require an institutionally independent air force.

The bomber faction dominated the Army Air Forces at the end of World War II, as they had prior to the war. It was the keeper of the faith in air power theory; it now possessed the instruments that had (in its eyes) been decisive in strikes at the heart of the enemy; and it would use the theory as a basis for postwar institutional independence. The other commands and interests in the Army Air Forces, as supportive adjuncts, could ride on the coattails of the bomber faction in its leadership of a new and independent Air Force.

The Strategic Air Command became the centerpiece of the Air Force and the ultimate embodiment of air power theory during the first decade of the new institution. If air power theory was not central to many who served in the Air Force, it was to those who were at the core of Air Force leadership. If the fighter and transport commands were not the mainstream of the Air Force, they at least supported a mainstream with a mission based upon a theory of air power.

In the previous chapter, I described two trends—the emergence of alternative technical means to the airplane and a new kind of leader in the Air Force—that coupled together to create adverse circumstances for the institutional development of the Air Force. It was under these adverse circumstances that two *events* then conspired—one technological and the other ideological—to cause the Air Force to neglect, if not abandon, air power theory during the late 1950s and early 1960s:

1. Alternatives to the airplane suddenly became competitive for the *ends* of air power (i.e., striking decisively at the heart of the enemy through the third dimension).

2. New national security theories—deterrence and assured destruction— emerged to dominate the design of strategic nuclear forces aimed at the heart of the enemy.

The Air Force response to these developments was accommodation rather than adaptation; the Air Force accommodated the new means and theories within the institution instead of adapting air power theory to encompass them. Air power theory became subordinate to deterrence theory instead of the other way around. The retention of airplanes and the dominance of pilots became the institutional imperatives and, thus, the seeds of institutional fractionation were sown.

Although several correctives have been proposed to reunify or reinvigorate the Air Force, the one advanced here focuses on air power theory as the heart of the institution—not air power as originally conceived more than 70 years ago, but air power theory as it should have been *reconceived* 30 years ago. What should have been done 30 years ago and what should still be done now is to redefine air power. Air power theory was the intellectual vehicle for creating the Air Force as an institution; it can be the vehicle for recreating it now.

The institutional problems now troubling the Air Force will not be resolved until it once again orients itself to a mission worthy of devotion by an independent military institution—not to *its* ends (more, better, higher, faster, farther), but to the ends of those it serves (cheaper, quicker, easier, safer). Redefining air power won't ensure the institutional health of the Air Force; but its health can't be recovered without it. Thus, fixing air power theory is a necessary, but not a sufficient, prerequisite to fixing the Air Force. The question now is how to redefine air power theory to meet the needs of the Air Force as an institution and the nation's security for the future.

Theory, Mission, Vision, and Strategy

To trace the role of air power theory in the evolution of the Air Force, we need to define and distinguish four related, but different conceptual terms—not to be pedantic, but to recognize them as different ideas with different uses. The definitions will be consistent with those that can be found in the dictionary; but their distinctions rather than their similarities will be emphasized to separate their meanings and uses.

1. A **theory** is a supposition or conjecture about the relationships between things. Theories explain *why*. Air power theory, when it was advanced as theory, supposed that air power could be applied decisively in war if applied to the heart of the enemy. The theory further supposed that such application would require control of the air and that such control would require independent control of air power. Until those suppositions were proven, air power was a theory.

2. A **mission** is a task or function that is assigned or adopted. Missions declare purpose. As originally conceived in air power theory, the mission of air power was to strike at the heart of the enemy. The theory said that such strikes could be decisive and, thereby, obviate the bloody stalemate of trench warfare. But the mission was to strike at the heart of the enemy. It was the theory that said, to make such strikes, it would be necessary, first, to seize command of the air and to provide for independent control of air power.

3. A **vision** is an imagined objective, a conception of what can and ought to be. Visions provide a coherent basis for future decisions. The early air power theorists envisioned large fleets of airplanes, like battleships of the sky, commanded by aviators, capable of controlling the air and striking swiftly and decisively at the heart of the enemy, breaking its will and destroying its physical means for fighting. An institutional vision is a conception of what the organization can and ought to be and be about.

4. A **strategy** is a concept for relating means and ends. Strategies show us how to connect means to ends. As originally conceived in air power theory, the ends were winning wars quickly, without great losses of life, like those sustained in the bloody stalemate of World War I. The means were airplanes. The strategy was to employ airplanes in independently controlled strikes against the heart of the enemy after seizing command of the air.

Of these four concepts, theory would seem to be the most fundamental; it supposes how things will or should work—if this, then that—and why we should care. Given a theory of how things might work, it is a much shorter intellectual step to suggest tasks that should be taken up (a mission), to conceive what can and ought to be (a vision), and to plan the relationships among means and ends (a strategy).

Yet these four concepts are markedly different intellectual tools: Theory is an explanation. Mission is a purpose. Vision is a dream. Strategy is a scheme. Air power has been all these things, separately and together, throughout the history of the idea. It will be useful to keep these four concepts distinguished from one another as we try to analyze what has happened to the idea of air power and what must be done if it is to be redefined and renewed.

Air power started out as a theory, an explanation of how to avoid repeating the nightmare of World War I. It turned into a mission when the clouds of World War II gathered and the theory was converted into the reality of air power. It became a vision for an independent institution even as the mission was undertaken. And, it became a strategy for coping with the stalemate of the Cold War.

As originally conceived, air power was a theory composed of the following three axioms:

1. Air power can be employed decisively in war by striking at the heart of the enemy.

2. To use air power decisively, command of the air (i.e., air supremacy or superiority) is a prerequisite.

3. To gain command of the air and to use air power decisively in war, air power must be centrally and independently controlled.

Only the first of these axioms was really disputed at the time the theory was first advanced; if one accepted it, the others followed. All this was unproven theory when the ideas were first developed and articulated during the two decades between the world wars.

When the theory had gained enough acceptance to be put into practice, air power theory turned into a mission to forge and employ the air forces that could seize command of the air and be wielded decisively as an independent instrument in war. Whether or not the theory was proven during the course of World War II—an argument that can easily be instigated and sustained even today—the arguments about its validity became academic to the American public with the advent of the atomic bomb.

If the atomic bomb made many traditional concepts of war seem archaic, it made strategic bombardment appear both farsighted and final. The Army Air Forces aviators—dominated by the bomber pilots—could declare the mission a success, the theory validated, and then turn the same ideas into a vision of an independent institution. The vision was nothing less than the ultimate expression of the third axiom of air power theory— the vesting of air power in an independent military service. The vision took credibility from the first two axioms—decisiveness in war (now validated beyond argument by the possession of atomic bombs) and command of the air which had been proven feasible in the contested skies over Germany and Japan. And the vision finally became a reality in the newly created Air Force.

The vision was that an intrepid band of aviators would control the decisive weapons of war—the airplane and the atomic bomb—in a force that would eclipse all other military forces in importance, size, funding, and esteem. As a vision, it contained the two essential ingredients—a unique sense of identity and a shared sense of purpose. The unique identity was vested in what had always been something of an exclusive club—the intrepid band of aviators, particularly military aviators. The shared sense of purpose was to wield the most powerful military instruments ever fashioned.

With the vision a reality, air power theory became the basis for the dominant strategy in the Cold War. The means were long-range bombers coupled with atomic bombs. The end was first coercion and then deterrence by the threat of massive retaliation and, later, assured destruction. The relationship between the means and end was the Single Integrated Operations Plan (SIOP), owned by the Air Force's bomber faction, the Strategic Air Command.

What had begun as air power theory had evolved by stages—through mission and vision—to air power strategy in the nuclear age. It was at this point that the original air power theory reached its ultimate expression, became frozen, and spawned a new and ultimately challenging theory to the Air Force. Deterrence theory, unlike air power theory, was a logistical theory of destruction rather than a theory of new means for waging warfare. Deterrence theory was indifferent to the means for transporting weapons except for the costs to provide delivered weapons. Deterrence theory was the domain of scientists and analysts, not aviators or pilots. The door had been opened to competitive means to the airplane for the delivery of nuclear weapons. Pandora's Box had been opened while the Air Force leadership had been preoccupied with acquiring its next generation of bombers.

The differences between theory, mission, vision, and strategy tell the story of the ascendency of air power: As a theory, air power was an idea and argument about what could and ought to be. As a mission, air power theory was a military trust to be fulfilled. As a vision, air power was an attainable dream of institutional independence, providing the unique sense of identity and the shared sense of purpose which have become associated with high-performing organizations. As a strategy, air power theory provided both the means and the end to the nuclear stalemate set up at the beginning of the Cold War. And with neglect of all four facets of air power—the theory, mission, vision, and strategy—the Air Force fragmented as an institution. To reunify and reinvigorate the institution, all four will need to be redefined.

What Broke and When?

If one could go back in time through the history of air power—as it evolved through theory, mission, vision, and strategy—what could now be viewed as broken, using 20-20 hindsight? The thesis presented here is that the Air Force neglected air power to its institutional detriment sometime in the late 1950s or early 1960s, when air power was being exploited mostly as a strategy. But were there flaws in the concept of air power earlier, when it was being exploited as a theory, mission, and vision? If there were—and I think there were—then they ought to be addressed in any redefinition of air power, even if those flaws were not central to its neglect and the consequences that followed. The search for prior flaws, even though the principal failure has been identified, is comparable to the philosophy of crash analyses.

Examinations for potential flaws in the concept of air power can be simply made at the intersections of its four historic uses—theory, mission, vision, and strategy—and its three axioms:

1. Air power can be employed decisively in war by striking at the heart of the enemy.

2. To use air power decisively, command of the air (i.e., air supremacy or superiority) is a prerequisite.

3. To gain command of the air and to use air power decisively in war, air power must be centrally and independently controlled.

Air Power as a Theory

As a *theory*, with 20-20 hindsight, it would seem that only the first of these three axioms was flawed. The claim of decisiveness should have been conditioned to certain kinds of war. The human disaster of World War I dominated perceptions of war at the time air power theory was first conceived. Indeed, air power theory took hold not just because of the advent of the airplane, but because it seemed to offer a way to avoid repeating the bloody disaster of stalemated trench warfare. It is understandable that the air power theorists were thinking about World War I when they said that air power could be employed decisively in war.

But that claim was flawed in two respects. First, it didn't contemplate different kinds of warfare such as we have seen increasingly in the last half of the 20th century—irregular wars that are not dependent on highly organized industry and transportation for the provision of their means—where there is no heart of the enemy which can be struck decisively. Could the theorists have foreseen such wars and the limitations of air power? DeSeversky did:

> Total war from the air against an undeveloped country or region is well-nigh futile; it is one of the curious features of the most modern weapon that it is especially effective against the most modern types of civilization.[3]

Second, the unconditional claim to decisiveness in war was correctly perceived as a direct assault upon the relevance of other kinds of military forces, particularly the surface forces of the Army and Navy. In their efforts to argue the importance of air power, the theorists went so far as to challenge the need for armies and navies. They could have been far less threatening if the first axiom had been qualified along the following lines:

1. Air power can be employed decisively in war *when the enemy's essential means for waging war are vulnerable to attack from the air.*

That phrasing leaves room for doubt about the decisiveness of air power depending upon the nature of the enemy's means for war and their vulnerability to attack from the air. Since, at the time air power theory first emerged, most perceived of war in terms of World War I, the essential means were seen as a nation's industry and transport. That would have focused the debate precisely where it should have been—on the vulnerability of war industry and transport to air attack rather than the relevance of armies and navies.

In their eagerness to make their case, the air power theorists probably overstated their claim to the decisiveness of air power; to have been equivocal on that point might have implied uncertainty about their cause. Qualifying the claim could have cost them some of the supporters they needed in advancing the cause of military aviation; but over the long run, they paid a price by sowing the seeds of the perennial debates between the American military services

The other two axioms seem appropriate to the theory. Under circumstances where air power can be decisive, that achievement will be predicated upon achieving command of the air; and both decisive use and command of the air will depend upon central and independent control of air power.[4]

Air Power as a Mission

When air power theory was converted into a *mission* and used as the basis for forging and employing air power, it is the second axiom, in retrospect, that seems flawed. Those who forged and initially employed air power in the late 1930s and early 1940s thought command of the air could be achieved by self-defended bombers. These would be the battleships of the sky. But others, like Claire Lee Chennault, foresaw a battle for command of the air, in which it would be necessary both to defend against the enemy's bomber attacks and to defeat the enemy's defenses against one's own bomber attacks.

In the scramble for limited resources in the 1930s, the bomber and fighter factions found themselves pitted against each other. The advocates of pursuit and interceptor airplanes for command of the air lost out to the advocates for seizing the offensive through daylight, precision bombardment from self-defended bomber formations. With 20-20 hindsight, the second axiom might have allowed for:

- the need to defend one's own essential means for war against attack from the air (as proven in 1940 over Britain and in 1943 over Germany); and

- the possibility of a separate battle for command of the air prior to the decisive or most effective use of air power against the enemy's essential means for waging war (as in 1944 over Germany and in 1945 over Japan).

These considerations could have been accommodated if the second axiom had been rephrased along the following lines:

(2. To use air power decisively or most effectively, command of the air (i.e., air supremacy or superiority) over all vital regions in the war, one's own and the enemy's, is a prerequisite.

To be sure, rephrasing the axiom—this way or any other way—would not have vouchsafed the forging of pursuit and interceptor aircraft capabilities as equal partners to the bombers. The bombers could even be rationalized as *defensive* weapons if necessary.[5] Bombers and the offensive were the intellectual embodiment of air power theory from the beginning. It would have taken more than word smithing of the axioms to have changed that predilection.

Air Power as Vision

When air power theory evolved into a *vision* for wresting the Air Force free as an independent institution, it was nearly perfect in its original form for the purpose. The atomic bomb made the claim of decisiveness plausible to all but the most skeptical (e.g., the Navy), but such skepticism was rooted more in the ends than the means. Command of the air could take strength once again in the offensive since the destructiveness of a single bomber penetrating to its target was evidently enormous. And if the first two axioms had been made obvious by the atomic bomb, then the third axiom—the real end of air-power-as-vision—was handed a walkthrough.

Thus, up through the birth of the Air Force as an independent institution in the aftermath of World War II and the atomic bomb, the concept of air power—conceived as a theory, applied as a mission, and exploited as a vision—served reasonably well. I can offer only slight adjustments on two of the axioms that might have improved them with the aid of hindsight. It was when air power theory was converted to a *strategy* for the Air Force as an independent institution, particularly for its dominant command, SAC, that serious flaws emerged at the hands of technology and ideology.

A Flawed Strategy

Recall that the vision of air power was the Air Force as an intrepid band of aviators controlling the decisive weapons of war—the atomic bomb and the big bombers needed to deliver them—in a force eclipsing all other military forces in importance, size, funding, and esteem. When the Air Force gained its freedom, the *only* means for delivering the few available atomic bombs were Air Force airplanes, although the Army and Navy were certainly scrambling to break that monopoly. The Army was exploring alternative means to the airplane for delivering atomic bombs, including ballistic missiles and guns. The Navy was working hard to acquire the means for atomic delivery from the sea—first with carrier-based aircraft and, as a longer shot, ballistic missiles. But until these alternatives proved to be competitive or even feasible, which took decades, the Air Force enjoyed a monopoly on the decisive weapons of war—the long-range bomber and the atomic bomb.

The monopoly was broken only ten years after the Air Force won its independence, not by the Air Force's sister services, but by the Soviet Union through its accelerated development of ballistic missiles. Alternative means to the bomber and airplanes, in general, for the delivery of atomic bombs could no longer be dismissed by the Air Force as theoretical possibilities in the future; the nation's mortal enemy had boasted perfection and possession of these new means for delivery.

If the advent of the nuclear-tipped ballistic missile shattered the Air Force strategy derived from air power theory, it was little noted at the time. The nation was preoccupied with a stunning challenge to its technical superiority; and the Air Force was confronted with more immediate challenges from its sister services which were arguing for their participation in atomic delivery by ballistic missiles. The result was an Air Force momentarily more concerned about its institutional dominance of ballistic missile development—to protect its missions domains and its attachment to airplanes—than it was about attending its air power theory. Bureaucratic imperatives took priority over theoretical foundations. *Like in so many accidents, the pilots had been distracted by an emergency from paying attention to their basic flight controls.*

Because of the highly competitive environment created by the Soviet *démarche*, the Air Force aggressively pursued programs to develop ballistic missile and space systems; but these new means for exploiting the third dimension of warfare were included as *adjuncts* rather than *alternatives* to the airplane. Just as the Navy, 30 years earlier, had accepted the aircraft carrier as an adjunct rather than an alternative or even a challenge to the big-gun battleship, the Air Force leadership would not admit to the possibility of missiles replacing aircraft. Ballistic missiles and spacecraft were seen a means for increasing the effectiveness and competitiveness of airplanes, not as their replacements. Unlike the battleship admirals, the Air Force aviators were never confronted with a wartime trauma, like Pearl Harbor, to clear their minds and overturn their dispositions. Consequently, the Air Force leadership accepted the missileers and "space cadets" into the institution as latter-day adjuncts to air power, as they had mechanics, navigators, and technologists before them. The missileers and space technicians could find a welcome home in the Air Force; but it would be in an institution run by aviators, particularly bomber pilots.

The strategy was flawed, not so much by what it drew from air power theory, but by its narrow focus on means (which were predominantly manned airplanes) and by its expanded interpretation of ends to include all uses of military airplanes. The Air Force and its air power strategy had been captured by its original means.

What could, and what should, the Air Force have done at that juncture to adjust its strategy, with 20-20 hindsight?

It should have seen that the air power theory which had brought them so far in 40 years was about unique ends and means, not about *all* uses of military aviation or airplanes. Air power theory proposed the unique end of striking at the heart of an enemy—at the sources of the enemy's means for waging war, before they could be used in combat. Air power theory proposed the unique means of carrying out such strikes *through the third dimension*, instead of engaging and defeating the enemy's surface forces.

In its zeal to promote military aviation, the Air Force implicitly broadened the end and narrowed the means of air power theory. The end, instead of striking at the heart of the enemy, became striking at the enemy anywhere, *including enemy forces which had been brought to bear in surface combat*. And the means, instead of strikes through the third dimension, had been narrowed primarily to the piloted airplane. Dirigibles and robot airplanes had been rejected early. Cruise and ballistic missiles and space systems had been accepted, but not with alacrity or with equality to manned aircraft. Missiles and space systems had been forced on the Air Force if it was to defend against encroachments from its sister services on its missions and budget slice.

Therefore the question is, in adapting air power theory to a strategy for the newly independent Air Force, should the end have been broadened; should the means have been narrowed? I think both changes undermined the theory as a strategy and then as a vision for the institution. The broadening of the end threatened the uniqueness of the Air Force's identity and the narrowing of the means threatened the shared purpose within the Air Force as an institution.

1. If the end of air power is striking at the enemy anywhere, not just at the enemy's heart, then the Air Force is not unique as an institution wielding air power: The Navy, Marines, and Army (to a lesser degree) also possess air power (and other means) to strike at the enemy's engaged surface combat forces and to defend their own surface forces against enemy air attacks.

2. If the means of air power are primarily manned airplanes, not missiles or spacecraft, then missileers and space technicians are not part of the mainstream of the Air Force and do not share in its institutional purpose. They would be better served in their own independent institutions or by being adjuncts to the other services.

The logical inconsistencies are (and have been) evident in a series of interservice and intraservice battles between the:

- Army and the Air Force over the close air support mission;

- bomber and fighter aviation communities over leadership of the Air Force;

- Army and Navy over ballistic missile developments,

- transport and combat aviation communities over their relative status within the Air Force;

- Air Force and the Navy over the targeting and control of strategic nuclear forces; and

- pilots and everyone else in the Air Force over their relative status.

All of these battles have their roots in the differences between air power theory, as originally conceived, and the Air Force strategy as it was implemented during the first decade of its independence as a military institution.

Notes

1. Sir Arthur Eddington, *Stars and Atoms* (New York: Oxford University Press, 1927), 41, as quoted in the frontispiece of *ICARUS, International Journal of Solar System Studies.*

2. Herman S. Wolk, "George C. Kenney: The Great Innovator," in *Makers of the United States Air Force*, ed. John L. Frisbee (Washington, D.C.: Office of Air Force History, 1987), 139, 140.

3. Alexander P. DeSeversky, *Victory through Air Power* (New York: Simon & Shuster, 1942), 102.

4. Col. John Frisby (in a letter to the author dated 11 March 1992) cautions that just "as the claim of decisiveness should be conditional to certain kinds of war, so should 'independent control' be conditional to certain missions." I would agree, but such conditions are specified in the third axiom of the theory: "*To gain command of the air and to use air power decisively in war*, air power must be centrally and independently controlled." Missions other than gaining command of the air or the decisive use of air power might not require central and independent control.

5. See Chapter 8, in the section entitled, "Camouflaging the Bombers."

PART VI

THE WEATHER AHEAD

19

Making Painful Choices

*In "American Icarus," Henry Murray outlines a
syndrome involving ascensionism (the wish to
overcome gravity, to rise, to fly, to be a spectacular
success) and an underlying fear of falling (of being
injured, of failing, of losing one's self-confidence).
The Icarus complex, Murray says, reveals itself in
fantasies of flying, floating, rising and falling, either
directly or through metaphors of success and
failure.[1]*

*Icarians seem to wish to remain children....
Basically, Icarians fear that they are in danger of
being destroyed.[2]*

Means and Ends Dilemmas

If air power is to be constructively redefined—as a theory and
strategy—to guide the Air Force toward its mission and vision as an
institution, some of the stark choices concern the means and ends of air
power:

1. Should the *ends* of air power be narrow or broad? Should they be striking
   at the heart of the enemy, or all military uses of air power, or something
   in between?

2. Should the *means* of air power be narrow or broad? Should they be
   primarily manned aircraft, or all means of striking through the third
   dimension, or something in between?

The extremes in these choices all imply costs to, or logical inconsistencies with, today's Air Force.

Nothing will more quickly go to the vital interests of the Air Force or influence its future than the choices about what is included or excluded from the Air Force's definition of air power. Exclusions risk divestiture of Air Force power, present or potential. Inclusions risk diffusion or dilution of the mission or vision and, hence, their utility in unifying the institution.

If the ends of air power are defined narrowly to striking at the heart of the enemy, then much of the Air Force investment in air transport and close air support simply doesn't fit. The Air Force should give the close air support mission back to the Army, as some have suggested; and the Army should also be allowed to get back into the air transport business, at least for its own airlift needs. For both missions, the Army has persistently worried that its needs would come second to the Air Force's consistent interests in strategic bombardment and air superiority.

If the ends of air power are defined broadly to include all military uses of air power, then the Air Force should logically have control of all Army, Navy, and Marine aviation which is presently focused on supporting their respective surface forces. Why should the Air Force provide close air support for the Army, but not the Navy or Marines? Why should the Army be permitted to use helicopters to support its ground forces, but not fixed-wing aviation?

If the means of air power are defined narrowly, primarily to manned aircraft, then much of the Air Force investment in missiles and space systems doesn't fit. Why shouldn't the missileers and space technicians argue, as the military aviators did before them, that these means should be independently controlled for their most effective development and employment?

If the means of air power are defined broadly to include all means for striking through the third dimension, then the leadership of the Air Force should logically include as equal partners those who have devoted much of their professional careers to the development and operation of missiles and space systems.

There is some cross-coupling between these choices: If both the ends and means are broadly construed, then the Air Force should also control tactical ballistic missiles as well as attack helicopters, for it makes no logical sense to control only the fixed-wing portion of the means for striking at enemy combat forces. If tactical missiles are seen as extensions of artillery, then how does one define the limits of artillery? What separates artillery from ICBMs or even bombers? If the Air Force is involved only with the fixed-wing means for engaging surface combat forces, then the basis for that division of labor is historical or institutional, certainly not logical or theoretical.

If the ends are narrowly construed, but the means broadly contstrued, then the Air Force should also control the sea-based forces designed to strike at the heart of the enemy through the third dimension. These would include the SLBM force at a minimum, since its only purpose is to strike at the heart of the enemy through the third dimension. The sea-based cruise missiles and carrier-based attack aircraft are problematical since they can be rationalized for striking naval targets in support of naval operations.[3]

It isn't obvious whether there is any satisfactory ground in theory or in logic for the Air Force to constitute itself as it has since gaining institutional independence. It has accumulated ends beyond air power theory from its World War II experiences as the Army Air Forces. It has accumulated means beyond those originally conceived by the military aviators because of technological developments and competitions with its sister services over roles, missions, and budgets.

Today's Air Force appears to interpret the ends of air power broadly, but is equivocal about the means. It shows a strong predilection toward manned aircraft and treats other means (missiles and space) as if they were somehow adjuncts to manned aircraft. While fiercely competing with its sister services over the possession of all its means, it doesn't even attempt to enforce all of its broad claims to ends.

The amalgamation which constitutes the current Air Force lacks that unique sense of identity and shared sense of purpose which are needed to make it a high-performing system.[4] The Air Force finds itself oriented on a diversity of means and ends by history rather than logic; it is the manager of the nation's military air transport and space assets by historical events rather than by design. The pragmatic questions now are these:

- Can an effective vision—a unique sense of identity and shared sense of purpose—be developed in the current amalgam of the Air Force?

- If the Air Force must change or be changed to arrive at an effective vision, which changes would be least costly to the institution?

Obviously, an affirmative answer to the first question has eluded many for some time, leading others to suggest that some surgery—in the divestiture of means or ends—may be necessary to bring coherence and integrity back to the Air Force as an organization. I am not convinced that such surgery is necessary; but the alternatives need to be explored, even if only to look into the abyss before redoubling efforts to find an effective vision within the current amalgam.

Is Triage Required?

If the Air Force had to relinquish one or more of its present missions or capabilities, what would they be and in what order of their priority? To ask that question of the Air Force would be much like asking a mother which of her children should be thrown to the wolves. Others, outside the institution are better able to suggest the answers—and have done so. Here are two missions that have been suggested for divestiture, along with their accompanying reasons:

1. **Close air support.** The Air Force has seldom embraced the mission with great enthusiasm; and the Army has usually been uneasy about the dependability and availability of close air support when needed. The mission is logically inconsistent with the Navy and the Marines since they both provide their own air support for their surface forces. The army should be permitted to provide its own air support, without the artificial restriction to rotary wing aircraft. In giving up that mission, the Air Force would not be denied an opportunity to contribute *additional* support to engaged Army forces, anymore that it is presently denied from providing additional support to Navy or Marine forces, provided the air commander has suitable forces that can be so assigned.

2. **Airlift for surface forces.** Although the Air Force has a need for airlift to support its own combat forces, it is less obvious that it needs to provide general airlift for all other surface forces. The Army has often expressed concern that its needs for intratheater airlift may have been sacrificed for the Air Force's interest in long-range transport aircraft. Splitting up airlift among the services would seem, at first, to invite inefficiencies in scale and duplication of capabilities; but the diversification of airlift might introduce some healthy competition and greater flexibility. Other capabilities, such as tactical air power and aerial refueling, have been split among the services with evidence of cross-service benefits in developments and employments.

These kinds of arguments are most often offered by civilian analysts, critics, or "reformers" of the American military. The military, however, has not been eager to reopen the debates over roles and missions between the services. The services would rather work these issues at the margin than risk the intervention of congress or the administration in what could be tantamount to a throw of the dice.

Obviously, there are *sotto voce* Air Force rebuttals to these arguments. If the close air support mission was given back to the Army, the following negative consequences can be foreseen:

- The Air Force would lose to the Army an important justification for some of its airplanes, particularly the dual-role tactical aircraft that can be used as fighters and attack aircraft.

- The Army would have its nose under the tent flap for an expansion of its fixed wing aviation into other roles such as air defense over the battlefield, at the expense of the Air Force claim on the nation's military aircraft assets.

- If the close air support role were returned to the Army, it might open up larger questions, such as the Army's control over its own airlift needs.

On the other hand, some in the Air Force would also quietly concede several positive consequences:

- The Air Force would be released from a role that has become vexing because:

    —of the subordination of air operations to the coordination and control by ground commanders;

    —of the susceptibility to fratricide of and by both ground and air force elements;

    —the aircraft requirements tend to be technically regressive (low, slow, and simple) and limiting in "mission"[5] flexibility (i.e., single role); and

    —the Army is steadily encroaching upon the role with its own helicopter and missile forces.

- The Air Force would have finally squared the circle on air power by freeing itself from the last vestige of control by surface warfare commanders and their concepts of war—one of the most basic principles or canons of the original air power theorists—leaving the Army, Navy, and Marines to shape aviation to their particular surface warfare ends while the Air Force pursued the *independent* ends of air power.

The same kinds of arguments and counterarguments can be developed around proposals for the Air Force divestiture of the part of the airlift mission[6] devoted to the lift of surface (army) forces, although they are not heard as frequently as those for the close air support mission.

The divestiture of means rather than missions isn't any easier. If the Air Force had to relinquish one or more of its present means or systems, what would they be and in what order of their priority? Again, here are some that have been suggested, along with their reasons:

1. **Space systems.** These have become national assets used to support all of the services. Surveillance, communications, and navigation support from space are essential now for all military operations. Although each of the services has special needs or priorities, these are converging rather than diverging over time. The increasing emphasis on joint service operations demands common frameworks and formats for communications, navigation, and surveillance information. Unless or until military *forces* are deployed into space—which seems unlikely in the near future—space systems should be treated as a shared infrastructure for all of the military services.

2. **Ground-launched missiles, both ballistic and cruise.** These Air Force weapons were all designed and deployed as alternative means for the delivery of nuclear weapons. With the virtual evaporation of the nuclear threat so long posed by the Soviet Union, these missiles now face declining prospects. Their original development was predicated upon a major nuclear war; and not only is the prospect for such a war declining, so is their prelaunch survivability in such a war. While these weapons have provided an important diversity in America's nuclear arsenal, that diversity was prized as a deterrent against a massive nuclear surprise attack, which is no longer an overriding national concern.

It could be argued that sacrificing one or all of the above two ends and two means would not take the heart out of the Air Force. It could also be argued that their divestiture by the Air Force would bring about a new coherence and focus which is now missing from the institution. Of the interservice and intraservice battles listed earlier, the following would be quieted between:

- the Army and the Air Force over the close air support mission;

- the Air Force and both the Army and Navy over ballistic missile developments;

- transport and combat aviation communities over their relative status within the Air Force; and

- the Air Force and the Navy over the targeting and control of strategic nuclear forces.[7]

The only battles that would be left from the earlier list would be those between:

- bomber and fighter aviation communities over leadership of the Air Force; and

- pilots and everyone else in the Air Force over their relative status.

But those two battles are precisely the ones that have persisted in the Air Force since the beginnings of air power theory; they are the ones that the Air Force has historically dealt with, although obviously not to the satisfaction even of its pilots.

Thus, a few hard choices of divestiture—choices that are admittedly too hard for the Air Force to make for itself, but which do not go to the heart of the institution—are beguiling to those who see the current contradictions in the Air Force. Sharing two missions with the Army and cutting the unmanned missile and space systems free could make for an entirely new landscape for the Air Force to consider what it means by air power.

However, participating in—let alone initiating—any part of this kind of radical surgery for the sake of coherence in the theory or vision of air power is simply unrealistic. Such amputations would ignore the circumstances of history and bureaucratics which have brought about the present predicament. The solution to the dilemma must not only make logical sense but must also be practically feasible. If a redefinition of air power as a theory, mission, vision, or strategy can only be found in divestiture of current Air Force missions and systems, the odds are against its being accepted, no matter how easily it might be found or argued.

Who Shall Be the Leaders?

However the mission and, hence, the vision of the Air Force may be defined or declared, they will only be words until they are turned into deeds by leaders. Leaders, by their deeds, may make a mockery of the words. It is the deeds, not the words, that ultimately define vision. When the record of the deeds is limited or mixed, it is natural for those who have a stake in the institution and its vision to look to the leadership for clues to the their future. If the leadership is perceived to represent special interests within the institution, then those interests, even more than the institution's mission or vision statements, will be seen by many as shaping the future.

The question and implications of leadership interests in the Air Force can be usefully examined in the light of contrasts with the Navy. The Navy leadership faction, like that of the Air Force, has changed during the past 50 years. The Navy, like the Air Force, is composed of many factions and interests, sometimes competing and jostling each other to be heard or to get their way within the institution. Unlike the Air Force, however, the Navy has had a clearly defined and declared mission throughout the past 50 (even 100) years, whereas the Air Force seems to have lost touch with its mission during the last 30 years.

The wrestling over the leadership of the Navy by the carrier aviators, the submariners, and the surface warfare specialists is appropriate: It is about where the future of the Navy lies and, therefore, whose perspective should *most* influence the future evolution of the Navy. The resolution of that leadership will not mean that the other dimensions of naval power disappear. Indeed, the Navy leadership—whatever its special interests— will be responsible, as it has in the past, for integrating all elements of the Navy, from carrier aviation to mine warfare, into concepts of naval power and its mission.

Similarly, the rivalry between bomber and fighter pilots for leadership of the Air Force (in the name of strategic and tactical air power) would be appropriate if it focused on where the future of the Air Force lies and on whose perspective should most influence its future evolution. But if the rivalry for leadership is restricted, by other institutional factors, to pilots or to combat pilots, then there is a danger that the future of the institution has been cast too narrowly. It would be the same as limiting the leadership rivalry in the Navy to the battleship and carrier admirals. That rivalry was pertinent to an earlier period of Navy evolution; but the future must now admit to other possibilities, such as the submarine, "surface-effects" ships, or the "stealth" cruiser as the cutting edge of the future Navy.

If the leadership rivalry of the Air Force has become limited to pilots, for whatever reason, then the Air Force may have tied its fate to one means and not the ends of air power. If the leadership rivalry has been limited to pilots mostly in the belief that the prerogatives or preeminence of pilots must be preserved within the institution, then even greater mischief may result, for such self-serving elitism sows the seeds of discontent among those whose contributions to mission have been denigrated and who have been excluded from any hope of leadership.

A symptom of the problem and a contrast between the Navy and the Air Force are illustrated by the assignments of mission commanders in the two services' surveillance aircraft. An Air Force officer who had served as the radar officer on the E-3 AWACS observed that the pilot was the mission commander; while on the Navy's E-2 Hawkeye the radar officer was the mission commander. He asked me whether I thought flying or surveillance was the principal mission of these aircraft.[8]

In a videotape describing the Air Force's organizational restructuring, General Merrill McPeak, Chief of Staff, concluded his briefing with the parting phrase, "See you on the flight line." A serving Air Force officer (and pilot) observed that probably only one in four or five Air Force people would see the flight line as a routine part of their working environment. Although the phrase probably should not be given any more significance than the exhortation to "have a good day," it could be an unfortunate one for those—perhaps a majority—who are already concerned about their status in an institution dominated by flyers and their airplanes. For an analog, one would have to imagine Admiral Kelso, the Chief of Naval Operations and a submariner by his origins, closing his remarks to all Navy personnel with the phrase, "See you in the control room on our next dive." The effect would be a chilling message to most in the Navy.

The Navy mine warfare specialist who is near the bottom of the Navy's exquisite hierarchy, sees his contribution in terms of naval power, not in terms of serving the carrier elites. Moreover, the mine warfare specialist is not excluded from leadership of the Navy *because* he has chosen the wrong specialty, but because of how his specialty is widely perceived throughout the institution to relate to naval power. If the perception of the importance of mine warfare to naval power changes, so do his chances of participating in Navy leadership.

If the leadership rivalry of the Air Force has been largely resolved in favor of fighter pilots over bomber pilots, then the future of the Air Force and its mission had better lie in the future of fighter aviation. If transport or tanker pilots really could not have aspired to the leadership of the institution, then the discrimination is even more than one of favoring pilots; it is in favor of certain kinds of pilots. If those who are not pilots or who are not associated with airplanes (e.g., missiles and space systems and operations) can never hope to assume the most senior leadership positions in the Air Force, then those who have been excluded must assume that one or more of the following apply:

- The leadership of the Air Force is reserved for certain kinds of pilots, regardless of the mission of the Air Force.

- The mission of the Air Force does not significantly depend on means other than fighters or, perhaps, bombers; and that is not likely to change in the future.

- The selection of the leadership of the Air Force has nothing to do with its mission or the future evolution of that mission.

None of these possibilities is attractive. One can only hope that none is accurate, although the past is far from reassuring.

However the mission of the Air Force may be defined, if the leadership of the Air Force is now in the hands of the fighter pilots then one would hope that the following are true:

- Fighter aircraft are presently the most important means for that mission to be fulfilled.

- At the beginning of the Cold War, bomber aircraft were the most important means for that same mission.

- If other means, such as space or missile systems, become the most important means for that same mission in the future, the leadership of the Air Force will shift accordingly.

The claims of the fighter or tactical pilots to the leadership of the Air Force would seem to be fairly grounded in the nation's wars since World War II. The contributions of air power to Operation Desert Storm, the Vietnam war, and the Korean War were dominated by tactical air power. Whether the contributions of air power in World War II were dominated by bomber aviation can be disputed,[9] but the dominance of the bomber at the end of that war and the beginning of the Cold War provided the basis for the bomber pilots' claim to the leadership of the newly independent Air Force.

That said, regarding the basis for claims in the past, what about the future? The claim of the carrier aviators to the leadership of the Navy was clearly laid down in World War II. Whether carrier aviation should have remained the future of the Navy—after nuclear submarines made their debut—can and has been disputed. Certainly, the submariner's claim to victory in the Pacific theater of World War II was as substantial, if not as evident or dramatic, as that of the carrier aviators. The role of carrier aviation in the application of naval power since World War II has been dominant; but it is not clear whether that dominance was natural or imposed by its proponents. One could speculate that if the Cold War had turned hot—if Soviet forces had engaged our Navy—the nuclear submarine might have proven itself over carrier aviation, just as carrier aviation proved itself over the battleship 50 years ago.

Thus, there is the risk that the dominant faction in the last war may persist in leadership positions, not as representing the true future of the institution, but by the inertia of the power acquired. The question for the Air Force today is whether fighter or tactical aviation is the center of gravity for the Air Force of the future. The inertia of power within the Air Force, gained from three conventional wars over the past 40 years, clearly favors tactical aviation as the dominant means for the application of combat air power. But there are trends, even within the past 40 years, which suggest that even that could change through:

- the rising importance of space systems and operations, not only for support air and land operations, but also for offensive and defensive tasks;

- the wider adoption of missiles by other nations as their primary means of attacking their adversaries;[10]

- developments in air defense technologies which make manned aircraft less attractive than robotic flight vehicles for most applications of force;[11] and

- the increasing demands for rapidly projecting infrastructures rather than force to assist allies and friends in a shrinking world of growing aspirations, expectations, and conflicts.

Thus, it is not inconceivable that the dominant contributions of air power by America over the next several decades could come from airlift, missiles, or space systems. Would the leadership of the Air Force change in ways that would reflect the dominant means of air power? If not, would the source of Air Force leadership remain fixed because of simple inertia or because the Air Force belongs to the combat pilots? If it is the former, then the institution is only vulnerable to being upset by unexpected events—as the Navy was by Pearl Harbor. But if it is the latter, then the institution will reap the whirlwind, for its real mission is not service to the nation, but to service one of its factions.

The Roots of Theory

Ultimately, the Air Force mission and vision must stand on a theory of air power—an explanation of how air power works and why it is important to those who must support it. The original theory of air power was about more than airplanes and air forces; it was every bit as much about the way the world and war were widely expected to work in the future. Embedded in the original air power theory were vivid images of a war just past, the prospects for another in the future, and of the rapidly developing transportation technologies. The theory explained how the aviation technologies might be exploited to avoid replaying the past war in the future. The theory was motivated and rationalized on a perspective of the future.

If air power theory is to be redefined, it must also be motivated and rationalized from some perspective of the future. That is why the next two chapters are devoted to a view of the future—a view of (1) how the world is coming to work and (2) the future nature of conflicts. Although the next two chapters stray far from air power theory, they are not a diversion; they provide an explicit example of the kind of conceptual foundations necessary for air power to be constructively redefined. To give this view of the future both force and integrity, I have had to draw upon what I see ahead, not what others may see or hope to see. Whether my view of the future is correct or incorrect will be less pertinent than demonstrating how important such perspectives of the future can be in reformulating air power theory. My view of the future is clearly evident as I try, in the last three chapters, to formulate statements of mission and vision for the Air Force and then a theory of air power for the future.

If the foundations of air power theory for the future are to be found in our perspectives of the future, then the pertinent perspectives are those of buyers and sellers of air power theory. It is not enough that Air Force leaders have a perspective of the future which suits them; if the theory—and all that flows from such a theory—is to be sold, their perspective must be shared by the buyers—those in the American public who must support (and pay for) implementing it.[12]

Notes

1. Robert May, "Fantasy Differences in Men and Women," *Psychology Today*, vol. 1, no. 11, (1968): 42–45, 69. May refers to Henry A. Murray, "American Icarus," chapter 28 in *Clinical Studies of Personality*, vol. II of *Case Histories in Clinical and Abnormal Psychology*, edited by Arthur Burton and Robert E. Harris (New York: Harper & Brothers, 1955), 615–641.

2. Daniel M. Olgivie, "The Icarus Complex," *Psychology Today*, vol. 2, no. 7, (December 1968): 30–34, 67.

3. The Navy has vacillated in its rationalization of carrier aviation. During the 1960s, when deterrence theory dominated the design of strategic forces and the Soviet's navy was not a sufficient threat to justify the carrier force, the Navy argued that the principal mission for carrier aviation was to project power over the land from the sea, including strategic (nuclear) strikes at the heart of the enemy. As the Soviets built up their "blue water" navy in the 1970s and 1980s, the principal rationale for carrier aviation returned to support of naval operations—protecting the fleet and striking naval targets.

4. The term, "high-performing system," and its association with distinct senses of identity and purpose are derived from the work of Peter B. Vaill, as reported in "The Purposing of High-Performing Systems," *Organizational Dynamics* (Autumn 1982): 23–39.

5. The term, "mission," here means the *role* of an aircraft, in contrast with the *purpose* of air power, as defined earlier in Chapter 18.

6. Again, the term, "mission," here means the *role* of military aviation, not the *purpose* of air power.

7. This interservice battle may be quieted, not by Air Force divestiture of means, but by the declining interests of both services in strategic missiles associated with the end of the Cold War and by the creation of a new joint command United States Strategy Command, (USSTRATCOM).

8. Equally revealing, this Air Force radar officer also asked me not to use his name when I suggested crediting him with the observation; such credit would not, he thought, be helpful to him in his Air Force career.

9. Tactical aviation played a dominant role in the application of air power in the Southwestern Pacific under General Kenney and in Europe, after the Normandy invasion. Strategic bombardment dominated the European theater before the invasion and the Pacific theater in the final attacks on Japan.

10. Missiles may become increasingly attractive to countries which are less endowed with the wealth and infrastructures required to maintain air forces. Missiles may also, in the wake of Operation Desert Storm, be perceived as less vulnerable to counterattacks than other forms of military force.

11. This could come about through a variety of developments in the continuous contest between offense and defense over command of the air. The proliferation of "smart" surface-based air defenses, like the proliferation of small arms in some urban areas, could make an increasingly hostile environment for intrusion by "outsiders." The loss of pilots, particularly if they are captured and turned into hostages, may be increasingly unattractive to political leaderships, even if the risks are acceptable to the military professionals. Manned aircraft could also become cornered for combat operations if the evasion of increasingly agile defenses requires intruders to bear acceleration forces (i.e., g-loads) that go well beyond human endurance. None of these possibilities is certain; and the contest for command of the air could also tip in the favor of the offense—and the manned aircraft. But the situation is in flux, and the possibility of change needs to be considered since the consequences could be profound for the Air Force.

12. The importance of buyer's and seller's perspectives in the market for national security services is developed further in Carl H. Builder, *Military Planning Today: Calculus or Charade?* RAND MR-293-AF, (Santa Monica, Calif: RAND, 1993), 21–23.

20

A Changing World

*Vision is in vogue…. [T]here is increased
recognition that some sort of guiding image of the
future is necessary…to steer…through the uncharted
contours of this new era….[1]*

*The world now taking shape is not only new but
new in entirely new ways. Something is happening
to the nation-state itself. Governments everywhere,
irrespective of ideology, appear inadequate to the
new challenges….[2]*

Getting the Future Right

The original air power theory evolved as it did and was widely accepted
by the Anglo-American publics because of a vivid perception of how the
world worked and what the future might hold. World War I had painfully
shown that:

- the nation states and their interests could clash on a global scale;

- nations could organize and bring to bear enormous industrial resources
  in their conflicts;

- science and technology were providing new and wondrous means for
  transport and destruction in warfare; and

- if allowed to stalemate, these conflicts could wipe out a generation of
  young men, terrorize the population, and devastate a nation's economy.

This perception of the world and the potential future provided a fertile bed
for the advocates of air power. If nations were, inevitably, going to clash

and unleash their full resources in "total" war, then air power, one of the premier products of science and technology, could provide the means to a quicker, more decisive end (victory) in war. Air power was the key to unlock the deadly dilemma of the future.

Not everything about that perception of the future was correct. Nations would clash again on a global scale and engage in total war; science and technology did continue to expand the means of transport and destruction, although not just through air power. But the nightmare of stalemates gave way to the fright of "blitzkrieg," lightning warfare, where mobility on land, sea, and air sometimes produced decisive campaigns in weeks or months. The slaughter of young men in battle was supplanted by the butchering of machinery more than men on the battlefield. And civil populations were more resistant than expected to terror from the skies, at least until the advent of the atomic bomb.

As they were when air power theory first emerged, our perceptions of the future are still dominated by the past, by the role of the nation-states in war, by the experiences of World War II, the Cold War, and, now, Operation Desert Storm. But, if air power theory is to be reformulated for the future, that formulation can be no better than the perception of the future on which it is based. To the extent that the original air power theorists were wrong in their perceptions of the future, their theory was at risk. Thus, the most important thing that air power theorists can do today is to try to get their perceptions of the future right.

The perception of the future presented in this chapter and the next has no claim to stature over others. It is developed in some detail here, not in the certainty that it is right, but to complete the principal argument of this manuscript—that air power theory needs to be redefined. If the original air power theory was rooted in a perception of the nature of the world and the future of conflict, so too will its redefinition. If nothing else, this perception of the future is an illustration of the kind of intellectual foundations needed to formulate and analyze security concepts for the future.

A Time of Great Change

Getting the future right at this time is an immense challenge. The conventional wisdom is that the world is going through a period of enormous dramatic changes in many dimensions—political, economic, social, and military. The momentous events which have taken place in the former communist bloc over the past several years have caused widespread speculation about a "new world order." These events were especially striking because neither their magnitude nor speed were anticipated by any of the affected governments, east or west.

Unfortunately, the enormity of those events is most often seen against the backgrounds of the Cold War (the past 40 years), the World Wars (75 years), and the Balance of Power (some 250 years), mostly centered on Europe.[3] One can detect those backgrounds as observers express various concerns about regional balances of power, about the balkanization of Europe in the breakups of the Soviet Union and Yugoslavia, and about the rise of a new European economic giant. According to the expressions of these concerns, the future problems of the world are to be found in models drawn from some part of the past 250 years of European-centered political history.

To assume, however, that the future of the world will remain rooted in the forces which have shaped Europe and, hence, the world over the past 250 years, while logical, is an important leap of faith. We may be at a break point in history not unlike that which occurred in Europe about 250 years ago—one where the dominant forces shift in their sources of power. In 1750, a projection of the future of Europe rooted in the previous 250 years would have understandably relied upon the histories of the monarchies which had dominated European events for centuries. It would, indeed, have required considerable prescience to perceive, then, the rise of nationalism and relative liberalism that would soon sweep Europe and dominate world developments for the next several centuries.

These considerations suggest that the recent stunning events in Europe and elsewhere (e.g., China) need to be examined not just in the light of the models which have prevailed for the past 40, 75, or 250 years, but against the possibility that these events are signs of a shift in the dominant forces shaping our world. New models may be required, not so much because the old ones are dead wrong, but because they may no longer describe the most important factors shaping the future: Monarchies didn't entirely go away in the revolutions of the late 18th century; they were just not as important thereafter in determining the face of the world. Nations and their political expressions are not going to go away in the revolutions of the late 20th century, but they may no longer be the dominant forces shaping the future of the world in the 21st century.

The past few years may be the harbingers of a new model for human affairs worldwide—of an era where *national* governments will experience declining control over those affairs. The future of the world may no longer be rooted in the political history of the past several centuries so much as it is in global trends being driven by profound changes in technology, principally those technologies associated with the current information revolution which has yet to reach its peak. And this suggests that national policies everywhere may have much less influence on the future world order than they have in the past.

Models for Change

Implicit in any perception of the future is a model of how the world works and, therefore, how it is expected to work in the future. Any model is a simplified explanation of why things work the way they do. Models, implicit or explicit, can be recognized in suppositions of the form, "If this, then that." A model is evident in the "domino theory" applied to American involvement in Vietnam: If America didn't stop the communists in Vietnam, all of the Southeast Asian nations would soon fall to communism, much like falling dominoes. That was a perception, a model, of how the world worked.

The prevailing model of political developments—the one which has dominated Western thinking for nearly 250 years—derives from these premises:

1. The most powerful forces shaping the world are those in the hands of national governments.

2. Those forces are manifested mostly in the form of political power, underwritten by economic and military powers.

3. The political, economic, and military powers are largely vested in national governments and wielded (or expressed) through government policies.

4. The leaderships of national governments, as the designers and implementors of government policies, can significantly shape the forces exerted by nations and, hence, the future development of the world order.

Those premises have endured for at least two centuries and would not be foreign to 19th or 20th century politicians. But they might have seemed strange—even alarming—to those attending 16th and 17th century courts; and they may come to be seen as dated or anachronistic to 21st-century observers.

The model that logically evolves from these premises places great weight on the qualities of national leaderships, their policies, and on the economic and military forces they control. This model says that good or bad leaders can have a profound effect upon the face of the world by the policies they adopt and by the way they employ the economic and military powers at their disposal. Alliances between nations can develop even more powerful forces for good or bad; and national leaderships have looked to them for ways to upset or to restore the balance of power. Since the future tenure or behavior of leaders cannot be assured, the military and economic powers under their control are important measures of future potentials.

For at least two centuries, this model has probably been a reasonably reliable guide to the future of the West, if not always for the rest of the world which it has dominated politically. It urges great concern about the qualities of national leaderships, about the ideologies they profess and which may guide their policies, and about the economic and military powers at their disposal. Where those concerns point toward the possibility of good or bad developments, the model urges further concerns about upsetting or restoring regional balances of power. That model is powerfully evident in such current questions as these:

- Will a reunified Germany represent an economic giant capable of once again dominating Europe, perhaps recreating the conditions leading to two world wars?

- Will the restoration of the Russian economy before the dismantling of its military power regenerate the threat it posed during the Cold War?

- Will the breakup of the Soviet empire result in the balkanization of Europe, thereby recreating the conditions that spawned the First World War?

Note that all of these question are a glance over the shoulder—all are concerns rooted in the history of the 20th century. More important, all of these questions contain within them the implicit, "if this, then that" relationship of a model of how the world works, might work, or is reasonably expected to work. None question the model or its premises.

They pose a world in the hands of statesmen, exemplified by Metternich and Kissinger and haunted by 1948 or 1939 or 1914 or 1870. Although the questions, themselves, cannot be faulted, their pertinency lies not in recent events but in the model that stimulates them and implies the possible answers.

The first premise of the prevailing model is key; if it fails, so easily may the rest. Is it possible that the most powerful forces now shaping the world are no longer those in the hands of national governments? The evidence for an affirmative answer is mounting. The following premises could be the basis for a different model and perception that may better describe the future of the world, if not the present:

1. The most powerful force shaping the world is the rapid diffusion of power into the hands of individuals, factions, corporations, and other non-state actors who are freely and independently associating themselves with shared causes, not necessarily or even mostly identified with nationalism.

2. That more diffuse power is manifested in a variety of forms—political, economic, and destructive—which are increasingly capable of effective challenges to those of the nation-states.

3. The source of that power is to be found mostly in information—its communication, processing, management, dissemination, access, and utilization—instead of the traditional sources such as military forces, territory, industrial production, or natural resources.

4. Traditional human hierarchies of all kinds—in governments, business, and even in families, wherever they have been erected upon the limitation and control of information—are increasingly being eroded, bypassed, or ignored when they do not serve the causes of those who are subordinated to them.

The evidence for these premises is found not so much in the past 250 years as in the present and over the past 40 and 4000 years. The past 4000 years is a story of the diffusion of power to individuals at the expense of elites through a series of revolutionary human developments, the latest of which is an information revolution, begun in the past 40 years.

Bronowski observed that all revolutionary forms of power—the horse, writing, gunpowder, and nuclear energy—initially vest with elites, who are later threatened as that power inevitably escapes their control and diffuses to individuals.[4] The horse-drawn chariot conveyed power to early community elites who were subsequently threatened when the horse was saddled by the nomadic raider. Writing conveyed power to the clerical elites; but the printing press threatened their authority as individuals gained access to books. Armored knights were horrified by the implications of crossbows and then firearms in the hands of unregulated individuals. While the implications of nuclear power under control of anything less than the nation-state are widely approbated, the inevitable diffusion of that power, even down to the individual, is only now beginning to be contemplated, but not really confronted.

The power of information is now diffusing rapidly to individuals throughout the world, especially in the most highly developed parts of the world such as Europe, North America, and East Asia. As Wriston has observed, the information technologies are eroding the traditional powers of the nation-state.[5] They are also eroding other hierarchical structures; but the nation-states are now the most vulnerable, for they have been historically erected and maintained on the control and limitation of information by their elites. Indeed, in the absence of adequate means for communications, the power derived from information *had* to be entrusted to elites in order to organize societies. Individuals and factions with free and abundant access to information and communication among themselves represent a new and obvious challenge to the authority and, hence, the power of the nation-state.

The power of information and the potential challenge to the nation-state of its diffusion were recognized even before the beginning of the current information revolution. The efforts of the nation-states to seize and control the sources of information and the means of communication are well documented in history and fiction. They include the efforts of the Nazis to destroy literature subversive to the state's interests and to exploit the centrally controlled means of communication for state propaganda. Orwell's vision of the future contemplated the extremes of such efforts. The communist bloc came close to (and in some places, may have achieved) Orwell's vision; but, judging by the events of the past few years, they were unable to persist against the expanding technical means for the diffusion of information.

In summary, there appears to be a significant shift in the locus of power, from the geographically defined nation-state to individuals and their free associations in factions and enterprises which are increasingly independent of geography. That shift is the result of developments in the information technologies, accelerating over the past 40 years, which have radically changed the speed, amount, and quality of information available to individuals. The power of that immediate, free, and abundant information in the hands of individuals is proving itself to be increasingly capable of challenging, undermining, or rendering impotent the traditional powers vested in the nation-state in all of its forms—political, economic, and military.

Of course, that shift is not yet complete. The developed world appears to be in a transition period where the sources of power—in things or in information—and the trustees of power—the nation-state or the individual—are still in the process of shifting. Nevertheless, more of the future of the world may be evident in the current trends of the information revolution than in the nationalism of the past two centuries.

Role of Information Technology

The current information revolution, which is only the latest major diffusion of power to individuals, can be traced back to the development of the telegraph and telephone in the last half of the 19th century followed by radio, television, and electronic computers in the first half of the 20th century. But it was the developments in solid-state electronics beginning in the 1950s that brought all of these devices into practical forms that could be mass produced for, distributed to, and used by individuals throughout the world. It is the worldwide spread of cheap, reliable, and powerful information devices that is truly revolutionary. Thus, the basis for the current information revolution is not in the advent of radio or television or even computers, but in their magical transformation by the silicon-based microchip in all of its many manifestations. Even the 100-year-old telephone has been recently transformed. That is what sets the past 20 to 40 years apart from prior history.

Since the 1950s, the means for communicating, processing, accessing, storing, managing, and exploiting information have exploded. No dimension of human affairs seems to have grown or changed so rapidly, including the much lamented growth in human population and its effect upon the earth's environment. In the past decade alone, measurement of the information revolution on almost any dimension—numbers (of telephone circuits, television receivers, videorecorders, videocameras, or facsimile machines), capacities (of transmission media, storage devices, or displays), speed, and cost—is described not in mere percentages, but in factors of three, ten, or more.

Coupled with jet transport, space satellites, and the concomitant spread of English as a common language, the electronic information revolution has netted and shrunk the world to the proportion of a village community. One can go almost anywhere in that world, taking videocameras and satellite uplinks, in the matter of hours. As in a village, one can now observe many world events in real time. Exploding volumes of information are exchanged daily through electronic mail, facsimile machines, and computer databases—between individuals who may never have met and whose nationality and location are nearly arbitrary. Global markets are the consequence of abundant telecommunications, which together with computerized means for utilizing voluminous data, have facilitated managing global enterprises.

That technology could accomplish such feats is no longer a great surprise to the publics of the developed world. Coming in an age of nuclear power and space travel, modern business and consumer electronic gadgets and their capabilities seem no different from other technical marvels in medicine, travel, and warfare. But unlike most of the other technical wonders, the information gadgets are *diffusing* power more than they are *concentrating* it. While the most spectacular technological developments in space, weaponry, and medicine appear to have concentrated power, the information technologies during the last 15 years have been marked and measured by the conveyance of capabilities directly into the hands of individuals.

Since the introduction of microprocessors in the 1970s, computer and communications technologies have moved rapidly away from centralized facilities and toward the broad distribution of information and computational power. The economic payoff of distributing computation and information resources is an enhancement of the creative productivity of the individuals given access. This economic benefit is proportional to the degree of distribution; cautious adopters of the technology can expect proportionately limited gains. But once the power of information is given to individuals, they will use it to serve their own ends, with little opportunity for effective control by authorities.

Because the information technologies are increasingly required for competitiveness in nearly all human activities, the transfer of power to individuals, even if unintended, is unavoidable. That transfer is having an effect on all aspects of human affairs: cultural, social, political, military, and economic. Perhaps the development having the greatest impact upon the affairs of nations is the practical networking of individuals through telecommunications. Print and broadcast media have traditionally allowed a privileged few to communicate to the many. These media have concentrated power in the hands of those who control the printing press or the television station. In contrast, electronic networking of the office, the nation, and then the globe, has for the first time permitted many to freely communicate with many—for almost any individual to be both a broadcaster and a selective receiver. The individual is no longer limited to a single source for information, and can now communicate information to as many as may have interest in that information. Although power elites may control the newspapers and television stations, personal computers and facsimile machines make every citizen a potential publisher or broadcaster. Moreover, the personal electronic media are proliferating much more rapidly than the traditional mass media.

Previously, the ability of individuals to freely communicate was limited by geographic proximity and especially by national boundaries. Now information flows freely around the globe and crosses national borders with increasing ease. Even where national governments may try to isolate their populations by limiting access to networks, information will cross national boundaries because it is easily accessible through satellite links. Italy made itself a magnet for the Albanians who were watching Italian television across the Adriatic. The impoverished in the east and south quadrants of the world are increasingly watching how those in the north and west are living; and mass migrations are the feared consequence.

Computer technology and the free communication of information have become the woof and warp of successful commerce in the world village. Computer technology is increasingly important both through its contribution to manufacturing and through processors embedded in products. A growing share of economic output is embodied in software, both in the programs that run the computers, and in the information that allows for the efficient management of human enterprises. The world is entering an information age, where the source of wealth and power is increasingly from information and human mental creativity, with physical resources and production declining in relative value. It is becoming increasingly difficult for any nation or society to keep pace with world affluence without embracing information technology.

But information technology introduced to improve economic performance ends up being utilized for other purposes. Regimes which once limited access to typewriters and photocopiers must now confront the challenges of computer terminals, printers, and networks. Attempts to limit the availability or use of such devices can only reduce the economic gains which motivate introducing them in the first place. Furthermore, to deny free communications is to be excluded from participation in a global economy that is growing much more rapidly than that of any closed national economy. To accept free communications is to grant the power of information to individuals who are then empowered to challenge the hierarchies which have been built on, and maintained by, the denial and control of information. The new personal electronic media (personal computers, fax machines, video and audio tape recorders and players, etc.),

> have brought geographically distant groups with like interests together for common activities and have allowed people around the globe to exert power against their governments, societies, and institutions. For the first time in history, these media have furnished the means for distributing individually crafted ideas and information on a massive scale, instantaneously, cheaply, and globally."[6]

National political hierarchies face a dilemma. For their nations to be economically competitive, they must allow individual citizens access to information networks and computer technology. In doing so they cede significant control over economic, cultural, and eventually political events in their countries. Symptoms of this devolution are discernible in the shift in control of public agendas between Western governments and the electronic media and in the gradual decline in authoritative regimes during the last 15 years. But a definitive impact of these trends on the fate of nations had not been seen until the last few years, in Eastern Europe and in China.

The role of telecommunications in the events of the past several years has certainly been noted and remarked on by many observers. But the effect generally ascribed by the media, to the media, is more that of *facilitating* change than *compelling* change. Telecommunications are still more likely to be characterized by the media as a new factor to be reckoned with in the old order of things rather than the manifestation of a completely new order. That distinction may be crucial to the future. Marshall McLuhan would probably have argued that telecommunications are not simply a new factor to be reckoned with but are the dominant force that will shape the decades ahead.

Opening Closed Societies

This model of the future of the world suggests that the communist bloc failed, not primarily or even fundamentally because of its centrally controlled economic policies or its excessive military burdens, but because its closed societies were too long denied the productivity of the information revolution that was developing elsewhere, particularly over the past 20 years. The centrally controlled economies were not obvious failures 40 years ago. What has changed so dramatically are not the communist economies (until their collapse) but the free economies of the developed Western nations, nurtured, fueled and made all too evident by the information revolution.

Absent the information revolution and its effects on the Western economies, it is not at all clear that the disparities between the Western and communist economies would have been so great. In only the last 20 years, the American economy has dramatically shifted to the information technologies—from an investment of about ten-percent of the total producer durables to more than 50 percent.[7] The role of the information revolution in the comparative growth of the Western and communist economies is striking and undeniable.

Absent the information revolution, the closing of the communist societies to protect the control of their elites might not have mattered. Indeed, the closing did not matter until the information revolution took hold as a significant world development in the 1960s with the development of solid-state electronics, space satellites, and the jet transport. Thereafter, closed societies paid a growing price for their isolation; they denied the economic growth inherent in information technologies and their progeny—world commerce and community. The fate of the communist societies provides a striking example of the importance of discerning the dominant forces shaping the future.

The information revolution has breached the walls of the closed societies—both physically and politically. They were breached not by military forces, diplomacy, alliances, or economic power, but by information spewing out of television sets, telephones, audio and video tapes, computers, and facsimile machines into the minds of individuals. It wasn't that the authorities couldn't prevent that flood of information—they could and did. In a few—like Cuba, China, and North Korea—they continue to a degree. But to do so is to deny themselves the benefits of the prospering societies they see all around them. Now the clock is ticking for them; probably none will continue as closed societies when their present leaderships die off.

Gorbachev chose to open his society and to risk his control over it. *Glasnost* was the strategic decision, not *perestroika*. Although he probably would not have put it this way, his choice was either to open the society and hope to secure the benefits of the information revolution or to close it and ensure its continuing backwardness relative to the open societies and the rest of the developed world community. Gorbachev's successors cannot escape the dilemma; they can only ratify or repudiate the choice. *Perestroika* was merely the undertaker that attempted, too late, to deal with the dead body of the hierarchy of elites that had been created in, and sustained by, a closed society.

The suddenness of the collapse of communist regimes must be explained by whatever model one subscribes to for world events. That the Eastern European satellites and captive republics of the Soviet Union were restive was certainly no surprise. If they had progressively gained greater political freedom from Moscow over the next decade or so, few would have expressed astonishment. But for all of these nations to come in from the cold, separately, sequentially, in the space of a few years, implies some common mechanism; and that mechanism was the sharing of abundant information. The publics throughout Eastern and Western Europe were acting on the basis of information that was increasingly available through non-governmental sources—through television, telephone circuits, facsimile and copying machines—as part of the global network of *commercial* (not state) electronic signals.

Remarkably, national governments and organized political bodies on *both* sides of the Iron Curtain acted to moderate rather than amplify the forces engendered by the information revolution. With few exceptions, national political power appears to be in retreat from events that governments either do not control or would control only at their own peril. Political leaderships appear not to have anticipated these events, but in their face, can only urge caution and moderation.

Are these temporary circumstances which the national political elites will soon accommodate and adapt to their traditional ends? The prevailing model for the past 250 years would predict so. But if that model no longer describes the emerging world, that comfortable prediction might not hold in any enduring or widespread way. The most important form of power seems to be diffusing beyond the control of the political elites; and technology, as it has before, is showing signs of changing from their mistress to their rival. The horse has slipped the chariot's harness and has been saddled by the nomadic raider. The implications for the future nature of conflict and national security are profound.

Notes

1. David Jablonsky, "Strategic Vision and Presidential Authority in the Post-Cold War Era," *Parameters* (Winter 1991–92): 2.

2. Richard J. Barnet, "Defining the Moment," *The New Yorker*, July 16, 1990, 46–60.

3. Much of the following draws upon Carl H. Builder and Steven C. Bankes, *The Etiology of European Change*, P-7693 (Santa Monica, Calif.: RAND, December 1990), A more complete development of these ideas can be found in Carl H. Builder, "Is It a Transition or a Revolution," *Futures*, vol. 25, no. 2 (March 1993): 155–168.

4. J. Bronowski, *The Ascent of Man* (Boston: Brown and Company, 1973), 78, 79.

5. Walter B. Wriston, "Technology and Sovereignty," *Foreign Affairs*, vol. 67, no. 2 (Winter 1988–89): 63–75. Wriston expands on these arguments in his *The Twilight of Sovereignty: How the Information Revolution is Transforming Our World* (New York: Charles Scribner's Sons, 1992).

6. Gladys D. Ganely, "Power to the People via Personal Electronic Media," *The Washington Quarterly* (Spring 1991): 5–22.

7. For a graphic representation of this growth, see Colin Norman, "Rethinking Technology's Role in Economic Change," *Science*, vol. 240, no. 4855, (20 May 1988): 977.

21

The New Security Environment

If a service does not possess a well-defined strategic concept, the public and the political leaders will be confused as to the role of the service, uncertain as to the necessity of its existence, and apathetic or hostile to the claims made by the service upon the resources of society.[1]

Altered Landscapes

If the dramatic changes now underway in the world are due, in large part, to an information revolution, the future may not be a new world order, but a period of world disorder until the transformation is widely absorbed or effectively accommodated in most of the world's societies. This is a revolution that is, among many other things, undermining the power of hierarchies, including those which have traditionally provided for our safety and security. The implications for security at all levels—personal, community, national, and global—are not likely to be mostly favorable.[2]

If the information revolution was a significant factor in the transformation of the communist bloc, then Western institutions may soon find themselves being challenged by the same information revolution, simply because hierarchies of all kinds are vulnerable to its effects. The authoritarian communist states were the most vulnerable to these effects because they depended, more than the democracies, on hierarchies and the control of information for their power and legitimacy. The democracies are less dependent on these things, but to the extent that dependencies remain, they will ultimately become vulnerable too. The difficulties of democratic governance in the age of television (and other mass media of communications) is increasingly acknowledged.

Some are concerned about renewed nationalism in the revolutions in Eastern Europe and in the breakup of the Soviet empire. There is certainly some evidence pointing in that direction. However, there are also signs suggesting something subtly different—not historic nationalism so much as the desire to reestablish self-governing cultural and ethnic communities which have been long suppressed by politically imposed nationalism. The revolutions so far demonstrate little interest in reestablishing authoritarian nation-states with the usual trappings of national power—particularly military power. Where there has been substantial organized violence, it has been at the hands of paramilitary factions more than the police. Thus, the current direction may not be one of nationalism so much as cultural and ethnic centrism—one for identification and affiliation with a common culture and local control within that culture.

Europe in the 1990s differs from Europe in 1914 in several critical aspects. Horizontal contacts between individual citizens of different nations through travel and communications provide a new rein on nationalistic aggression. The propaganda effort required for central governments to convince their citizens to forfeit their lives through state-organized warfare is now being undermined by the availability of independent sources of information. This effect is now strong in Western Europe, and can be expected to grow stronger in the East as restrictions on the flow of people and information are eased.

The economic interdependencies that were supposed to prevent war in 1914, but did not, have also changed. The growing economic interconnectedness between societies is different than that which existed prior to the information revolution. Before, it was mostly in trading connections, now it is in the business enterprises themselves—in the ownership, management, financing, and production. The risks of large-scale, organized warfare have become more than a threat to future trade profits; they now jeopardize existing capital and its purposes. Furthermore, in the information economy, the sources of wealth and power are increasingly dominated by human knowledge and creativity as material resources decline in importance. Wealth based on information cannot be acquired through the conquest of territory. Thus, information technology erodes both the motivation and the capability for nationalistic conquest. Violence of various kinds will remain, probably even grow, but the likelihood of wars of national conquest appears to recede as states lose the ability to dictate either the use or the availability of information.

The leaderships of national governments everywhere are being challenged to stay ahead of their increasingly international publics and commerce, whose access to information and communications are no longer so disparate from that of their leaders. The Cable News Network (CNN) now appears to be more pertinent than the CIA for current White House intelligence, judging by what the White House staff monitors most continuously. Of course, the intelligence-gathering resources of CNN, while considerable, do not rival those of the CIA. The significance of CNN to the White House is that it represents the information which is in the hands of the public and which must be reckoned with by the political elites. CNN can, by default, set the political agenda. Similarly, the move toward a European community seems less one of bold leadership than the ratification of directions and practices that have been adopted by the publics and businesses of Europe.

Where national governments are already weak or subject to powerful ethnic and factional forces, the information revolution is likely only to increase the prospects for disorder. Parts of the Islamic world appear to be particularly vulnerable—in North Africa, the southern tier of the old Soviet Union, the Middle East, south-central Asia, and perhaps even into the Western Pacific. Although we do not yet adequately understand how different cultures will adapt to, or exploit, the artifacts of the information revolution, there appear to be important differences in how the information technologies will be absorbed between the Islamic cultures and those in the West and Orient.[3] Instead of helping some of these nations or their societies participate in the new prosperity enjoyed by the developed world, the proliferation of the personal electronic media may be used mostly to challenge authority, and to overturn order rather than open new opportunities.

Making Choices

The significance of these developments for national security is not altogether promising. Organized warfare may decline in frequency, scale, and scope; yet conflicts in the form of riot and disorder may increase on all three dimensions. Whether we shall be better off or worse off will not be obvious. In general, the United States government may have less control over the future of the new world order (or disorder) than it would like to think, even as the American culture and commerce may have been the most influential forces in shaping these developments. As its domain of control shrinks, the American government may respond by emphasizing its national interests and its superpower status, with the risk that it may reduce, rather than enhance, the respect and influence it seeks. The audience for American foreign policy may be changing; it may be less other national governments and more their publics—who are watching and listening and to whom the power is shifting.

The information revolution now underway has transformed the world; but the final form of that world is not entirely clear. It seems unlikely to be a more peaceful or kinder world. If violence organized by the nation-states declines, factional violence of all kinds may well increase. Many of the effects of this revolution will be unwelcome, particularly within hierarchical institutions; certainly not all of the information available will be uplifting to those watching or listening. What does seem clear is that the world has shrunk to a global village or community where many voices can be heard and where information is abundant, both for the first time. The United States has been the leader and role model in this revolution, through its culture and its commerce. It remains to be seen whether its government and policies will serve and support that cultural and commercial leadership or will, as the relative powers of the nation-state decline worldwide, simply try to conserve those previous powers as long as possible.

For many Europeans, the corner has already been turned, and the new landscapes are more evident. Here are a few voices from Europe: Helmut Kohl, German Chancellor, has said, "I believe there can be no return to the nation-state of the nineteenth century." Francesco Speroni of the Lega Lombarda[4] observes,

> Europe has three levels now—the EC, the state, and the region. The weakest of these is the state. The state may well disappear. You can't tell me that states really represent the people in the new Europe. Often they were formed for the wrong reasons, by diplomats and generals.

And Eric Hobsbawn of London University notes the shift of power which is bypassing the governmental hierarchies: "The nation-state has lost control. The world economy became so transnational that the state was bypassed."[5]

More than 30 years ago, in commenting on Henry Kissinger's *Nuclear Weapons and Foreign Policy*, Robert Oppenheimer saw the shadows of what can now be seen so much more clearly:

Of course Kissinger is right in conceiving the problems of policy planning and strategy in terms of national power, in rough analogy to the national struggles of the 19th century; yet I have the impression that there are deep things abroad in the world, which in time are going to turn the flank of all struggles so conceived. This will not happen today, nor easily as long as Soviet power continues great and unaltered; but nevertheless I think in time the transnational communities in our culture will begin to play a prominent part in the political structure of the world, and even affect the exercise of power by the states.[6]

The Future of Nuclear Deterrence

Even before the end of the Cold War, it was apparent that the role of nuclear weapons and deterrence theory was rapidly mutating. By the 1970s, some had begun to argue that there was no significant military utility to nuclear weapons when confronting a comparably armed opponent. Any marginal tactical utility was simply swamped by the enormous shadow of the end-game which is inherent in their possession and largely divorced from policy, strategy, weapon numbers, or technical virtuosity.[7] When all the arcane technical details of nuclear arms control, deterrence, and strategy were stripped away, nuclear weapons, by their inherent destructive capacity in modern societies, became political instruments of terror, not military instruments of war:

...nuclear weapons serve no military purpose whatsoever. They are totally useless—except to deter one's opponent from using them.[8]

While that statement flatly denies any military utility for nuclear weapons, it does not assure us about their adequacy for the political purpose of deterring an opponent from using them, because achieving that purpose also rests upon the respective *vulnerabilities* to nuclear weapons. An opponent cannot be deterred by the threat of nuclear weapons if that opponent has no definable society to threaten. This is the terrifying asymmetry that now yawns ahead: Some who will come to possess nuclear weapons will not be comparably vulnerable to their use. That possibility first surfaced with concerns about civil defense in the Soviet Union, then with primitive societies in Asia and Africa, and now, most ominously, with radical factions distributed throughout several societies.

As political instruments for terror against modern societies, nuclear weapons will come to be most effective in the hands of political terrorists who do not have a modern society at stake. Modern societies have more to lose than to gain through their use. Thus, nuclear deterrence as a strategy or policy is increasingly an empty observation of the state of affairs. The simple facts of nuclear weapons and modern societies will serve to deter those who have something to lose. We are moving from an era where the question was "who has the most or best nuclear weapons?" to one where the question is "who has the most to lose?" The political power of nuclear weapons is shifting from the strong to the weak.

Military programs will have less effect on the future of nuclear deterrence than the political and social changes now being wrought by the information revolution. The greatest implications of that revolution for nuclear deterrence are the same as those for state-organized warfare—the decline in the sovereignty or political power of the nation-state and the rising power of transnational factions or groups. These changes will have several profound implications for the future of nuclear deterrence:

- The information necessary for the development of nuclear weapons will inevitably spread beyond the control of the nation-states.

- The transnational nature of commerce will make nuclear materials or the means for their production (or recovery) increasingly available worldwide.

- Global access to information will facilitate transnational factionalism based on interests—religious, economic, or political—that transcend the nation-state.

- Free access to information will augment the political power of individuals and transnational factions even as it detracts from the power of nation-states.

One consequence, but by no means the most important, will be a wider distribution of nuclear weapons in the world, not only among the nation-states, but even to factions and, eventually, to individuals. Although this will result in a larger number of nations seeking to possess nuclear weapons for deterrence, it will also result in some—particularly factions—possessing nuclear weapons to coerce (terrorize) others, including the nuclear-armed nations who are likely to be much more vulnerable to the effects of nuclear weapons. Thus, while the numbers who seek to acquire nuclear capabilities for deterrence will increase, the number who seek them for *coercive* purposes may increase even faster and become a much more preoccupying concern for the nation-states.

Thus, the most important consequence of the information revolution for nuclear deterrence will be the rise of transnational factions that oppose or threaten the nation-states and which, because of their dispersed or commingled nature, cannot be effectively deterred from terrorist or subversive actions by nuclear threats. Although nuclear weapons will remain the premier means for nation-states to deter one another, they will not be an effective deterrent to a faction which presents no target for nuclear weapons. If such factions possess nuclear weapons, even in very small numbers, then they may be able, not only to terrorize nation-states, but to deter them as well. Indeed, nuclear weapons in the information era may become the bane rather than the power symbols of the nation-states.

At that point, nuclear weapons will finally be recognized, even by the nation-states for what they have always been since the moment of their creation at the zenith of the technology era—political instruments of terror. Their initial use against Hiroshima and Nagasaki may have been justified, at the time, in military terms; but the strategic bombardment theories which they finally validated had long before become campaigns of terror against the civilian populations, whether of Rotterdam, London, Berlin, Dresden, or Tokyo. Despite sincere efforts to find military utility for nuclear weapons throughout the Cold War, they remained, at the core of their possession and justification, political instruments of terror. Despite the elaborate theories of the deterrence theologians designed to portray them as the exclusive and exquisite military instruments of power for the nation-states, nuclear weapons will soon become, instead, brutal political tools in the hands of those who will be eager to demonstrate the vulnerability and, hence, the impotency of the nation-states. Then the nuclear trappings of the nation-states—the numbers or the technical virtuosity of their nuclear delivery vehicles—will count for little; and the relative vulnerabilities of the antagonists will count for everything.

The New Security Environment

The above perceptions—of the way the world is changing in how it works, how it is increasingly likely to work in the future, and the shifting sources of power in that world—logically lead to a number of premises about the future security environment with which the American military will have to cope and be tasked.

From the foregoing, it should be clear that the dramatic, on-going changes in the global security environment have a much deeper source than the reductions in the Soviet threat or the U.S. defense budgets. They reflect a fundamental revolution in the global conduct of human affairs as a result of the shrinking, crowding, and netting of the world because of the explosive changes in the information and transportation technologies. The global mobility of information, commerce, and people has created worldwide markets and communities and is generating new cultural and environmental stresses, and, more importantly, will be changing the nature of conflict.

For the developed nations, both the traditional means and ends of international warfare are becoming increasingly impertinent to their political, economic, and social interests. First, the available technical means for destruction (i.e., nuclear weapons) now overwhelm any reasonable ends for the developed nations. Second, the traditional ends of aggressive warfare—national control over territory, natural resources, industry, or people—have become less important in a world where economic power is increasingly derived from the innovation of free peoples with free access to the world markets in commerce and information. Thus, the probabilities for international conflict between the most developed nations will decline, even as the frequency and scope of *factional* conflicts will increase throughout the world, especially (but not exclusively) in the least developed regions.

The crowding of peoples and cultures in the world is both actual and virtual. The actual crowding, due to population growth, while substantial, may be less than the virtual crowding now being brought about by the explosive increases in the mobility of information and people associated with the technological revolutions in microelectronics, space, and jet transportation. The shrinking, netting, and, hence, virtual crowding of the world are exposing long-standing disparities between cultures, bringing long-separated or isolated cultures into collision, and providing a worldwide stage for their conflicts. These conflicts are increasingly about egregious disparities in political and economic power and about preserving deep differences in racial, ethnic, and religious practices.

These factional conflicts are not being fought with regular forces or traditional means; they have the character of civil wars, insurrections, and riots; and they are being exported in acts of terrorism anywhere in the world. These conflicts will increasingly disturb the security and commerce of the developed nations; and it will be in their interests to intercede and quiet such conflicts. These disturbances to the security of the developed nations may be indirect, as in the Arab-Israeli conflicts. They may involve the interests or concerns of factions in other nations, forcing their political leaderships into taking sides when they would just as soon stay out and avoid widening the conflict. Such conflicts may not be resolvable by the application of any reasonable amount of force; and the intercession of the developed nations will often be predicated on ways that do not make them parties to the conflict.

The need for the developed nations to retain traditional military forces for nuclear deterrence, strategic, tactical, and combat support missions will not disappear; but the size of the active forces retained for those missions will almost certainly decrease as the prospects for large-scale, regular international wars requiring those forces recede. At the same time, the conflicts and missions involving the rapid projection of infrastructures (transport, communications, surveillance, rescue, medical, humanitarian assistance, civil emergency and security) are likely to increase disproportionately. Evidence of that can be seen in the three largest theater or tactical airlifts conducted during 1991, one of them being an integral part of Operation Desert Storm. As shown in the accompanying table, two USAF humanitarian and relief operations in 1991 were comparable, by any measure, to the tactical airlift required to support the "left hook" of Desert Storm.[9]

Three Theater Airlifts During 1991

Airlift Operation	Sorties	Passengers	Cargo (tons)
"Left Hook" in DESERT STORM	1,175	13,843	9,395
Kurdish relief in PROVIDE COMFORT	1,100	14,421	40,000
Mt. Pinatubo evacuation in FIERY VIGIL	1,726	23,400	44,440

Source: Air Force Secretary Rice, *A New Air Force: Reshaping for the Future*, undated testimony during 1992, pp. 20, 25.

While the ready capabilities to project traditional forms of military force will remain in reduced quantities, the needs for rapidly projecting security and civil infrastructures of all kinds, particularly into the less developed regions of the world, will be expanding. Security infrastructures will include the enforcement of civil order, such as imposing curfews, separating adversaries, and deterring the casual resort to force by the presence of obviously superior force.

While the existing Air Force capabilities for projecting infrastructures are significant and will be increasingly exploited in the future, the eventual demands for these capabilities may call for changes in Air Force structure, organization, equipment, and training. However, as the Air Force is compelled in the near future to reduce its force structure under the pressure of budget reductions, there will be a strong tendency to preserve those forces which *have* dominated the mission spectrum in the past rather than those which *might* dominate in the future. To be explicit, there will be a natural tendency to preserve the fighter and bomber forces at the expense of the supporting forces, such as those for transport, communications, surveillance, rescue, and so forth. This tension between institutional proclivities and perceptions of the future illustrates the importance of the latter to the evolution of air power theory.

Nothing in the perception of the future security environment presented here suggests a lessened importance for air power. It does, however, suggest a shifting balance between the projection of *force* and *infrastructure* in air power in the future, just as it has been steadily shifting in the past. Jeffrey Record puts the imperative this way:

> If present and anticipated developments portend neither the demise of manned aircraft nor a diminution in air power's contribution to U.S. security, they do portend significant alterations in the character of U.S. air power as we have come to know it since 1945—at least if air power is to remain a major and effective component of American military power as a whole.[10]

The positive resolution of that last conditional phrase is the burden of the chapters which follow.

Notes

1. Samuel P. Huntington, "National Policy and the Transoceanic Navy," *U.S. Naval Institute Proceedings*, vol. 80, no. 5, (May 1954): 483.

2. This chapter draws heavily from Builder and Bankes, *The Etiology of European Change*. A more complete development of these ideas can be found in Builder, "Is It a Transition or a Revolution?"

3. For a discussion of our need to understand how the information revolution will impact different societies, see Carl H. Builder and Steven C. Bankes, *Artificial Societies: A Proposal for Basic Research into the Societal Implications of Information Technology*, RAND P-7740 (Santa Monica, Calif.: RAND, April 1991). For an excellent discussion of the contrasts between Islamic cultures and the West, see William Pfaff, "Islam and the West," in *The New Yorker*, January 28, 1991, 83-88.

4. Lega Lomarda refers to the Lombardi League of Northern Italy.

5. All three quotes are from David Lawday "My Country, Right...or What?" *The Atlantic*, vol. 268, no. 1, July 1991.

6. J. Robert Oppenheimer in a letter to Atomic Energy Commissioner Gordon Dean, dated May 16, 1957, as quoted by Richard Rhodes, *The Making of the Atomic Bomb* (New York, Simon & Schuster, 1988), 788.

7. This discussion draws from Builder, *The Future of Nuclear Deterrence*.

8. Robert S. McNamara, "The Military Role of Nuclear Weapons: Perceptions and Misperceptions," *Foreign Affairs*, vol. 62, no. 1 (Fall,1983): 79, (emphasis in the original).

9. However, the presentation of the data on these three airlifts clearly showed the greater pride or importance the Air Force associated with the airlift for Operation Desert Storm. The other two airlifts were mentioned later in the testimony among miscellaneous good deeds and could have easily been lost in a casual reading.

10. Record, *The Future of the Air Force*, 158.

PART VII

SETTING THE COMPASS

22

Mission Desiderata

Perhaps we have been floating on the stream of history but need to begin paddling, as did the air power prophets.[1]

But an air force is more than an agglomeration of aircraft, bombs, and bullets. It needs several other elements: a clear understanding of its purpose or mission; a body of ideas (concepts and doctrine) governing in broad terms how it will carry out its mission; strategy and tactics for the efficient use of its equipment; a system for supplying its material and human needs; a research and development organization to keep ahead of potential enemies; experienced leaders; and sound organization to coordinate and direct its activities.[2]

The challenge in redefining the mission of the Air Force is daunting. The desiderata are many, but so are the constraints. The Air Force mission must:

- embrace an Air Force which is an amalgam of historical means and ends more than logic;

- unify rather than fractionate the diverse interests and endeavors of people within the institution;

- justify an independent military institution for its fulfillment;

- inspire a commitment to purposes higher than those of the interests of the institution[3] or its people;

- provide a clear basis for discriminating choices and for collective decisionmaking;

- endure through the foreseeable changes in technology, threats, and the interests of the American society; and

- enlist broad support from the American public and its government.

The constants or boundaries of that mission are rooted in history and law: It must be consistent with the heritages of the Air Force, the American military services, and the American institutions. Hence, it must be a *military* mission and prominently feature aviation as an instrument. It would be inconsistent with the heritage of the Air Force if military aviation were no longer central to its mission. Similarly, it would be inconsistent with the heritage of the American military services for the Air Force mission to be defined apart from service to the nation as that service may be defined by duly constituted civilian authorities. The trick is to define the mission broadly enough to capture the scope of the institution's greatest aspirations without losing the focus and reality essential for incisiveness and credibility.

If the mission of the Air Force is to remain centered on air power, then air power must somehow be defined as more than force, airplanes or pilots:

- Air power must be more than force because the problems of the world must increasingly be addressed by the military with more than force. Many of the crises and conflicts in our shrinking world are no longer highly susceptible to resolution through the projection of force, but—as in protection of the Kurds in the wake of Operation Desert Storm—will require the projection of infrastructures such as security, medical care, communications, and transportation.

- Air power must be more than airplanes because the power to be projected through the third dimension is also increasingly derived from critical space and ground support systems.

- Air power must be more than pilots because the power to be projected through the third dimension can often be more effectively derived from self-guided missiles, remotely-piloted vehicles, and unmanned platforms.

- Air power must be defined as more than combat, since the nature of conflict is changing worldwide. Regular warfare between nations is becoming less attractive, while irregular warfare between factions—ignoring national boundaries—is becoming more so.

Indeed, the precise destructiveness of modern weapons supported by modern infrastructures—as demonstrated in Operation Desert Storm—may accelerate the shift from regular to irregular warfare. If grievances cannot be resolved by resorting to conventional military force, frustrated causes will be resolved through other, less conventional means. Dealing with conflict may increasingly require Air Force provision of infrastructures to friends or allies to help them deal with unrest, riot, insurrection, insurgencies, terrorism, and subversion.

Lieutenant General Charles Boyd, commander of the Air University, has described this broader conception of air power with these words:

> ...I use the term *air power* in its most comprehensive sense of air and space power. Such inclusive air power values every role and mission, as well as all the support, services, and—most importantly—all the people the Air Force needs to be a fully capable service.[4]

If air power is what the Air Force is about, then air power must be defined inclusively—to include every person in the Air Force and every one of their diverse contributions to air power.

If air power is a spear, then the point of that spear is the strike systems which deliver the "fire and steel" (i.e., the bombs, missiles, and gunfire); and the shaft of the spear is all those support systems (i.e., the surveillance, communications, navigation, jamming, refueling, logistics, transport, medical, weather, security, etc.). The point of the spear is getting sharper, better aimed, and more deadly every day because of technology; but the shaft is getting longer and more important as well. With every passing year, with every advance in technology, the point of the spear gets smaller, while the shaft of the spear gets bigger. Significantly, it is not the point of the spear that has become the measure of global reach and global power, but the shaft that carries the point.

The long-term trend in the balance between spear point and shaft is obvious; and the shift is not limited to the Air Force: When the principal form of firepower was musketry, and soldiers could live off the land upon which they fought, it was important that most soldiers be at the front line—with the infantry, artillery, or cavalry—where they could bring fire and steel upon the enemy. Now, a single soldier can, at the press of a button, bring to bear the firepower equivalent of thousands of muskets; but to do so requires the support of tens, even hundreds of specialists to locate the targets, maintain the complex equipment, and provide the myriad supplies and services for a modern, mobile army. While many soldiers express concern about the balance between "teeth" and "tail" in their armies, the teeth are now more than sharp enough; it is the tail that marks the difference between world-class armies and local militias.

During Operation Desert Storm, we took great pride in our combat aircraft and the weapons they carried. Yet they are not what our allies envied or our enemy regretted most. It was our infrastructure. They had combat aircraft and weapons that might not have quite matched ours; but they felt naked and lost without our surveillance, communications, and navigation capabilities. Indeed, one of our allies was reported to have sworn never again to be utterly dependent on American intelligence capabilities, even in coalition warfare. It was not our combat aircraft that set us so apart from our allies or enemy in capabilities; it was our projection of essential infrastructures for modern, precision warfare.

In addition to what air power is, there is the issue of what air power does—the claims for air power. In the wake of Operation Desert Storm, some air power advocates have felt vindicated in their long-disputed claim of decisiveness, only to find that the dispute has not ended. Air power may have finally revealed and proven itself, not as independently decisive in all wars, but as *definitive* in shaping most conflicts, decisive in some, and therefore demanding independent conception and use. The unqualified claim of decisiveness for air power has always been contentious and created headwinds. However much the claim may have helped to rally the early advocates and supporters of military aviation, history has overridden their theory and conjecture with more tangible and credible counter claims.

It is enough that air power can be decisive in some conflicts—most accept that it would be decisive in an all-out thermonuclear war—and to be definitive in most. Whether or not air power was decisive in World War II can still be disputed;[5] but it certainly defined the remainder of the war on land and sea.

In Korea and Vietnam, it is generally accepted that air power was not decisive; but there are some air power advocates who would go on to argue that it could have been if it had been employed properly—that the problem was with the political leaderships, in their understanding of how to use air power decisively. The political leaderships involved might well respond that the decisive use of air power may involve a price that the nation should not have to pay—in the prospects of too much "collateral damage" to innocent civilians or in the prospects for a much wider and violent war.

However the debates over the employment of air power in the Korean and Vietnam wars may be resolved, air power did define the nature of the land wars that were fought there; air power limited the enemy's means and therefore the pace of those conflicts. In Operation Desert Storm, air power dominated the entire conflict and defined the ground war on very favorable military terms; but it may not have been possible to make air power independently decisive in that war on terms acceptable to the American or world's publics—to be independently decisive, air power might have had to be more destructive than the war's audience would tolerate for the goals at hand.

Candidate Mission Statements

How might the early advocates and practitioners of air power have defined the mission of the Air Force? Douhet, Mitchell, or Arnold might have put it this way:

> The mission of air power and, hence, the Air Force is to strike decisively at the heart of the enemy through the third dimension.

With hindsight 60 years later, it can be argued that this statement neglects the other important uses of air power besides striking the enemy, other places and things to strike besides the heart of the enemy, and other important outcomes beside decisiveness in war. This statement may have been the right one in the 1930s when airmen were struggling for recognition and independence, but not the 1990s. It is too narrow for what the Air Force has become and for what 60 years of air power history have revealed.

During the apogee of air power theory in the 1950s, the Strategic Air Command (SAC), as the centerpiece of the Air Force, adopted the slogan, "Peace is our profession." It was a way of saying that SAC considered its mission to be successful if its terrible instruments of destruction did not have to be employed—if it kept the peace. It was a means for addressing the dilemma for SAC and its people that for the first time in the air power history, its full employment against an enemy signified the nation's worst nightmare. Although not intended as a mission statement, the slogan could be reasonably interpreted as one. The problems with it were several: Peace was the hope and purpose of *all* military forces, not just SAC; there was nothing unique to the Air Force in saying "Peace is our profession." Moreover, peace was not the profession of those professionals who had to forge the instruments of nuclear deterrence; their profession was to build and maintain the most credible (i.e., ready and survivable) and awesome means for destruction that the world had ever known.

Air Force Chief of Staff, General John P. McConnell,[6] reportedly endorsed the now-familiar slogan:

The mission of the Air Force is to fly and fight.[7]

Sometime later, the next Chief, General John D. Ryan, took pains to put it more gruffly:

The job of the Air Force to fly and to fight—and don't you ever forget it.

Again, these slogans were not intended as mission statements, but as a reminder of where the Air Force, as an institution, should keep its focus. They were intended as sharp counters to the administrative and management attitudes that seemed increasingly to be dominating Air Force concerns and decisions.

But if the job or mission of the Air Force was to fly and to fight, the slogans sent an uncomfortable signal to many in the institution. Only a favored few in the institution were flyers; and even a smaller fraction of people in the institution, including pilots, would ever be called upon to fight. It could and was interpreted by many as a reminder of who was running the Air Force, not what the Air Force was really about.

In October 1991, when General Merrill McPeak was interrogated by the press on the implications of the Air Force reorganization for the career prospects of non-rated (non-pilot) officers, he noted that:

The Air Force does not exist for any other purpose except to defend the United States.[8]

From the context and negative structure of his observation, it is clear that General McPeak was not providing a mission statement for the Air Force. Yet, it is equally clear that this was an excellent opportunity for the Air Force Chief of Staff to restate clearly and concisely the mission of the Air Force. The leadership of an institution should never lose any chance to invoke and restate the mission and vision of their institution. It is the means by which the membership can be reminded of their institution's unique identity and shared purpose. Such invocations can bring the institutional mission and vision to life, relate them explicitly to decisions being made, and unify the membership in their common cause.

The reason that General McPeak did not exploit this opportunity to restate the Air Force mission probably had less to do with the context (press questions about the Air Force reorganization) than with the absence of a coherent and concise mission statement for the Air Force at that time. In the Air Force white paper, *Global Reach—Global Power,*[9] which then served as the institution's highest level and most comprehensive perspective of itself, one cannot find a statement of the Air Force mission but only a recitation of Air Force capabilities. Since the explicit purpose of the white paper was to relate the Air Force to U.S. national security, one would expect it to state somewhere the Air Force mission as a contribution to national security.[10]

Although it would be unfair to hang General McPeak's observation around his neck as a mission statement, it isn't unfair to look for signs of the Air Force mission when he talked about the purpose of the institution, even in passing. Those listening to General McPeak might have been excused if they tried to interpret his words by restructuring them in the form of a positive mission statement along the following lines:

The mission of the Air Force is solely to defend the United States.

The problems with this strawman statement, of course, are that it is neither correct nor unique. The mission of the Air Force is clearly more than defending the United States, no matter how broadly the word, "defend," is construed. And if the word could be stretched to cover everything the Air Force does, then that mission is not unique to the Air Force—all of the military services could lay claim to the same mission.

(General McPeak subsequently came forward with an explicit statement of the mission of the Air Force, acknowledging that,

...strictly speaking, we have never been given a clear statement of the mission.[11]

But that important recognition and its correction came after the third draft of this manuscript and, therefore, is more appropriately addressed in the final chapter.)

Notes

1. Lt. Gen. Charles G. Boyd and Lt. Col. Charles M. Westenhoff, "Air Power Thinking: 'Request Unrestricted Climb,' " *Airpower Journal*, vol. 5, no. 3, (Fall 1991): 9.

2. John L. Frisbee, "Introduction: Men with a Mission," in *Makers of the United States Air Force* (Washington, D.C.: Office of Air Force History, 1987), 2.

3. It is not a contradiction to ask that an institution be committed to purposes higher than itself, anymore than it is to ask a human being to be committed to higher purposes. Although we accept that institutions, like human beings, should have a great interest in their survival and fortunes, that may not be all that we ask of either. The profession of arms asks that an individual be dedicated to the military mission assigned, even, if necessary, unto life itself. Likewise, military services—as implied by the words—are expected to dedicate themselves to their assigned military missions above and before their own survival and fortunes. If a military service is not committed first and foremost to the missions assigned by the nation it serves, then it has become a contradiction in terms.

4. Boyd and Westenhoff, "Air Power Thinking," 5, (emphasis in the original).

5. See Chapter 10 for some of the conflicting views.

6. General McConnell (1908–1986) was Air Force Chief of Staff from 1965 to 1969, during the expansion of the American involvement in the Vietnam War.

7. According to a subsequent chief of staff, Gen. Merrill A. McPeak, in an address, *Does the Air Force Have a Mission?* at Maxwell AFB, Alabama, 19 June 1992.

8. As reported in a correction in *Aerospace Daily*, October 23, 1991, 129B. Two days earlier, in the same publication (p. 110), General McPeak had been reported as setting

...reporters straight about his widely-reported desire to put fighter pilots in all key positions in the Air Force. The service's purpose, he says, is to generate combat capability that protects the country, and not necessarily to "provide equal career opportunities" for those who fly heavies, or, heaven forbid, don't wear wings at all.

The corrected remarks read as follows:

The Air Force does not exist for any other purpose except to defend the United States. It doesn't exist to provide equitable career tracks for everybody in the Air Force. That's not our mission.

9. USAF White Paper, *The Air Force and U.S. National Security: Global Reach—Global Power*, Office of the Secretary of the Air Force, Washington, D.C., June 1990.

10. A closer examination of *Global Reach—Global Power* is undertaken in the next chapter, in connection with the Air Force vision.

11. McPeak, *Does the Air Force Have a Mission?* 3.

23

From Mission to Vision

> *In general, an occupation pays enough to fill the job and to get it done—no more. An effective manager in an occupation prevails on workers to do what they are supposed to do; an effective leader in an institution motivates members to do more than they are supposed to do.*[1]

> *Policies and strategies must be consistent with the vision articulated by leaders, and leaders must build commitment to that vision among members at all levels. [T]he key question is whether that vision approximates the institutional or the occupational image of military culture.*[2]

Is It Global Reach—Global Power?

Just before Operation Desert Shield, the Air Force fired the opening gun in its own restructuring process—a process that continues as this is being written. The first shot was an Air Force white paper, *The Air Force and U.S. National Security: Global Reach—Global Power*, dated June 1990. Several things made the paper stand out against the background of its time:

- It came from the highest levels of Air Force leadership[3] as a statement of its perceptions and policies.

- It served to fill, partially, the apparent vacuum identified in *A View of the Air Force Today* about the fate of the Air Force as an institution.

- Its short title, *Global Reach—Global Power*, caught on as an apt motto or slogan for the Air Force and its role in the future.

- It was decidedly up-beat at a time of fiscal bleakness and institutional uncertainty.

At the very least, it was a soothing and reassuring balm to a troubled Air Force constituency. At best, it was a bold bid to define the Air Force's central role in the future of the nation's security.

Under the circumstances, it is not surprising that *Global Reach— Global Power* should be seen differently by different people, in and out of the Air Force. Some saw it as the long-awaited vision for the Air Force. Some saw in it the Air Force mission defined. More expansively, some could see an emerging strategy for the nation's future security. Perhaps others could find in it a new theory of air power—a nation with global interests would need to reach out globally and exercise its power; and that could best be accomplished with air power.

Given that potential, *Global Reach—Global Power* deserves careful examination. Has it redefined air power? Does it hold the seeds of a new theory for air power? Does it provide a new vision of the Air Force? To answer those kinds of questions, I will resort to analysis rather than summary judgments of the paper. Hence, I have undertaken a content analysis of the paper identical to those I have previously made for *The Maritime Strategy*[4] and *A View of the Air Force Today*.[5]

Here, then, is an abstract of the ideas found in *Global Reach—Global Power*:[6]

THE AIR FORCE & U.S. NATIONAL SECURITY:
GLOBAL REACH—GLOBAL POWER

The world security environment is changing dramatically, requiring that we rethink the role of military forces in the future. Although the future security environment is highly uncertain, it is not likely to be tranquil. The nation's interests are global in a world where weapons are proliferating and becoming more sophisticated. Thus, the prospects for U.S. military forces to be employed in a lethal environment is high, but the time and place are highly uncertain.

U.S. NATIONAL SECURITY STRATEGY

The U.S. security objectives, the instruments to support them, and the elements of our defense strategy remain unchanged. The *National Security Strategy of the United States* (March 1990) places deterrence of nuclear attack as our first priority; but our worldwide commitments and interests in Europe, the Pacific, the Persian Gulf, and around the world will drive our force requirements.

The risk of global war will remain low; but in balancing our forces we can not assume that nothing or everything has changed. Stable nuclear deterrence will depend upon arms control; but that stability can be threatened by nuclear proliferation. Our conventional forces will be focused on deterring and containing local conflicts rather than continuous presence or occupation in the world's trouble spots.

Quality Forces: Quality forces, particularly quality people, are our first priority. Advanced technology rather than large forces has been the hallmark of American military forces; we will continue to exploit technology to maintain our decisive advantage, reduce our casualties, and avoid being surprised. Investing in our aerospace technology also helps the nation compete economically.

THE U.S. AIR FORCE & THE EVOLVING SECURITY ENVIRONMENT

Each of our services contributes unique capabilities; but the Air Force is committed to orchestrating its forces and operations so as to complement those of the other services. The focus on a European conflict during the past 40 years may have obscured how the Air Force contributes across the spectrum of conflict. Across the spectrum of conflict, from wartime to peacetime, the Air Force works independently and in concert with the other services, allied forces, and security partners.

The strengths of the Air Force are its inherent speed, range, flexibility, precision, and lethality, which will be drawn upon and exploited to support the following objectives as a planning framework:

- sustain deterrence,
- provide versatile combat force,
- supply rapid global mobility,
- control the high ground, and
- build U.S. influence.

SUSTAIN DETERRENCE—NUCLEAR FORCES

Although strategic nuclear forces will be limited in size by treaty, the Soviets are vigorously modernizing theirs, so we must continue to develop and deploy forces that can sustain our confidence in deterrence into the future. A balanced and modernized triad of strategic nuclear forces is fundamental to effective deterrence because of the unique and complementary character of each leg. A fundamental goal is stability against first strike; therefore, we are modernizing our bomber force, reducing the warhead densities for our fixed base missiles, and pursuing strategic defenses.

Theater nuclear forces extend nuclear deterrence and provide for flexible response and air launched capabilities.

PROVIDE VERSATILE COMBAT FORCE

Our objectives in the conventional conflict arena will increasingly require that our forces be fast, flexible, and powerful so that we can deal with regional conflicts effectively. Although the threat of a major European conflict with the Warsaw Pact is diminished, the instabilities in Europe could produce other kinds of conflicts which will argue for our continued involvement in the European security framework.

Reserve components are an economical hedge against the emergence of a major threat from the Soviets or elsewhere; but they are no panacea; and adequate active forces of the highest quality will be required.

THEATER OPERATIONS & POWER PROJECTION

The speed, range, and flexibility of the Air Force allows it to concentrate force in a responsive manner over great distances, thereby changing the military and/ or political conditions that necessitated the response.

Joint/Combined Operations with Ground Forces: The main objectives of joint surface-air operations are to impair the enemy's resistance, freedom of action, and scheme of operations while enhancing ours and shaping the battlefield to our advantage. As their first priority, however, theater air forces carry out those functions which afford the greatest opportunity for conclusive accomplishment of the theater mission.

In theater operations, the Air Force conducts air superiority, close air support, battlefield air interdiction, and interdiction. Because of their flexibility and striking power, air forces can be decisive and have a strategic impact on theater operations. Theater airlift provides flexibility to deliver, reinforce, and resupply forces where they are most needed. The Air Force may also support allied ground forces, whether or not U.S. ground forces are engaged.

Presence and Direct Application of Force: Although the other services will be required for power projection, the Air Force will usually provide the President with the quickest, longest range response available. Long range bombers can project massive power within hours anywhere on the globe with precision and low risks of losses—and, if necessary, without forward bases or overflight rights. Long range bombers may be the only means for projecting power or enhancing presence quickly in many places on the globe.

Forward-based tactical air forces are also capable of providing a day-to-day presence and projecting power anywhere in the world on short notice. Although land-based tactical fighters require forward bases to sustain power projection, such bases have historically been made available by our allies in crises.

The rapid response capabilities of the Air Force also enable other forces to respond quickly, as in the movement of airborne troops, contributing to their success and reducing casualties.

Complementary Air Force and Naval Operations: The Navy and Air Force can complement each other in establishing presence and projecting power—with respect to relative advantages in responsiveness and endurance or in the provision of air defense capabilities. They can also complement each other in providing defense suppression, air superiority, and offensive strike capabilities.

Land-based air provides unique capabilities in maritime operations in the form of long range surveillance and mine delivery. History has shown that land-based air has a significant potential to contribute to sea control.

Special Operations/Low-Intensity Conflict: The Air Force is committed to supporting special operations and providing certain specialized assets; many Air Force conventional capabilities are essential to special operations and low-intensity conflict. The Air Force is committed to supporting the anti-drug effort with a variety of assets and capabilities.

SUPPLY RAPID GLOBAL MOBILITY—AIRLIFT AND TANKERS

As forward-based forces decline but global interests remain, the importance of airlift will grow. Airlift and sealift are complementary, not competitive. When operations must be carried out quickly, airlift will be the key player, as exemplified by OPERATION JUST CAUSE. The importance of timeliness is illustrated by the airlifted resupply of Israel during the 1973 Arab-Israeli War.

With reduced forward bases, aerial tankers are increasingly important assets, not only for Air Force operations, but also for those of sister services and allied air operations. Air Force aerial refueling capabilities during OPERATION EARNEST WILL (the Tanker War in the Persian Gulf) permitted the Navy carriers to stand off farther from potential threats; and during OPERATION JUST CAUSE they accelerated the airlift by reducing or eliminating transport refueling times on the ground at their destinations.

CONTROL THE HIGH GROUND—SPACE & C3I SYSTEMS

Technology has made air the high ground over the last 75 years; in the future, it will increasingly be space. Space technology provides for global knowledge and situational awareness. Space systems are vulnerable to only the most sophisticated threats; and even those vulnerabilities are declining with the changing relationship between the United States and the Soviet Union. The reliability, endurance, survivability, and autonomy of space systems make them cost-effective for many warfighting capabilities.

We need to insure our access to space with space launching capabilities, to deny space to our adversaries with anti-satellite capabilities, and achieve wide area surveillance capabilities for support of our global military operations. The Air Force is well postured to provide, as it has in the past, most of DoD's space systems.

Airborne surveillance and communications capabilities, such as AWACS and JSTARS, complement our space capabilities for the battle commander.

BUILDING U.S. INFLUENCE:
STRENGTHENING SECURITY PARTNERS & RELATIONSHIPS

The Air Force is well postured to contribute to security assistance by supporting the operations and supplying the equipment needs of our security partners. Training and logistics aid are often acceptable security assistance even when other forms of influence are not; training other nation's pilots is a cost effective way to provide influence and to keep our training base ready to surge, if necessary. Our airlift is an important tool for good will and humanitarian assistance in disaster relief, with dividends in strengthening our allies and influencing security-related events.

Long-range surveillance aircraft provide for deterrence even when other forms of presence or force are not appropriate or possible. Land-based aircraft have proven to be the most effective than any other kinds of force in resolving crises without war; and aerospace forces will become even more important in the future.

CONCLUSIONS

The Air Force is focusing on changing security needs, not just on changing fiscal constraints. The United States is the world's foremost aerospace power; and the Air Force is a partner with the nation's aerospace industry in that power. The Air Force is building the forces and capabilities—complementing each other and those of its sister services—as needed for the future nation's security. The Air Force sees a window of opportunity to become even more useful to the nation through its unique capabilities to provide global reach and global power.

What Is Global Reach—Global Power?

On the basis of this abstract of *Global Reach—Global Power*, what can be said about the nature of the document?

- Most of all, it is about *current* Air Force *capabilities* and air power *attributes*—not so much about what they should be as about what they are.

- Strikingly, it presents a perspective of the nation's interests and security needs which are extensions of the past, but projected into a future world environment that is admittedly, uncertainly different.

- It briefly declares priorities only with respect to Air Force people and technology—aspects whose importance is not reinforced elsewhere in the document or supported by its balance.

- It declares the attributes of air power that should be revered and preserved.

- It devotes most of its attention to restating the traditional spectrum of Air Force missions.

If there is a vision of the Air Force in *Global Reach—Global Power*, it is one of an institution which:

- identifies itself proudly in terms of its present spectrum of capabilities and

- sets its purposes on retaining and improving those capabilities for an uncertain world where it will play an even more central role in the nation's security.

If *Global Reach—Global Power* redefines air power, it is air power doing what it has done before, only better and more essential to the nation's security in the changing world environment. The missions undertaken by the Air Force in the future will be what they have been in the past, but their balance may shift with the reduction in overseas presence of U.S. forces and the changes in the Cold War threat. No missions will go away; no new missions will be assumed by the Air Force.

Perhaps the short title of the document will be its greatest, most durable contribution. *Global Reach—Global Power* captures something that seems new and pertinent to air power in the future. Air power has finally achieved evident and routine global reach—not just through the aerial refueling of bombers, fighters, and airlifters, but also through the reach of intercontinental ballistic missiles and global nets of spacecraft. And the desire to apply such power anywhere on the globe, if not simultaneously globally, seems to be independent of the uncertainties about the changing world and the nation's interests.

The Quest for an Air Force Vision

Just as a theory can be the basis for a mission; a mission can be the basis for a vision. The original institutional vision of the Air Force—evolving from air power theory and the mission of forging air power according to that theory—was that an intrepid band of aviators could control the decisive weapons of war—the airplane and the atomic bomb—in a force that would eclipse all other military forces, in importance, size, funding, and esteem. That vision fractured with the advent of alternative means (missile and space systems) to provide decisive weapons of war and with the realization that the atomic bomb was not, after all, a politically usable weapon short of Armageddon.

Recognizing the importance of a vision to the institutional health of the Air Force, its Chief of Staff, General Merrill McPeak, addressed the subject at a meeting of the Air Force's senior leadership (i.e., the "CORONA" conference) in November 1991. General McPeak defined a vision as "a compelling image of the future...advanced by leaders," who share it with the community they expect to support it, with the purpose of determining direction. Such a vision, he argued, should answer three questions:

1. What is the purpose and meaning of our efforts?

2. What do we really want to be?

3. What's important around here?

In addition, it had to be "developed by leaders, shared and supported, and positive and inspiring." General McPeak argued that "It is not enough to have a vision. You must *intend* to carry it through. Intention involves having the stomach to bring a vision into reality. Intention is a sheer act of will." He then proposed the following statement for an Air Force vision:

> Air Force people building the world's most respected air and space force...global power and reach for America.[7]

Secretary of the Air Force, Donald B. Rice, in amplifying this vision statement, distinguished between visions, slogans, and missions:

> A vision is a picture of the future—more than a slogan, it's what we want to be. Our mission describes what business we're in and why. The vision determines our direction. It's the way things could be, our best possible future, and tells the organization what to care about in order to reach that future.[8]

The vision statement set forth by the Air Force leadership contains the two essential elements uncovered by Peter Vaill in his study of high-performing organizations:[9] A unique sense of identity (who are we?) and a shared sense of purpose (what are we about?). The unique sense of identity and shared sense of purpose are both to be found in the same phrase, "people building the world's most respected air and space force." But *effective* visions demand more than those two minimum essential elements.

In a study of the role of visions in helping military organizations to adapt to changing environments, Setear, et al.,[10] offered four additional criteria for effective institutional visions:

> First, a vision must be *inspirational*: The sense of identity and purpose provided by the vision must be one that is inherently attractive to those that the organization would like to enlist as its converts or benefactors. Such a vision draws suitable personnel to the organization, and inspires them to excellence after they have joined the organization. In addition, a suitably inspirational

organizational vision presents a positive image to those outside the organization (such as...members of a congressional subcommittee) who determine what external resources (such as...budgetary appropriations) the organization will have available.....

Second, an organizational vision must be *relevant* and *realistic* with respect to the challenges and opportunities that confront the organization. A vision that does not help to solve the problems members of an organization face each day will be discarded as sloganeering. A vision that clearly cannot be fulfilled or, if fulfilled, cannot contribute in the prevailing circumstances, will also ultimately fail to serve the organization..... Selecting a vision that is appropriate to (or slightly ahead of) its time...is one of the hallmarks of great leadership.

Third, a vision must be *clear* and *distinctive* in its discrimination of the unique identity and purpose of the organization. If the sense of identity and purpose provided by an organizational vision does not set the organization apart from others—from its competitors and even from its companions—then there is no reference frame for the organization's decisions. Every blur of distinction in identity and purpose invites mimicry and, hence, a loss of the opportunity for leadership.

Fourth, a vision must be *pervasive* and *stable*, *widely shared* and *understood* inside (and, ideally, even outside) the organization. If the vision is not known or understood, it cannot be the basis for decisions and actions. An inspiring and relevant vision that exists only in the mind of the organization's leader may be useful under ideal conditions; but the power of an organizational vision lies in its ability to serve the organization under less-than-ideal conditions, particularly in those times of stress when an organization must depend on all of its members to detect and implement change. At the same time, a vision that changes each month with the mood of an organization's top leader will not be able to soak through the ranks of an organization to guide the myriad of decisions that are made by those far from the...Pentagon's outer ring.

All four of these attributes are essential. We can imagine circumstances where all but one of these attributes would be satisfied, and yet the vision would not be suitable. We cannot imagine any suitable vision where one of these attributes could be missing.....

Some of these four additional criteria are specifically addressed by General McPeak when he says that a vision must be "developed by leaders, shared and supported, and positive and inspiring;" but it is less clear that they will be met by the Air Force's proposed vision statement. The Air Force is without any doubt already "the world's most respected air and space force." The Air Force already possesses global power and reach. Thus, the image projected is not one of the future, but of the present. Yet would the vision be inspiring if it read, "Air Force people *maintaining* the world's most respected air and space force...global power and reach for America"?

Secretary Rice acknowledges that problem when he says of the vision statement:

> We are the best Air Force in the world today. But we want to keep improving the definition of the best, then beat it and define it anew. If we are to stay the best, we must keep striving for new ways of becoming the best, most respected Air Force. We must continually improve and innovate because we know potential adversaries are doing the same thing.[11]

In the above quote, if one replaced the words, "Air Force," with "computer company," it would sound even more appropriate as an exhortation to the company's employees. This sounds like a fill-in-the-blank business manager's speech, not one from the leader of a military institution to military professionals. The call is to be better, do better, at what we already are and have done. This is a call for workers to do the best possible job against the competition, not a call for an altruistic devotion or commitment to the profession of arms which transcends the institution. This is a businessman's vision of the Air Force.

The deeper problem with the vision advanced by Secretary Rice and General McPeak is that it focuses on *internal* purposes more than external or altruistic purposes. Being the world's most respected air and space force may serve the ambitions of the Air Force more than the American public which must support it. Contrast that ambition with the one offered by the original air power theory—to strike decisively at the enemy through the third dimension—thereby avoiding the public's nightmare of a bloody, stalemated ground war. That was a noble purpose which might justify risking an airman's life—the ultimate sacrifice of the profession of arms. Should we, would we, ask Air Force people to risk their lives to build "the world's most respected air and space force...global power and reach for America"?

Possessing global power and reach, while appealing to the Air Force, may or may not always be what America wants most from its Air Force or wants to pay for. There may be times when the American public will want to be protected or to protect a nearby friend much more than it wants the global power or reach *already* provided by the Air Force. Thus, the proposed vision poses several risks:

- It may not be sufficiently visionary (future oriented) because its aims could be seen as having already been achieved.

- It may not be sufficiently inspiring because it focuses more on the ends of the institution than the ends of those who must support it. It lacks the kind of altruism that enlists people in higher causes than the survival or betterment of their own institution. Such altruism may not be necessary in a commercial enterprise, but it is essential to the profession of arms.

- It may not be stable against the changing interests of the American public which the Air Force serves. It presumes that what the American public will steadfastly want most from its Air Force in the future is global power and reach—the same capabilities from which the Air Force currently draws its pride and ambitions.

(Subsequently, these indictments of *Global Reach—Global Power* and the Air Force vision seem to have been at least partly sustained by General McPeak when he acknowledged:

> So, *Global Reach, Global Power*, and the Air Force "vision"…may have caused confusion become some will have concluded that one or the other of them is a mission statement for the Air Force. But that is not the case. They were not meant to be mission statements and they do not, in fact, describe in a clear, simple, straightforward way, what it is that we are supposed to be doing.[12]

That explanation clarifies what the two documents are not, but it does not explain how they could be written without addressing the Air Force mission. Indeed, if the Air Force vision was to meet the first of the criteria for visions set forth by General McPeak—What is the purpose and meaning of our efforts?—the Air Force mission could hardly be avoided. The answer, of course, is that the two documents were written before General McPeak directly confronted the question of the Air Force mission.)[13]

Notes

1. Charles C. Moskos and Frank R. Wood, eds., *The Military: More Than Just A Job?* (Washington, D.C.: Pergamon-Brasseys, 1988), 5.

2. Frank R. Wood, "At the Cutting Edge of Institutional and Occupational Trends: The US Air Force Officer Corps," in Moskos and Wood, *The Military*, 46.

3. The paper was written in the Secretariat and coordinated through the Chief.

4. See *Masks of War*, 82–85.

5. See Chapter 1 of this manuscript.

What is the HF vision ! mission ?

6. The headings are as found in the original. The abstract has been reviewed by one of the authors of the original paper to ensure that its ideas have been fairly represented.

7. This statement of the Air Force vision was subsequently published over the signature of Donald B. Rice, Secretary of the Air Force, in *Policy Letter*, from the Washington D.C. Office of the Secretary of the Air Force, Department of the Air Force (December 1991), 1.

8. Ibid.

9. Vaill, "The Purposing of High-Performing Systems."

10. John Setear, et al., *The Army in a Changing World: The Role of Organizational Vision*, RAND R-3882-A (Santa Monica, Calif.: June 1990), 19–21, (emphasis added here).

11. Rice, *Policy Letter*, 1.

12. McPeak, *Does the Air Force Have a Mission?* 4.

13. *Global Reach—Global Power* was published in June 1990. The Air Force vision appeared in December 1991. General McPeak finally addressed and proposed an Air Force mission statement in June 1992.

24

A Theory to Fly By

*Understanding our mission will help by giving us a
steady compass bearing to get through this heavy
weather and into the clear.[1]*

*Professionals from all the services will increasingly
study air power as a catalyst and prerequisite to
other military means, just as policymakers will view
air power as a key that opens and closes the doors
of many strategy and policy options.[2]*

The Burden of Mission

The central problem for Air Force leadership today is dedication to
mission above all things—above the institution, its budget, force structure, airplanes, pilots, people, or occupations. Those are all means to the
end of the institution, which must be its mission. And it is the leadership
that must be dedicated to mission if they expect the rank and file to be
professionals at arms.

The profession of arms can not flourish in an institution whose first
priorities are budgets, maintaining force structure, acquiring and flying
airplanes, personal relationships and loyalties, or a particular avocation.
If there is to be a profession of arms, there first must be a total and resolute
commitment to the military mission, above all other things. And that
military mission must embody service to others, beyond one's self,
and—for the American military heritage—beyond one's own institution.

The foremost challenges for the Air Force and its leadership today
center on its mission, not its budget, force structure, or modernization
programs, important as they may be. The mission needs to be defined (or
redefined), then nurtured (developed and kept viable), and finally enshrined (revered and honored).

If the Air Force mission is effectively redefined so as to be rationalized with history and future trends, less chauvinistic in its claims and demands, and embracing rather than discriminating among its contributors and practitioners, then the Air Force leadership has a fair chance at creating a vibrant, committed military institution. General McPeak put it this way:

> We need a mission that unifies all our people, that defines what makes us special, that can inspire, can make sacrifice seem worthwhile.[3]

To seize that opportunity, however, the Air Force leadership will have to adopt a demanding regimen:

- It must consistently attend to the alignment of the mission with a changing world of technology and military challenges.

- It must be loyal to the mission above things or people.

- It must associate or identify its actions and decisions with the mission.

- It must promote and reward people according to the mission.

If that regimen can be adopted, then the profession of arms should find a flourishing climate.

Defining a profession, let alone the profession of arms, can be more frustrating than revealing. It may be sufficient to separate the profession of arms from other professions on but one aspect: on the unreserved commitment to a lawfully assigned mission, *even at the risk of deliberately giving and taking human life*. Even those in the military whose lives are not directly at risk in hazardous or combat operations, but who support those who are at risk, should be professionals at arms, for their actions, too, ultimately may lead to the deliberate giving and taking of human lives.

Given that awesome responsibility, the true professional at arms, regardless of position or specialization, regardless of proximity to the hazards, cannot be deflected from the commitment to mission above all else—if necessary, even above personal safety, career, and associations. To be sure, not all military personnel will choose to be professionals at arms, but that choice has nothing to do with their skills, specializations, or assignments; it is about their acceptance of a prior and overriding commitment to mission. There may be places in modern military institutions for people who choose not to be professionals at arms—perhaps because of some technical specialty—but those places are not in the military institution's leadership; their responsibility is too high for anything less than a total commitment to mission.

If the leaders are not committed to mission, they can hardly complain if their followers are not. Thus, the trustees of the state of the profession of arms in the military are properly its leaders; they fulfill that trusteeship by their evident commitment to the institution's mission over everything else, including their careers, avocations, friends, and even their institution itself.

The distinctions between the imperatives of business and the profession of arms in defining the military ethos are nicely summarized by Frank Wood:

> Attempting any specification of a military ethos...would be inappropriate here; one can only offer some general observations regarding a desirable emphasis. National contingencies and traditions vary considerably but, whatever the specifics, the emphasis would be on a morality of military service that is
>
> - nation-centered, not organization-centered;
> - mission-centered, not career-centered;
> - group-centered, not individual-centered;
> - service-centered, not work-centered.
>
> Traditionally, these values have been emphasized in military creeds and culture. Military leaders have always sought to bring them to life in the armed forces, and the best leaders are still seeking them today.[4]

Those values are centered on a commitment to mission—a mission of national service—not on the institution, career, or self. It should be apparent that the Air Force has its institutional work cut out for it, because

> ...absent a clear understanding of overarching purposes, some people give their loyalty to the next best thing—their particular job or their equipment...., We all recognize this problem as occupationalism. It's what can happen when an institution does not convey a sense of mission to its people.[5]

A Proposed Mission Statement

Considering all that has been said up to this point, I would offer and defend the following mission statement:

The mission of the Air Force is the military control and exploitation of the aerospace continuum in support of the national interests.[6]

On seeing these words, one active Air Force officer observed, in part:

Few would disagree with your statement; but this looks like an academic's idea of the Air Force mission. Most people won't relate to a word like "continuum." It doesn't have the simplicity of *Global Reach—Global Power*.

I could only agree with him. I am an academic; I am concerned with precision in conveying ideas, not with how they should be phrased for popular appeal. I must leave the packaging to others who are better qualified in such things. What follows is an academic defense of the ideas and choices of words in my proposed mission statement.

The central idea behind my mission statement is that each of the military services serves the nation by controlling and exploiting a particular medium. For the Navy, that medium is the maritime environment. For the Army, it is the land environment. For the Marines, it is the land-sea interface. And for the Air Force, it is the aerospace environment.

I deliberately chose the word, *continuum*, instead of environment to stress the unity of the air and space environments in Air Force operations.[7] It represents my explicit intent to integrate air and space operations in the mission of the Air Force; space has been a stepchild too long. By the word, *aerospace*, I would avoid any separation or distinction between air and space in priorities, preferences, or budgets—the things people will look to for clues about favoritism.

The verbs, *control* and *exploit*, include, but go well beyond combat operations. They admit that the Air Force may serve the national interest—as expressed by the president as commander in chief of the nation's military forces—by operations that have nothing to do with combat, such as humanitarian and disaster assistance. Control and exploit admit both defensive and offensive combat operations. Those verbs also admit air and space operations by the Air Force in support of its sister services and of friends or allies.

Is it necessary to qualify those verbs with the adverb, *military*? I would argue that some of the nation's interests in controlling and exploiting the aerospace continuum might also be served by commercial ventures, such as the nation's airlines, aerospace industries, telecommunications utilities, and civil institutions (e.g., NASA and COMSAT). The Air Force, as a military service, provides for *military* control and exploitation of the aerospace continuum, a mission which is and ought to be distinguished from *civil* control and exploitation of those media.

Is the mission of the Air Force media-specific (the aerospace continuum) rather than task-specific (strike, defend, etc.)? I would argue that it is or ought to be. The tasks or the operations of the Air Force should be open-ended and changing over time, limited or constrained by only four parameters:

1. **Media:** Tasks or operations that are associated with control or exploitation of the aerospace continuum.

2. **National interest:** Tasks or operations that serve the national interests— survival, security, well-being, prosperity, etc.

3. **Military:** Tasks or operations that require military personnel and their equipment because of dangers, risks, or unique assets.

4. **Law:** Tasks or operations that conform to the American constitution and domestic laws governing the military, as well as to the international treaties and laws governing the military.[8]

Is that mission statement so broad that it would dilute the focus of the Air Force? I would argue that the Air Force has been over-focused on airplanes—on *combat* airplanes, on *manned* combat airplanes, on *fast* manned combat airplanes—to the detriment of many systems and capabilities it should have if it is truly committed to serving the nation's interests rather than the interests of military pilots. The nation's interests in the future, as in the past, are likely to be better served by the diversity than by the scale of capabilities offered by the Air Force.

(Subsequently, General McPeak offered this mission statement: "Our mission is to defend the United States through control and exploitation of air and space."[9] I like the verbs, "control and exploitation," and the brevity of the statement. I think that "defend the United States" is too narrow a definition of military missions now and, increasingly, in the future; but, interpreted broadly, General McPeak's statement can be helpful to the profession of arms within the Air Force and, hence, to the institution.)

A Proposed Vision

Would my mission statement—the military control and exploitation of the aerospace continuum in support of the national interests—provide a better basis for an Air Force vision? The essential elements of a vision for a high-performing organization—i.e., a unique sense of identity and a shared sense of purpose—can both be found within this mission statement:

- As to the sense of unique identity as an institution, the Air Force is the only American military institution *exclusively* devoted to military operations in the aerospace continuum. The other military services may indeed conduct operations in the air environment while pursuing their surface-oriented missions, but only the Air Force is devoted to controlling and exploiting the aerospace continuum for the nation's interests—where those interests can best or only be pursued through the aerospace continuum.

- As to the sense of shared purpose within the institution, the purpose of the Air Force is to provide the nation with an unsurpassed spectrum and quality of capabilities it may need to pursue its interests through the military control and exploitation of the aerospace continuum.

It is as this point that the Air Force's white paper, *Global Power— Global Reach*, could contribute to the vision by describing the spectrum and quality of Air Force capabilities. To be complete, however, it should also include some statement of mission or purpose.

Military control and exploitation of the aerospace continuum in support of the national interests is not the same as "global power and reach for America." Global power and reach may or may not be necessary to control or exploit the aerospace continuum in support of the nation's interests, depending on what the nation's interests may be at any point in the future. Some of the nation's interests may require only local power and reach in controlling and exploiting the aerospace continuum. My formulation of the Air Force mission:

- allows that the nation's interests may vary over time and region;

- ties the Air Force to any degree of control and exploitation of the aerospace environment demanded by its supporters, the American public; and

- does not limit the nation's interest in the Air Force to its abilities to exercise global power or reach, neither of which are fundamental to why nations all around the world have air forces. Nations have air forces because they enable those nations to do something they could not do with any other kind of force—control and exploit their air (if not aerospace) environments to the ends of their governments.

This reasoning leads me to a vision statement something like the following:

> The Air Force is America's only military service exclusively devoted to military operations in the aerospace environment and is, therefore, dedicated to providing unsurpassed capabilities for the nation to pursue its interests through the military control and exploitation of the aerospace continuum.

This leaves the question of "Why?" Why should anyone care whether or not the "Air Force is America's only military service exclusively devoted to military operations in the aerospace environment"? Why should anyone care about dedicating themselves "to providing unsurpassed capabilities for the nation to pursue its interests through the military control and exploitation of the aerospace continuum"?

It is at this point that theory pays off. Suppose one were to have asked the early air power theorists why anyone should care about striking decisively at the heart of the enemy through the third dimension. The answer would have been instant:

> Because that is the way to avoid your worst nightmare of a stalemated, bloody war. To strike at the heart of the enemy without fighting your way across the ground, without inviting the nightmare, you have to strike through the third dimension, and that means air power. And if the strike is to be decisive, it must be centrally and independently controlled by airmen, not by surface commanders.

That answer flows directly and easily from a theory—from the theory of air power as it was formulated in the 1920s. It explains what air power does that is unique, why that form of power is important to those who must support it, and how that form of power must be organized and controlled. That is the enormous contribution of theory; and that is why air power theory is so important to the fate of the Air Force as an institution.

Thus, if a vision is to invite dedication to some higher mission or purpose, there has to be some theory (or hypothesis) that justifies the enterprise. The original vision of air power was underwritten by a theory which justified air power, which made the enterprise worthwhile, which made it worth caring about, *whether one was a buyer or seller*. If air power is to be redefined so as to provide an effective mission and vision for the Air Force of the future, it will have to have its roots in a theory—in a reason why anyone should care about the Air Force, its mission, and its vision.

A Theory to Fly By

If the mission of the Air Force is the military control and exploitation of the aerospace continuum to support the nation's interest, then an air force would seem to need, among several other things, global reach as a means for applying global power to national ends. But it might need much more than that; and the relative importance of "speed, range, flexibility, precision, and lethality" (or other, less frequently cited attributes such as presence, visibility, resolution, capacity, etc.) may vary considerably as world events unfold.

The future may or may not unfold as implied by *Global Reach—Global Power:* a world which changes more than our nation, but still a world dominated by the nation-states in the model of the past two centuries. Even if that were the *most probable* future, it will probably not *be* the future. Where there are many possible futures, the most probable future is less likely than the advent of *any* one of its many alternatives.[10] The alternatives include changes in the interests of the American society and nation and in the nature of the world order or disorder now evolving, but not contemplated in *Global Reach—Global Power.*

The possibilities of great changes in the interests of the American society, in the political structure of the world, in the nation-state as the locus of power in the world, and in the degrees of chaos or order in the world seem too high to ignore in redefining air power at this time. Air power needs to be redefined independently of these uncertainties. It needs to be a truth about the nature of power in the world that transcends the directions of the American society, its nation-state, and the future order of the world. It ought to be a form of power whose attributes become only more valuable as the world becomes more uncertain. Air power should be the most attractive instrument for dealing with a world that could spin off in almost any direction—one that is more orderly or more chaotic, one in which power blocs form or dissolve, one in which wars are more or less likely, and even ones in which the American society's interests are more truculent or pacific than in the past.

If air power were to be redefined on a single perspective of the future, then a wager has been made. If the perspective turns out to have been prescient, then the wager could have a high payoff. History offers many examples of leaders who perceived the future correctly and made their wagers. Those who saw the future incorrectly have largely been lost to history, and their failures relegated to the dustbins of history instead of its pedestals. Air Force leadership, in redefining air power, must adopt a perception of the future. The more narrow and specific that perception, the greater the risks of failure, but the greater the payoffs if they get it right. Hap Arnold was one who got it right for the 40-year Cold War that followed his leadership of the Air Force.

My views of the future and its uncertainty have been presented in Chapters 20 and 21. Two aspects of that future stand out for me as realities rooted in the present: Commerce has gone global and nations have lost control of their borders. I would be willing to bet on those aspects—much more than the constancy of American security interests—in redefining air power. I believe that those two aspects will dominate the shape of the future, making a much more disorderly, chaotic world which the United States can neither completely control nor completely avoid.

Such worlds, even if not attractive to national leaderships or accepted by them, are likely to make air power the military instrument of choice for those who retain and exercise military power. In a chaotic world, the aerospace continuum will offer power elites three unique attributes not available through any other military force: *universal access, vantage point,* and *speed* to bring military power—both force and infrastructures—to bear upon situations and adversaries, both of which may know no borders. This kind of access, vantage point, and speed can not be afforded through either the land or sea media. Controlling and exploiting the aerospace continuum will become the most omnipresent and omnipotent means for the exercise of power for peace or war where the imposition of neither is any longer certain.

It seems to me that a theory of air power should not rest upon the fate of the nation-state, the preferences of national leaderships, or the attractiveness of the future to the American (or any other) society.[11] To let it so rest would be to mortgage the theory to wishes. It should rest upon the broad outlines of what is evidently happening to the world and what air power will bring to that world in the ways that military power can be wielded in the interests of those who possess it. That theory should appeal to those who have the resources and courage to convert it into practice—quite irrespective of history or heritage. Thus, my candidate for a theory of air power goes something like this:

> In the emerging, less controllable world of global commerce and borderless nations, the military medium of dominance and, hence, of choice to power elites will be the aerospace continuum because of its universal, rapid access and unique vantage point. Hence, the control and exploitation of that medium, more than any other, will offer the widest range of military options and the highest degree of military power.

Will the aerospace continuum *really* be the dominant military medium? After all, most of the world's commerce, including military logistics, moves by sea, and nothing implies that will drastically change in the foreseeable future. But the dominant medium for the *military*, is not necessarily the dominant medium for *commerce*, just as the dominant terrain for the soldier may be the high ground rather than the valley floor where the commerce or fertile field is found. For the military, the preferred medium will be the one that affords the most favorable access and vantage point for bringing military power to bear in all of its pertinent forms.

In a world where access to other points on the surface may be increasingly jeopardized by intervening regions of disorder or hostility, the third dimension may be the most confident, secure, and rapid means for access. In a world of widespread political disorder and conflict, the third dimension may also be the most confident and secure vantage point for observing and then discriminatingly applying military power. Thus, even as the relative powers of the nation-states decline, there is more rather than less to suggest that air power has become the military instrument of choice for coping with the new disorder of a world undergoing revolutionary change.

I began this manuscript with praise for theory and now would end it with a different kind of praise: Theory does not have to be absolutely correct or timeless to serve human enterprise well. Theory is seldom completely correct or immune to the new knowledge that time brings. But theory provides a basis for directed action that can benefit human enterprise even though it is not quite correct or permanent. The fields of science and technology are defined by such less-than-perfect theories as the stepping stones to progress.

By today's standards, the original air power theory was not completely correct or enduring. But it made a powerful and, I believe, an essential contribution to several successful human enterprises, including the winning of wars and the independence of air power from surface forces. A redefined theory of air power need not be perfect or permanent, but it should inspire people to join in a directed human enterprise that they can and want to believe in—one that is worthy of the profession of arms and, if called upon, the risking of lives. That is the most important legacy of air power theory. When redefined, that will be its greatest promise.

Notes

1. McPeak, *Does the Air Force Have a Mission?* 9, 10.

2. Boyd and Westenhoff, "Air Power Thinking," 9, 10.

3. Ibid., 11.

4. Wood, "At the Cutting Edge of Institutional and Occupational Trends," 53.

5. McPeak, *Does the Air Force Have a Mission?* 3.

6. I am indebted to my friend and colleague, David J. Stein, now with the Department of Energy, for advancing the essentials of this formulation while commenting upon the press reports of General McPeak's observations in October 1991, on the purpose of the Air Force (see Chapter 22, fn. 8). This was not the first time David had, through his casual comments, provided me with intellectual keys to an analytical problem which was vexing me at the time (see my *Masks of War*, n. 24, 215).

7. Per Webster: continuum: 1: a coherent whole...["air" and "space" form an indivisible operational medium, a continuum best described as aerospace—Martin Caidin].

8. The military is constrained by international laws, such as the laws of armed conflict, even though civilian legislators may not be so obligated. See Carl H. Builder and Morlie H. Graubard, *The International Law of Armed Conflict: Implications for the Concept of Assured Destruction*, RAND R-2804-FF (Santa Monica, Calif.: RAND, January 1982), 45–53.

9. McPeak, *Does the Air Force Have a Mission?* 9.

10. I am indebted to my colleague, Jim Dewar, for this observation from his research on futures forecasting for the U.S. Army. The truth of his observation can be seen from the following analog: In the card game of Blackjack, the most probable count of a dealt card is ten (the value of all face cards and the ten-cards). Yet, one is more likely to be dealt something other than a card with value ten because the other cards are more numerous. Thus, the highest probability *event* (being dealt a card with a value of ten) is not necessarily the most probable *outcome* (which is being dealt a card with a value *other* than ten).

11. The original conception of air power theory did not rest on any such limited purviews. It was a universal theory, available for exploitation by any nation or society or government with the foresight and courage to seize upon it. It was an emerging truth about how the world and war would soon work.

Index